Praise for
*Guerrilla Marketing for Job Hunters 3.0*

"This book will teach you how to sell yourself. That knowledge will change your opportunities and can change your life."

—**Carl Albert, Chairman, Boise Inc.**

"As with all things in business, in a job search, only results matter. David Perry's tactics deliver!!"

—**Jim Rulseh (#1000) Chief Operating Officer, Tulip Corporation**

"Rarely do I read a business book that leaves me with actionable suggestions that are truly original. From the first pages, *Guerrilla Marketing for Job Hunters* does just that—it provides both a concrete plan and a wealth of tips for serious job seekers that are new but eminently logical and extremely effective. And having seen David Perry in action, I know he sets the bar in teaching that failure is not an option. He and Jay Levinson provide a game plan that is both powerful and practical."

—**Eric W. Golden, President & CEO, Equipois Inc.**

"A literary Trilogy ... they're rare—due to the difficulty in delivering a sustainable message, or worthless—due to lackluster content. Now Perry/Levinson join the ranks of C.S. Lewis & J.R. Tolkien and deliver a masterpiece every job hunter must have in their Guerrilla arsenal. This edition, more than the others, defines commando concepts and tactics already proven to work by scores of people who have mustered the courage to approach their search using the Force Multiplier Effect. The paradigm shift in the job market is forcing change. Get this book—you need to be battle ready."

—**Rudy Richman, Vice President of Sales, Protus IP**

"The current state of the global job market is more challenging than it has been in over 25 years. The magnitude of job force reductions is unprecedented. *Guerrilla Marketing for Job Hunters 3.0* is the most important and critical tool to use as a competitive advantage. When you think about the quantity of people who are vying for the few job openings that might exist, the job hunter must be clever and think outside of the box. This book provides ample ways to stand out head and shoulders beyond all others in a very crowded job market."

—**Steven O'Hanlon, President & COO, NumeriX**

"If you are a job seeker, an educator, career practitioner, this is the best resource anyone can have to find the work you love! It is all about branding the individual and giving you step-by-step strategies and tools that really truly work. BRAVO again!"

—Janet Uchacz-Hart, Executive Director,
Saskatoon Industry-Education Council

"*Guerrilla Marketing for Job Hunters* is an excellent source of information for job seekers and for job developers. The combination of creativity, practicality, and action makes this the 'must-have' book for people who are seeking new ways to spark their job search. The ideas included in this text are imaginative and have relevance, even under the most adverse economic conditions. Use this book to stand out from the crowd, to make a difference, and to get moving in some new directions."

—Norman E. Amundson, author of *Active
Engagement*

"There's never been a more important time than now for the unconventional, Guerrilla job search methods in this book. To cite just one example: You'll learn how to build a compelling new network in days that gets you sit-down meetings with decision makers who can hire you for jobs that aren't advertised or don't even exist yet. You will literally have no competition if you use these proven methods for creating a Guerrilla Resume, picking your target employers, and convincing them to hire you. What Jimi Hendrix was to the blues, David Perry is to job hunting. I cannot recommend this book highly enough."

—Kevin Donlin, Creator, TheSimpleJob
Search.com, Co-Creator, The Guerrilla Job
Search Home Study Course

"Most business books are b-o-r-i-n-g. However, you know from the minute you crack open *Guerrilla Marketing for Job Hunters 3.0* this book is different. David Perry has done it again. It's everything you need to know to land the perfect job for YOU using the most creative and up-to-date methods. In fact, I challenge any reader to open this book to any page and try to *not* find something that helps them with their career (you can't do it)."

—Lee Silber, author of *Career Management
for the Creative Person* and 14 other
popular books. www.leesiber.com

"*Guerrilla Marketing for Job Hunters 3.0* is a comprehensive resource that works in today's job market. The ideas shared are nontraditional, innovative, aggressive, and most importantly they provide results. The step-by-step process is easy to understand and implement. I would recommend this book to anyone serious about finding or changing their job!"

—Barbara J. Bruno, CPC, CTS, author,
speaker, entrepreneur, Good as Gold
Training, Inc.

"Full marks to author David Perry, the Peter Drucker of the executive search industry. *Guerrilla Marketing for Job Hunters* provides powerful and unique insights into how to take complete control over your next career move. After reading this book you will do just that, take control, using a road map that gives you the confidence to succeed."

—**John Reid, President, Canadian Advanced Technology Alliance (CATA) Alliance**

"*Guerrilla Marketing for Job Hunters* is the first practical battle plan for a new, empowered workforce—one that is ready to go to war over talent—their own. Jay Levinson and David Perry take you to the front lines and tell you how to survive and prosper. Not for faint-hearted whiners looking for an easy road. These guys show you how to build underground tunnels, find back doors, and infiltrate the opposition."

—**Gerry Crispin, SPHR, Chief Navigator, CareerXroads**

"The Relationship Edge. Are you on it, in it, or over it? In business and in personal relationships of all kinds, trust is the critical element. It's the glue that bonds all the other elements together. Without it, the relationship will diminish or die. David Perry is a trusted advisor. His book openly discusses the approaches to making right decisions and building the relationship edge. I highly recommend this read."

—**Steve Gordon, CEO, The Regional Group of Companies Inc.**

"Can you believe it? A book on job hunting that is a page turner! David manages to turn job hunting into an energizing activity. Follow the methods laid out in David's book, and you will actually look forward to your job search! Even if you are not looking for a job, you will want to read this book. In today's fast-moving knowledge-worker economy, everyone needs to know how to brand and market themselves—this is exactly what David teaches you to do. One last thing: If you are an employer, you will want to try to keep this book out of your local bookstores—this is not a book you will want your employees to read—it will give them too many door-opening ideas."

—**Ron Wiens, Senior Partner, Totem Hill Management Consulting Group**

"We're all Guerrillas now."

—**Allan Hoving, Founder, TheFrequency.tv**

"When you are looking for help in landing that position you dream about, *Guerrilla Marketing for Job Hunters 3.0* is the resource to turn to."

—**Doug Smith, International speaker and author of *Thriving in Transition***

"There are lots of ways to job hunt but not lots of smart ways. If you want to go smart, then go with David Perry and buy this book."

—**Penelope Trunk, author of *Brazen Careerist***

"We're in a new world. Resumes alone won't do it. Take it from someone who stood on a street corner wearing a sandwich board of his resume in the mid-1990s—the ideas in *Guerrilla Marketing for Job Hunters 3.0* are a heck of a lot easier to implement—and you won't get laughed at anywhere near as much. Recommended reading."

> —Peter Shankman, Founder of Help a Reporter Out and author of *Can We Do That?! Outrageous PR Stunts That Work— and Why Your Company Needs Them*

"Job hunters don't need to be told the 'what' of job hunting; they want and need to know the 'hows.' They are all in here and then some and, just as important, conveyed with the energy and passion of someone who not only knows what he's talking about, but truly believes it. You will, too."

> —Dave Opton, Founder and CEO, ExecuNet

"This new book lays out a straightforward and detailed plan of attack for every step of a job search from planning to negotiating the offer. The insights and insider knowledge of the recruitment industry that *Guerrilla Marketing for Job Hunters 3.0* offers establishes it as an indispensable tool for job seekers to land the interview and secure the job of their dreams. Going into a job search without this book would be like going into battle unarmed."

> —Gautam Godhwani, CEO, SimplyHired .com

"This book is brilliant. Packed with stories, examples, and tactics to help you at any point in your job search—this book is all about landing a real job with intense competition in a minimal amount of time. An absolute must-read."

> —Jason Alba, CEO, JibberJobber.com

"If you're a college student looking for an internship or a recent graduate looking for an entry-level job, then you'll understand from even a quick skim through *Guerrilla Marketing for Job Hunters 3.0* that it will be as indispensable to your job search as your textbooks were for your classes. In tight job markets, the competition for the best positions is especially fierce, and every candidate will be looking for an edge. If you want to get the edge over your competition, then you need to get this great new book."

> —Steven Rothberg, Founder, College Recruiter.com job board

"Perry and Levinson truly understand how changes in information and communication technologies have created new opportunities and pitfalls for the job seeker. Stand out from the crowd and truly shine by illuminating your most important talents to the broadest audience—in a cost-effective fashion. Stop wasting time and start with this book."

> —Sam Zales, President, Zoom Information, Inc.

"If you are ever tempted to think, 'I know all that' when it comes to the job search, read this book. As a former director of Career Services at a major university, this book is a humbling reminder that even 'experts' need refreshers and new insights to stay relevant. Thanks to technology, the tools and techniques to assist with self-marketing strategies are constantly changing (evolving). This book not only allows you to stay in the game, but it helps you get ahead of the game when it comes to marketing you."

—Dawn Brown, author of *That Perception Thing!*

"David Perry calls his co-author, Jay Levinson, the 'five-star general of Guerrilla Marketing.' Perry is the drill sergeant. He kicks butt. In the army, his squad would lose the fewest men. In the job wars, his men and women beat the opposition and gain the position. If a career victory is what you're after, follow Perry."

—Tony Patterson, Editor and CEO, SCAN

"This book provides readers with valuable information that will enable them to stand above the crowd and secure the best suitable employment. A wealth of information extends into areas that I will be able to utilize in my business, because in a way, I am always applying for the 'job' of being a trusted advisor to potential clients."

—Milan Topolovec, BA, TEP, CLU, RHU, President & CEO, TK Group, www.thetkgroup.com

"*Guerrilla Marketing for Job Hunters 3.0* is a must-have manual for the serious career professional. David brings his strong sales perspective to the job hunt strategy. Follow his process. Don't compromise. Leave your emotions in the bedroom and let his system do the work. David leaves out the fluff and academics, leaving us with fast-paced advice and lots of free go-to resources that he uses to execute the system himself. I'll be providing a copy of *Guerrilla Marketing for Job Hunters 3.0* to all my sales clients. David's approach applies to the deal hunter as much as it does the job hunter."

—Terry Ledden, Sandler Training

"This much-needed sequel to *Guerrilla Marketing for Job Hunters 2.0* puts the tools of the Internet at the fingertips of the searcher! Advice on social networks, blogs, special web sites, and interactive promotion is laid out for all to use. In today's troubled economy, it would pay every employee—not just those who are currently looking for a job—to become familiar with this book. One of the benefits of the process is that it will help you appreciate your own strengths and skills and your value as a person—not a bad side effect from an exercise that is, after all, devoted to your future!"

—Barry Gander, Senior Vice President, CATA Alliance

"When the first *Guerrilla Marketing for Job Hunters* was published, the content was original, game changing, and outrageous. In just four years, the recommended tactics have become absolutely, undeniably necessary for success. Candidates who don't adopt this plan are handing over their new career opportunity to the competition."

> —Debra Feldman, Executive Talent
> Matchmaker: Part Sleuth, Part Networker,
> JobWhiz

"David has looked at the process of job hunting in a completely out-of-the-box approach, and why not? The automotive industry says this is no longer your father's car, so your approach to looking for a job is no longer the way your father looked for one, either. It's about the two-way street of value. Your future employer needs to value your skills just as you need to value their appreciation of them, and David's book is about the whole process."

> —Allan Zander, CEO, Data Kinetics

"A must read. A useful and effective tool for all economic times. Once you start reading, it's hard to put it down."

> —Rick M Sabatino, Financial Director,
> Camp Fortune/Mont SteMarie

"Dave never ceases to amaze me with his ability to adapt the latest marketing trends to the job-search procedure. Bravo, Dave! This book is even better than the last one."

> —Mark Hanley, Director of Operations,
> Kingston Economic Development
> Corporation

"The job-search paradigm has shifted, and you can either play by the new rules or go the way of the dinosaurs. The bold, cutting-edge search strategies found in *Guerrilla Marketing for Job Hunters 3.0* will position you to exploit the system and demolish the competition. I know, because it's how I coach my clients to win!"

> —Cindy Kraft, CPBS, CCMC, CCM, CPRW,
> JCTC, The CFO–Coach

"It doesn't matter how brilliant you are or how exceptional you are at your job. If you are not getting yourself in front of the right people, the hiring decision makers, you will be overlooked. David Perry and his *Guerrilla Marketing for Job Hunters 3.0* will give you the ammunition to get noticed. Don't get lost on the battlefield; win the war."

> —Donato Diorio, CEO, Broadlook
> Technologies

# GUERRILLA
# MARKETING
FOR
# JOB HUNTERS
# 3.0

# GUERRILLA
# MARKETING
## FOR
# JOB HUNTERS
# 3.0

## How to Stand Out from the Crowd and Tap Into the Hidden Job Market Using Social Media and 999 Tactics Today

### JAY CONRAD LEVINSON
### DAVID PERRY

WILEY

John Wiley & Sons, Inc.

Published by John Wiley & Sons, Inc., Hoboken, New Jersey.
Published simultaneously in Canada.

For general information on our other products and services or for technical support, please contact our Customer Care Department within the United States at (800) 762-2974, outside the United States at (317) 572-3993 or fax (317) 572-4002.

Wiley also publishes its books in a variety of electronic formats. Some content that appears in print may not be available in electronic books. For more information about Wiley products, visit our web site at www.wiley.com.

*Library of Congress Cataloging-in-Publication Data:*

Levinson, Jay Conrad.
  Guerrilla marketing for job hunters 3.0 : how to stand out from the crowd and tap into the hidden job market using social media and 999 other tactics today / Jay Conrad Levinson, David E. Perry.
    p. cm.
  Includes index.
  ISBN 978-1-118-01909-2 (pbk.); ISBN 978-1-118-06136-7 (ebk);
  ISBN 978-1-118-06170-1 (ebk); ISBN 978-1-118-06127-5 (ebk)
  1. Job hunting.   2. Social media.   3. Career development.   4. Vocational guidance.
I. Perry, David, 1960 Jan. 12–II. Title.
    HF5382.7.L4654 2011
    650.14—dc22

                                                                          2010051280
Printed in the United States of America.

10  9  8  7  6  5  4  3

You know who you are, David Perry, and you know how much heavy lifting and fiery hoop diving you've had to do. I also owe acknowledgments to Frank and Ginger Adkins, who are currently walking the walk; to Jeremy Huffman, who has reached his destination already; to Christy Huffman, who has the journey ahead of her and will benefit from the words in these pages; and to Joshua Huffman, who searched for the perfect job and found it while looking in the mirror.

J.C.L.

To my darling wife Anita: Wow, our 30th year together. I love you. You are an inspiration as a wife; mother to Christa, Corey, Mandy, and Shannon; and business partner.

D.E.P.

# Contents

# Foreword

Do you know why Jay Conrad Levinson and David Perry use the word "Guerrilla" in the titles of all their books and talks? The answer is that Guerrillas pursue conventional goals in unconventional ways. Guerrillas, like the achievers who read *SUCCESS* magazine, have a better perspective on reality than their conventional opponents who tend to pursue their dreams by the book.

Never before have Guerrillas had such a competitive advantage. In the job market, doing things "by the book" is a fairly certain path to disaster and frustration—unless you operate according to the principles and insights in this book. This book ushers you into the land of conventional goals attained, to reality as it is, rather than as it was. It guides you to a new world that remains unknown to other job hunters—a world in which Guerrillas reign supreme. It has been said that in a dog-eat-dog economy, the Doberman is king. We're in that kind of economy right now—and the Guerrilla is king.

It takes a lot to be a true Guerrilla, and this book provides a lot to accomplish that goal. Wanting to be a Guerrilla is part of the job, but the heavy lifting of becoming a Guerrilla is in being a master of details. Where do you learn those details? The answer is in the pages ahead. It's not necessarily an easy answer, but it's a correct answer.

You absolutely must be aware of how the job market has changed dramatically just in the last decade. This is not your father's generation; it is yours. But it only belongs to you if you have the wisdom and awareness of the Guerrilla. You'll gain those invaluable attributes if you soak up that wisdom and become aware of today's realities. This book was written both to help you open doors to jobs others dream about and to show you how to get one.

To many, getting the job of their dreams is close to impossible. But Guerrillas are experts at learning the art of the impossible. Their knowledge of what is really happening in the job market transforms the impossible into the probable. Lightning has been captured in these pages. Minds will be changed. Lives will be changed. Light will illuminate the way.

Can all that really happen with just a book? It's a beginning. If you're not a Guerrilla job hunter, we wish you success, but if you are a Guerrilla job hunter, we predict success.

Are you ready to design your life on purpose and live the best years ever? Start right now!

To your SUCCESS.

DARREN HARDY
*Publisher*
*SUCCESS magazine*
*www.SUCCESS.com*

# Acknowledgments

Sage Schofield knows what she's done; Seth Pickett is our Official Man on the Streets; and Natalie Smith continues to lead by spirit.

Acknowledgments are also due to Steven, Michelle, Heide, Elexa, Hayley, Zachary, Austin, Blake, Ava, Alyssa, Leighton, and John Thomas for being so darned cute.

And, of course, my life and my search are more fruitful because of my new bride, Jeannie Levinson, and my constant daughter, Amy Levinson.

JAY CONRAD LEVINSON

Writing a book truly makes you appreciate your friends and colleagues. It takes many people to bring a book to life, and it is my honor to recognize them now.

When I started Perry-Martel International Inc. with my wife and business partner Anita Martel, my marketing budget for the entire year was $20. As luck would have it, I stumbled across an interesting book called *Guerrilla Marketing* by Jay Conrad Levinson (Boston: Houghton Mifflin, 1989) that promised to reveal hundreds of ways to stretch my marketing budget and get results. Indeed, I owe my early successes in marketing to Jay's ideas. Little did I know that 17 years later Jay would write the Foreword for my first book, *Career Guide for the High-Tech Professional* (Franklin Lakes, NJ: Career Press, 2004), and ask me to co-author *Guerrilla Marketing for Job Hunters*. To Guerrilla Marketers, Jay Conrad Levinson is a five-star general. He is also a true gentleman.

Kevin Donlin helped to expand the offering with the formation of Guerrilla Job Search International. A great business partner, he's a pleasure to work with—save for all the excess energy.

Mark J. Haluska, my friend, colleague, and business partner in recruiting, contributed his blood, sweat, and smarts to the first two editions of the book. Following a remarkable career in the military and in public service, Mark has become a first-class headhunter and life-long friend.

Wayne Eells dogged me daily to ensure I focused on the end-user needs of the reader to make certain that the book would make an immediate impact.

All the people at John Wiley & Sons were a pleasure to work with, including Shannon Vargo, my editor, Elana Schulman, and Linda Indig. I want to single out Shannon for stewarding it through the editorial process. What a breath of fresh air she has been.

I have Christa Martel-Perry to thank for providing the drill-instructor-themed original art work.

Many thanks to Megan Quinn at Google for steering me through the permissions process so we could use all the Google screen shots, which make the book easier to follow. Google is a trademark of Google Inc.

To my father, Fred Perry, who patiently read and reviewed all my first drafts in spite of having a life of his own . . . thanks!

The recruiting industry, by its very nature, attracts mavericks, evangelists, and pioneers. It has been my good fortune to work alongside and share ideas with some of the finest in the business, including many who contributed to this book. Thank you, Wayne Eells, Chris Perry, Gerard le Roux, Steve Duncan, Grant Turck, Rob Mendez, Skip Freeman, Adam Swift, Barbara Ling, Animal, Martin Buckland, Gail Neal, Tom McAlister, Bill McCausland, Steve Cobain, Mary Berman, Kenrick Chatman, Cindy Beresh-Bryant, Chad Lemke, Erica C. Jade, Jeff Donaldson, Jeff Kruzich, Lauryn Franzoni, Bill Humbert, Beth H. Kniss, Ross Macpherson, Shari Miller, Jim Moens, Dave Opton, Sally Poole, Paul Rector, Jill Tanenbaum, Deanna J. Williams, John Sumser, David Braun, Anita Martel, Dennis Smith, Dave Howlette, Gary Smith, Daniel Houle, Patrick McConnell, Allan Place, Allison Doyle, Mark Haluska, Jim Stroud, Jim Reil, James Durbin, Penelope Trunk, Kevin Watson, Willy Franzen, Peter Clayton, Glenn Gutmacher, Donato Diorio, Jason Alba, Matt Massey, Harry Joiner, Steve Panyko, Joseph Nour, Dave Mendoza, Steven Rothberg, Simon Stapleton, Cindy Craft, Stephen Forsyth, Rayanne Thorne, Jason Davis, Michael Kelemen, Tom Weishaar, Darryl Praill, and Allan Zander.

And finally, to the tens of thousands of job hunters and hundreds of clients I have worked with over the years—thank you. Without you, my life would not have been nearly as interesting.

DAVID PERRY
DAVID@GM4JH.COM

# Disclaimer

## ■ JOB HUNTERS

If you really want to get a new job and you are willing to do the work necessary to stand out from the crowd—buy this book! Grab a highlighter and mark it up. Devour it. Dog-ear the pages that are of most interest. Try everything that doesn't completely knock you out of your comfort zone and then try those ideas that do. By studying our book and applying the ideas, you will always be able to get a job no matter what the economic conditions. You will never again be dependent on anyone but yourself.

## ■ SMART PHONE USERS

Adoption of mobile technology is growing at a faster pace than the Internet. Because Guerrillas recognize new opportunities to differentiate themselves, portions of this book leverage Quick Response technology from Microsoft to deliver exclusive content. To encourage you to embrace and use this technology, watch for "Tags" like the one below for extra bonus content. Go get the free application for your smart phone.

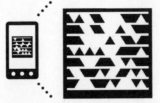

**Get the free mobile app at**
## http://gettag.mobi

## ■ HEADHUNTERS

Please don't buy this book! I haven't responded to any of the hate mail from the recruiters who have accused me of trying to put them out of business, and I won't respond to yours.

BTW: Smart recruiters have adopted the tactics in this book to help them close more deals.

## ■ LAZY PEOPLE

*Do not* buy this book if you're unemployed and happy to stay that way. You won't do what's necessary to get "unstuck" and no one can do it for you. Save your money.

## ■ PAID PROMOTIONAL CONSIDERATION

Zero. The people and products/companies profiled in *Guerrilla Marketing for Job Hunters 3.0* are here based solely on merit, just as those featured in the first two editions were.

# Introduction

## The Winner's Edge

Through my illness I learned rejection. I was written off. That was the moment I thought, Okay, game on. No prisoners. Everybody's going down.

—Lance Armstrong

I was waiting in line at the airport, minding my own business when suddenly my BlackBerry started to vibrate—vigorously. It was my oldest daughter Christa Martel-Perry (she's in university studying advertising and design) who just wanted to say "hi!" Right! I'm the proud father of four, high energy, impatient, just get it done, future leaders of the new world. But I digress . . . .

Texting is a great communication tool. It avoids long-winded conversations and the need to make excuses for not calling. Most important is its brevity. What follows is my entire texted communication.

Time: 1501 hrs.

Location: Detroit

Christa: Dad, I need help with a homework assignment for my advertising class. Need to design a new media campaign to find a job. I have to present it in two days—Friday. Ideas?

Me: Launch a chain letter e-mail and a Facebook ad campaign targeting your top 10 companies.

Time: 1647 hrs.

Location: Philadelphia

Christa: Dad—have top 10. Need your credit card number for Facebook ad.

Me: K here's # ******** PIN follows in next txt.

Me: PIN ****** spend $10 max w .25 per click.

[Action: I agreed to a $10 maximum spend for the Facebook ads with a suggested cost per clickthrough of $0.25, giving Christa a potential test group of 40 people. E-mailed credit card number with PIN—I know what you're thinking, but hey! In for a penny . . . ]

Time: 2215 hrs.

Location: Ottawa

Christa: It worked!

Me: What worked?

Christa: E-mail chain letter. Got two replies already.

Me: Already! From who?

Christa: Friend's father knows the executive director at X. She's sending me details and passing on my message.

Christa presented her campaign to her class Friday. A day later she received an e-mail invitation to interview with one of her targeted organizations and shortly thereafter (days) she agreed to head overseas.

## ■ EVER HAD ONE OF THOSE DA. . . MOMENTS?

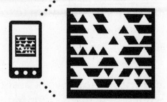

**Get the free mobile app at**
**http://gettag.mobi**

Think about what just happened. I interacted with Christa for mere minutes between flights:

➤ By the time I landed in Philly, Christa was ready to execute.

➤ She used free software on her laptop to create an ad and upload it to Facebook.

➤ By the time I cleared customs in Ottawa, Christa was seeing results.

➤ Her message went viral.

➤ Christa closed an offer days later.

... never having read a newspaper, surfed a job board, gone to a networking event, or spent a penny (of her own money)!

Can job hunting be this easy? Yes. For most people, starting the conversation is the hardest part, but once they're talking, they can get the offer. This book will help you start more conversations with people who can hire you.

## ■ JOB HUNTING HAS CHANGED

Let me contrast Christa's experience with those of the audience we presented to earlier in the day, at the SAE World Congress (Society of Automotive and Aeronautical Engineers). Kevin Donlin (my business partner in Guerrilla Job Search International) and I were in Detroit to present "Guerrilla Job Search Secrets Revealed." The audience: engineers between opportunities (job hunters).

As background, let me just say that when Kevin and I present it's a lively interactive event—best described by one attendee as a "good old-fashioned revival meeting!" We know holding an audience's attention for 90 minutes requires that we grab attendees by the throat and shake them to their very core—figuratively speaking, of course.

We begin every talk by playing "Stump the Recruiter." This is a fully interactive game that allows me to whip the audience into a frenzy by telling them that they can win a copy of *Guerrilla Marketing for Job Hunters 2.0* or a *Commando Tactics* DVD . . . (wait for it!), further informing them that "no one ever wins." "So I brought just one copy of each because a box of books is heavy, and I know I'm just going to have to lug them home—again." But that day I went just a little farther saying, "but maybe, because I'm in a room filled with engineers, and I'm just a "simple BA, it might be the first time."

Got their attention? You bet.

So up goes Slide #1, which is blank save for these two sets of numbers standing 16 feet tall: 24,297,000 and 2.6. I ask the audience, "Can you tell me what those numbers stand for?" A flurry of answers is shouted out, running the gamut from: the number of unemployed people in America to the daily consumption of Starbucks coffees.

Sadly, none are correct. "Looks like I'll be lugging the book home again," I say.

## ■ WANT TO TRY?

What do you think these numbers stand for?

24,297,000

2.6

Give up? Come on, try!

Okay, let me tell you. The 24,297,000 number comes from the U.S. Bureau of Labor Statistics and represents the "Hires levels and rates by industry and region, seasonally adjusted" for the 6 months from September 2009 to February 2010. The 2.6 stands for the number of jobs that went unfilled—2.6 million in January of 2010. By November 1, 2010, that number had grown to 25.5 million people hired. Do you remember seeing 24 million job postings? Me neither.

## ■ INTUITIVELY THAT MAKES NO SENSE

We've been bombarded with news to the contrary for nearly four years. But it's a fact. How can that be?

One of the great underreported/unreported stories about the recession is that American employers have jobs they can't fill. What statistics reveal in the midst of the weakest economy in several decades, and a national unemployment rate hovering around 9.7%, is that employers have jobs that can't be filled. How many last month? Just go to this U.S. Bureau of Labor Statistics link to see: http://tinyurl. com/nku3d9. These numbers indicate that the problem is more than a simple supply/demand mismatch.

Here's the real problem. More than 95% of jobs are not advertised anymore because employers are ill equipped to deal with the avalanche of resumes, each one of which has to be filed, tracked, and replied to for Equal Opportunity Employer reasons. This consumes hundreds of hours of time that few can afford. The vast majority of jobs remain unadvertised—they are invisible to ordinary job seekers. However, millions of people are being hired, and if you want to know how many, just load this URL into your web browser:

www.bls.gov/news.release/jolts.t02.htm.

Are you surprised? Think I'm fibbing?

## ■ LOGIC PREVAILED

It took me just two minutes to explain why employers were hiding jobs and how attrition and "casual labor" affected what openings job hunters actually saw. It was quickly clear to them why, how, and where they were looking wasn't working. Conventional tactics like job boards, newspapers, and networking have their place, but they are largely passive tools and nowadays employers are only looking to talk to a handful of the "most qualified" people, and they are using a brand new suite of tools and tactics to reach them. What they needed to understand was how employers' recruiters and headhunters filled positions.

We then showed them how a recruiter, given the task of finding an engineer with brake and exhaust system experience, for example, would go about their task. The recruiter could:

1. Run an ad and hope the person they're looking for sees the ad and applies.
2. Create a Boolean search string using keywords and run it through Google.

Hint: the keywords solution takes two seconds and returns *only* exactly qualified people. It was obvious which route the recruiter would take. I showed them exactly how it would be done. The search strings I used and the number of hits returned (figures in parentheses) are below.

➤ intitle:resume brake.system | exhaust.system education -jobs -apply -submit mechanical (84)

➤ site:linkedin.com inurl:in brake.system | exhaust.system mechanical ~engineer (290)

➤ ("brake system" OR "exhaust system") engineer inurl:profile (occupation OR "about me") (72)

By the way, you can cut and paste each of these search strings into Google to see the results—do not include the numbers in parentheses.

## ■ CURRENT REALITY

Every day there are hiring managers, recruiters, and headhunters searching for people with your skills. They want to find you. They're looking to fill jobs that aren't advertised. You want to come up in those searches but you only come up in those searches if your profile has the exact same words that they're searching for. The big question we asked the audience was, "Would you have been found if I had run a similar search using your skills and abilities?" The answer was a resounding "no!" "Well, if the people who are looking for you can't find you, then your job may go to a lesser qualified engineer and you are going to miss out on many opportunities," I said.

For the next 90 minutes Kevin and I explain why the traditional methods job hunters have been coached to use are not sufficient for today's new reality. We explain why newspapers and job boards (passive mediums) are rapidly being replaced by Boolean search strings (keywords) on LinkedIn, Facebook, and Twitter. It was clear no one in the audience realized how proactive employers are when they have a problem to solve, or that hiring managers are 1,000 times more likely to reach out to candidates selectively themselves, before ever using a headhunter, recruiter, employee referral, or advertisement.

## ■ THE EUREKA MOMENT!

You can reverse engineer the same search techniques to be found or to find employers who have problems you can solve and create a job for yourself.

What's your takeaway?

1. The economy has changed and every organization has had to change the way it does business, and that means changing how it hires.

2. Looking for problems you can solve is easier than looking for a job—one implies value (employers will pay to have a problem resolved), the other simply implies a payroll cost.

The audience quickly figured out that an "opportunity" was a chance to solve a problem and that's what engineers do best. This is the most competitive job market we've ever seen, but there are jobs out there, lots of them. They're still aren't enough jobs for everyone though, so it is no longer good enough for you to just be the most qualified. That's not who gets the job. And you probably already know that. The person who gets the job is the one who can find the job to begin with and then maneuver the job search process.

Finding and maneuvering to the offer stage are a Guerrilla Job Hunter's competitive advantage.

## ■ GUERRILLA TACTICS WORK

There are jobs in the "hidden job market"—lot's of them—but hidden they will stay. To get at these opportunities, you need to relearn how to search for opportunities and articulate your value to employers in terms they can understand.

Guerrilla job search methods have already passed the test in some of the toughest cities in America, like Detroit where one man landed a six-figure job just eight days after hearing us speak. Three others landed jobs just seven weeks later. That's 76% faster than the national average of 32.2 weeks. You will be reading of many more examples.

Our strategies and tactics will empower you to be found and start a conversation that will lead to you getting hired. When you learn about the way interviews have changed, you can adapt and win every time.

The Great Depression, two World Wars, the Cold War, putting a man on the moon—each generation of Americans has met, and conquered, its own seemingly impossible challenges. Now is the time for us to conquer ours—and to put America back to work—one Guerrilla at a time!

## ■ SO WHY THE THIRD EDITION?

For job hunters, a lot has changed since the book debuted. For example:

➤ There are two job search strategies that always work no matter the economy:

1. Being found is now the best way to guarantee you're always working. You need to understand how employers think and look for people so that you can be found.

2. Finding a job in today's overcrowded, hypercompetitive job market requires that you understand how to cut through the noise and get in front of a decision maker who can hire you.

➤ When I first wrote about an upstart social networking site with lots of promise named LinkedIn, it barely had 125,000 members. I was member 113,709. Today it's a household word with 80,000,000-plus members and is used by recruiters daily—but not in the way you think! No other job-search book teaches you that recommendations you post on LinkedIn can entice recruiters to read your profile and call. (Of course, there's more to LinkedIn success than this, and we cover it all.)

➤ Likewise, ZoomInfo had fewer than half a million profiles. Today, a successful job search starts with you claiming your Zoom-Info profile or creating one. And of course, it's *free*. But did you know that ZoomInfo has far more to offer than just passive registration? We tell you how to turn it into a research tool on steroids.

➤ Googling was a novel tactic, used only by recruiters. Now Google must be a major weapon in your job search arsenal.

➤ In the "old days" (pre-2009), blogs were "the voice of the people" and a minor annoyance to mainstream media. Nowadays, professional journalists troll blogs for story ideas.

➤ Monster and CareerBuilder were the largest jobs boards (and still are). Now there are also 55,000 microboards, and you need an efficient way to use them (introducing SimplyHired.com, Indeed.com, and NatsJobs.com).

➤ MySpace and Facebook were mildly interesting to recruiters. Now, headhunters and corporate recruiters source and hire—or not—based on what they find there.

On January 1, 2011, Facebook had more than 500 million users. If Facebook were a country it would be the third largest by sheer population, eclipsed only by India and China. When compared to Facebook, the two best-branded job boards, CareerBuilder and Monsterboard, have dismal web site traffic. Go to Compete.com, plug the sites in, and you will see for yourself.

Yet in the midst of all this change, most people are still looking for opportunities on job boards and networking the way they did five years ago. This has serious implications when you're trying to find a job and/or be found.

You must think and you must act—differently. Don't worry. We will show you:

➤ What to do.
➤ How to do it.
➤ Why you're doing it (knowledge is power!).

What's different in our job search approach?
There are two key breakthroughs:

1. Our step-by-step marketing-based approach
2. The Force Multiplier Effect

## ➤ Step-by-Step Marketing-Based Approach

Every job search is a sales and marketing campaign. The successful job hunter identifies prospective companies; contacts them by phone, uses mail and/or e-mail; and meets in person to convince them to make a job offer. This is no different from what an insurance agent or mortgage broker does to get new clients—it's sales and marketing. Intuitively we all know this.

Yet, the vast majority of job-search books are written by people with *no* background in sales or marketing—academics, HR professionals, and career coaches.

By contrast, Jay and I have forgotten more about sales and marketing than most job search "experts" will ever learn. This is not to brag—being tops at sales and marketing in the career space is like being the tallest midget in the sideshow.

Yet, Jay and I do stand out with our sales and marketing backgrounds, unlike any other writing team in the career space today.

Jay is the father of *Guerrilla Marketing*, the best-selling marketing series in history, while I started a successful recruiting practice by making up to 150 cold calls per day, telephoning busy executives and handling rejection after rejection. My prospecting and closing skills were forged after a years-long baptism by fire, and this has helped me negotiate more than $184 million in salaries since 1986.

## ➤ The Force Multiplier Effect

In the first two editions of *Guerrilla Marketing for Job Hunters*, job hunters were introduced to the Force Multiplier Effect, the military discipline of using multiple tactics at the same time to create synergy—and overwhelm the target. In modern warfare, it's a proven process of dominating the enemy to win.

*Guerrilla Marketing for Job Hunters 3.0* is the sequel designed to help you organize and launch your own Force Multiplier Effect. It explains in step-by-step detail how to use the newest social networking sites and digital tools to perform a precession-guided job search and all-out job hunting assault on a targeted list of ideal employers. Every tactic in the book has been put to the test, based on feedback from job hunters who bought the book and/or attended an event or Boot Camp as well as the newest techniques used by recruiters and employers.

*Guerrilla Marketing for Job Hunters 3.0* gives you access to worksheets and exercises that make it drop-dead simple for you to find a job fast. There are detailed before-and-after sample resumes and cover letters, as well as proven ideas you can use to tailor tactics to your situation. You will use these tools to beat out your competition, to find jobs (opportunities) first and be the most prepared so you get the offer.

There is extensive supplemental material and "Special Reports" available *free* for people who expressly purchased the book at www. GM4JH.com.

## ■ THE KEYS TO LANDING YOUR DREAM JOB

What's in it for you? *Guerrilla Marketing for Job Hunters 3.0* shows you how to take full advantage of strategies and job-hunting techniques that are not available as free information on the Internet and were previously only known by a handful of insiders.

Employers will literally be lining up to hire you because the book:

➤ Guides you through a simple method to pick your most marketable skills, in 30 seconds or less (as a result, every resume, cover letter, and conversation you send will cut through the noise in any job market, like a hot knife through butter).

➤ Leads you through the process of crafting a resume that connects directly to your ideal employer (based on 100 years of principles used in advertising copywriting).

➤ Shows you how to build a ZoomInfo, LinkedIn, Twitter, and/or Facebook profile that gets found and read and makes the phone ring with interview offers.

➤ Demonstrates how to use innovations like Google Local to identify employers.

➤ Details more than a dozen alternate ways to land an interview.

➤ Shows you how to "start work before you're hired" and prove your ability by demonstrating your skills right there in your next interview.

Because you will discover how to:

➤ Articulate your unique strengths in resumes, letters, e-mail, and interviews (while avoiding the typical "resume speak" or "interview babble" that causes hiring managers to guffaw).

➤ Leverage ZoomInfo, LinkedIn, Facebook, and other social networking sites to take advantage of "the secret lives of top recruiters."

➤ Build a specialized resume that's fun to read, speaks the language of employers, and proves every claim you make.

➤ Target a job that plays to your strengths and abilities—a job you would do for free, if you weren't getting paid!

➤ Design, launch, and execute a multimodal job-hunting campaign based on the same success principles used by General Norman Schwarzkopf in Operation Desert Storm.

➤ Learn how to present your skills in creative new ways that stand out in today's hypercompetitive job market.

➤ Employ little-known search engine optimization tricks used by top headhunters (who have to make placements or starve).

➤ Zero in on the best jobs at the highest salary—fast—because you'll know exactly what hiring managers really want (this transforms you from "pest" to "guest" in the minds of employers).

## ■ HOW THE BOOK IS SET UP

The book has four sections. Each chapter in a section builds on the last and prepares you for the next.

The quickest way to success is to read the entire book from cover to cover—twice. The first time is so you appreciate how all the ideas can fit together and understand why some tactics are strategy-specific. The second read is where you start to combine strategies and tactics to customize your personal Force Multiplier Effect. You can't do this piecemeal.

Of course, you could jump from chapter to chapter like a stereotypical male driver who wastes time "looking" for his destination, instead of pulling over and asking for directions. Pull over now because you've got the map in your hands, and in this economy you don't have time to waste. Read this manual from cover to cover as directed. It's faster!

| | |
|---|---|
| **Introduction: The Winner's Edge** | *Key Concepts: Why the job market has drastically changed. The importance of keywords.* |
| **Chapter 1: Why You Need to Become a Guerrilla Job Hunter: The New Global America** | *Key Concepts: The #1 secret to a successful job search. Details the elements of your successful plan.* |

## Part I Your Guerrilla Mind-Set

**Chapter 2: Personal Branding Guerrilla Style: Shape Up Your Brand with Attitude**

*Key Concepts: The skills employers seek. How to build your brand for free and make employers call you.*

**Chapter 3: Attitude Check: Upfront and Personal**

*Key Concepts: How to stay focused. How to right the typical mistakes job hunters make.*

**Chapter 4: Your Guerrilla Strategy: Think Like a General—Execute Like a Sergeant**

*Key Concepts: How to crack the hidden job market. Tools and tactics for staying on top.*

## Part II Weapons That Make You a Guerrilla

**Chapter 5: Your Research Plan: The Guerrilla's Competitive Edge**

*Key Concepts: How to locate opportunities before your competition does.*

**Chapter 6: Resume Writing and Cover Letter Boot Camp: Overhaul Your Personal Marketing Materials**

*Key Concepts: Creating your marketing materials: cover letters and resumes that will be read instead of tossed.*

**Chapter 7: Guerrilla Networking: A Radical Approach**

*Key Concepts: Effortless networking that really works in any market.*

## PART III Tactics That Make You a Guerrilla

**Chapter 8: LinkedIn—the 800-Pound Guerrilla: Your "Be Found" Epicenter**

*Key Concepts: How to use LinkedIn to be found and other strategies.*

**Chapter 9: Digital Breadcrumbs: Plugged In—Turned On—Tuned In**

*Key Concepts: How to leverage social media and social networking.*

**Chapter 10: Commando Tactics: 15 Breakthrough Strategies That Work**

*Key Concepts: How to get in front of the people you want to meet with.*

**Part IV Your Guerrilla Job-Hunting Campaign**

**Chapter 11: The Force Multiplier Effect in Action: 12 Sample Campaigns**

*Key Concepts: Case studies of ordinary people who achieved extraordinary results by taking control of their job search.*

**Chapter 12: Hand-to-Hand Combat: Winning the Face-to-Face Interview**

*Key Concepts: What to do and say before, during, and after the interview to land the offer.*

**Chapter 13: Negotiating the Deal: How to Bargain with Confidence**

*Key Concepts: How to get what you want without fighting.*

**Chapter 14: Career Lancing: All—Ways—Ready**

*Key Concepts: What's next?*

## ■ SPECIAL FEATURES

To help keep you focused and interested, there are several special features in the book:

1. Drills: must-do exercises to put you on the fast track to getting hired.
2. Downloads: scripts and worksheets are organized by chapter and can be found at this url: www.gm4jh.com/g3downloadpage. Please type it into your browser.
3. War Stories: anecdotes about regular people employing Guerrilla Marketing techniques to land their dream jobs.
4. Guerrilla Tactics: dozens of tips and tricks to hasten your hunt.
5. Guerrilla Intelligence: vignettes by prominent bloggers/authors and career coaches.

   ➤ These pieces are graciously contributed by the best minds in the industry. Their names are household words in the recruiting world. Each is a thought leader. Many are speakers; some are trainers and successful authors in their own right. We have brought them together for the first time because of the unprecedented changes in the employment market. You will quickly learn about new tools and tactics and how you should apply them to your job search.

6. Software: links to free software and other special offers designed to accelerate your being hired.

7. Web site and blog: state-of-the-moment tactics and articles on social networking at www.GM4JH.com.

8. Job Alert System: fully functional and completely anonymous – compliments of NatsJobs.com.

9. Expanded References: because there is no way for us to know what type of learning best suits you, there are videos on www.GM4JH.com.

10. Online Bonuses: Register online at www.GM4JH.com to access even more content. Special reports on working with recruiters, and warm-calling, as well as exclusive video and audio portions. Follow the instructions on the last page of the book.

## ■ STATE-OF-THE-MOMENT CONTENT

Nonfiction books go stale quickly, but you need the best information possible to succeed. So we are using cutting-edge tools to bring it to you.

This symbol is called a QR (Quick Response) Tag. You will very likely be seeing them in stores, magazines, and advertising venues soon. They are used to deliver rich media content to people who have smart phones. We are using them throughout the book to bring you state-of-the-moment content. If you have a smart phone, go to http://gettag.mobi and download the application needed for your device, then use the application to scan the Tag below for a special notice.

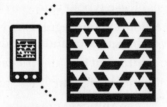

**Get the free mobile app at**
**http://gettag.mobi**

## ■ WELCOME TO YOUR FUTURE

*Guerrilla Marketing for Job Hunters 3.0* is about managing your career as a professional services provider: how to brand yourself, increase your value, and build a rewarding career. With our help, you can mount a multipronged plan of attack that outflanks the competition and that will separate you from the pack quickly and put you on top always.

Guerrilla, this is your Super Bowl—get out on the field now—because there can be only one winner. Play with your head and your heart. Give it everything you've got, and then some. Celebrate your success with us. Send your victory story to G3@perrymartel.com.

This book is your fast lane to success.

---

### GUERRILLA INTELLIGENCE

*Hiding in Plain Sight*

**John Sumser**

Things have really changed. Knowing exactly what you want is more important than ever. In the last generation, you could "parachute" into your new job. Today, it's a Guerrilla war . . . clear, focused, targeted, and opportunistic.

While you weren't looking, job hunting became a direct-marketing exercise. "Who you know" matters less than "who knows you." The transition between one job and the next is a matter of how quickly you can acquire and harness attention. You are now required to know what you want and where to get it. You are in charge of manufacturing your own luck.

Employers are buried in a sea of resumes they don't want or like. If they acquire yours from a job board, they may consider you an "active job hunter." That's a bad thing. Huge volumes of unwanted and indistinct resumes mean that you have to simultaneously stand out and look like you're not trying to be seen.

That is the essence of a Guerrilla job-hunting campaign.

Have you noticed that it gets harder to make sense out of the world every day? The Internet created explosive growth in information sources. Each offers an opinion screaming for your attention. Survival depends on choosing among the sources. Information overload affects everyone. Our organizations know more and more about themselves. They are less and less able to utilize that knowledge.

*(continued)*

(*Continued*)

The workplace contains members of four generations. Differing preferences for differing communications technologies drive the vast gulf between them. Collaboration and file sharing, the favorite tools of the young, look like cheating and stealing to their elders. The ever-present texting and social networking seem rude and unproductive to the technologically illiterate.

Several things make the workforce older with each passing day. The United States (and the entire industrialized world) produces fewer offspring than it takes to keep population constant. As a result, the average age of workers in the economy rises continuously. More elders stay at work. Changes in finance, housing, and pensions raise the real retirement age. The differing generational perspectives cloud the certainty needed to make productive decisions.

New technology flows relentlessly into our lives. Cell phones became ubiquitous in less than a decade. Universal Wi-Fi dominates public spaces, including your car. Computers merge with phones to create an omnipresent connectedness. Old media dies. New media replaces it. Disruption and change define the era.

Amid all of this, we find our work. The orderly processes of the last generation are evaporating as quickly as newspapers. Old industries disappear while new ones explode on the scene. Looking for work means finding people we want to work with. It means helping them find us. Guerrilla job hunters stand out from the crowd with purpose.

The goal is disarmingly simple. Identify and build relationships with the kind of people who either do what you want to do or want you to do it. Let them know you are available, better than competent, creative and persistent. Demonstrate your value. Demonstrate it again.

The problem is always the opportunity. Today, so much has changed, from demographics to technology, that getting simple things done can be confusing. An environment like that rewards people who are clear about what they want. It pays big benefits to people who persist. Environments with great potential are confused and noisy.

You are on your own. Exhilaration, autonomy, and self-direction are now the necessities, not the consequences. You find your next engagement by being distinct from the noise.

John Sumser is the editor of HRExaminer, an online newsletter devoted to HR strategies and people. Visit him at www.hrexaminer.com. See him on LinkedIn at www.LinkedIn.com/in/johnsumser.

# GUERRILLA MARKETING

FOR

# JOB HUNTERS

## 3.0

# Chapter 1

# Why You Need to Become a Guerrilla Job Hunter

## The New Global America

It's not the strongest of the species, nor the most intelligent, that survive; it's the one most responsive to change.

—CHARLES DARWIN

The world is in the midst of a profound business transformation. America is under siege from layoffs, outsourcing, offshoring, rightsizing, downsizing, and bankruptcies. This is a result of developments in information and communications technologies, changing human values, and the rise of the global knowledge-based economy. The sheer complexity and technical sophistication of business has also transformed the job market. We are at a major crossroad in our history.

According to the U.S. Department of Labor there are 50 million employment transactions annually. Already reeling from the struggling economy, competition for the remaining jobs is tougher than ever, the rules for getting them have changed, and global competition ensures that the rules will change again tomorrow.

The current "jobless" recovery is a consequence of the economy's rapid evolution from a natural resources- and manufacturing-based economy to a knowledge-based one. We are witnessing firsthand the information economy's first *full* economic recovery.

You see, for most of the twentieth century, a recession was a cyclical decline in demand—the result of excess inventory that needed to

1

be sold off. People were temporarily laid off—inventory backlogs were reduced and demand would snap back quickly. As product demand increased and shelves were once again filled, workers returned to their preexisting positions in factories—that, or they found an equivalent job with another company.

Over the past few years, dramatic advances in information technology have allowed companies to establish tightly integrated demand and supply chains and outsource manufacturing and low-end service jobs to save money and increase shareholder returns. Rightly or wrongly, many of the jobs that have entirely disappeared from North America have reappeared in India, China, and Latin America. This time, though, rather than getting furloughed, many people were let go, forcing them to switch industries, sectors, locations, or learn new skills to find a new job.

At the same time, job growth now depends on the creation of new positions; you should expect a long lag before employment rebounds because employers incur risks in creating new jobs and require additional time to establish and fill positions. Investment in new capital equipment is no longer a pendulum swinging from recession to recovery and back again.

Instead of resources or land, today capital means human capital. It doesn't take a store to go into the shoe business—just ask Tony Hsieh, CEO of e-tailer Zappos.com. Nor do you need raw materials, a factory, or fleets of trucks. Nike became a shoe industry leader by concentrating on the value-producing capacity of its employees for design, marketing, and distribution know-how.

---

The real capital is intangible: a person's knowledge level, combined with an aptitude for application.

---

## ■ OFFSHORING AND AMERICA'S FUTURE AS A GLOBAL INNOVATOR

Politicians always have a lot to say about the future of offshoring and what the practice of shipping jobs overseas means for the U.S. economy—especially when they want to get elected. But the rhetoric often dies after Election Day.

Politicians, economists, and futurists will argue the macroeconomics of today's upside-down economy for years, because it makes good press. As a Guerrilla job hunter, you need only interest yourself in the microeconomic impact of offshoring and how it affects you and your career—in short, which jobs are likely to disappear over time and what industries are likely to benefit.

Your job is at risk for offshoring if:

➤ It can be broken down into many smaller tasks that can be redistributed to lower skilled, lower paid workers.

➤ Your company's profits are under constant assault by low-cost competitors.

➤ Someone else with a high school education can do your job with less than a week's training.

Here's what you can bank on:

➤ The offshoring trend won't stop anytime soon.

➤ Companies will continue to maximize profits and reduce costs.

➤ The government will not solve your career problems—at best it will provide limited retraining assistance.

## ■ THE PEOPLE WHO BEST MARKET THEIR TALENT WIN!

With a radically smaller pool of skilled workers and the increased demand for profits, the original War for Talent of the late 1990s has morphed from a quantitative to a qualitative one, best described as the War for the Best Talent by author Peter Weddle in *Generalship: HR Leadership in a Time of War* (Stamford, CT: Weddle's, 2004). The old "bums on seats" mentality of many employers in the late 1990s is quickly being replaced by "brains on seats."

Faced with stiffer competition and tougher hiring requirements, companies are single-minded about productivity and bottom-line performance. Consequently, competition for jobs is increasing as management seeks out and hires only those people who appear to have the most potential for helping to boost the company's profits. For many companies, employees are now viewed as a variable cost—hence the term human capital—to remain on the books only as long as they continue to produce.

Looking for an old-fashioned job like the one Dad used to have is a waste of your time. All jobs are temporary in the new economy—henceforth you always need to be looking for the next opportunity.

# ■ WHY YOU NEED TO BE A GUERRILLA

The most qualified job hunter is rarely the one who wins. I can tell you from personal experience. The positions invariably go to the person who does the best job at positioning himself or herself as the solution to an employer's problem.

The dramatic changes we are witnessing in the marketplace mean that the tried-and-true methods of finding a job will no longer suffice. They should remain a solid part of your plan, but they don't provide an adequate amount of exposure to potential employers.

In 1997, Tom Peters introduced the concept of Brand U in his book *Re-Imagine!* (London: Dorling Kindersley, 2003). At the time, self-branding was an assertive marketing concept best reserved for high-flying techies and senior executives who wanted to maximize the financial returns of their biggest asset—their career. Today, personal branding is a matter of survival.

Becoming a Guerrilla job hunter is the only way to consistently move your career forward. The market is geared toward those who effectively brand and market themselves as the ultimate commodity across multiple distribution channels.

# ■ THE #1 SECRET TO GETTING HIRED

Have a plan *and* follow it. To succeed in today's hypercompetitive job market where you are competing with the millions of unemployed people and millions more employed but dissatisfied people, you must have an awesome plan. Your plan must be clear and detailed in every way.

# ■ THE #2 SECRET TO GETTING HIRED

Are you ready for it? Show an employer that you are worth much more to them (value) than you cost (salary and benefits).

Too simple? Well, think about it for a minute. Do you know any sane person who wouldn't trade a nickel for two bucks? Everyone wants a deal. As a Guerrilla job hunter you are going to learn how to package and promote yourself as a blue-chip stock—to appear like money in the bank to an employer. This is achievable when you plan every step, and that's what we're going to show you.

## ■ YOUR GUERRILLA PLAN

Your plan will include your:

- ➤ Top 10 target companies
- ➤ Guerrilla resume(s) and cover letter(s)
- ➤ Guerrilla tactics
- ➤ Follow-up activities

In short, everything you need to do to land a great job and guarantee a steady stream of future opportunities.
It will be:

- ➤ Clever
- ➤ Marketing oriented
- ➤ Inexpensive
- ➤ Realistic
- ➤ Results driven

## ■ GUERRILLA JOB SEARCH FLOW CHART

Download
available

This flow chart shows you visually what you need to do and in what order you need to do it, so you can be successful in your job search. This flow chart is an integral part to all Guerrilla Job Search Boot Camps and presentations because it easily organizes what otherwise appears to be sheer chaos—the vastness of tools, tactics, and techniques available. Download the flow chart from the book's web site. Print it. Hang it on your wall. Refer to it often to stay on track.

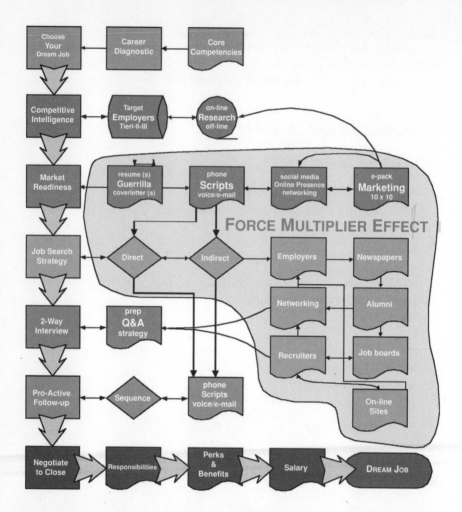

---

tools for success. If I say "cola," the majority of you will say "Coke."

The wise Chinese General Sun Tzu said, "Victorious warriors win first and then go to war, while defeated warriors go to war first and then seek to win." He understood positioning hundreds of years ago.

At a recent historical battle reenactment focusing on the period around the mid 1700s, I saw General Tzu's quote become reality. The battlefield was full of noise and militia on both sides. Dozens of cannons were pounding at each other like they were playing a giant game of tennis. Hundreds of men with muskets took turns firing at each other, sounding like large claps of thunder. While this was going on, officers were yelling orders to the soldiers. It was a loud, smoky, haze covered, semiorganized, free for all. No one knew who would win.

Suddenly, in the distance you heard the sound of bagpipes over all the sounds of the battle. You could hear them coming for some time before you could see them. As the colonists heard the bagpipes you could see their fear. They knew hundreds of trained men in bright red coats were about to hit them head on. The best fighting machine in the world was about to take the field. When the lines of soldiers with flags flying high in the wind finally arrived and fired two volleys, the colonists were in chaos. The British fixed bayonets and began their push. It is amazing how quickly they cleared the field.

Searching for a job is just like that battlefield. It is full of chaos, shots from all sides, smoky haze, and everyone trying to be heard. A position is announced and the employer receives hundreds or even thousands of resumes. You need to approach your job like the British approached the battlefield. They were well researched and trained. They made mistakes and learned from them. They turned all of that into their brand, "the world's best army." Then they drove that position into the minds of everyone. They backed it up with bright red uniforms so you could see their well-trained army units through the smoky haze of battle. They would blow their bagpipes loud and proud before they arrived, knowing that the sound of those instruments could be heard above the yelling, guns, and cannons. It announced their

*(continued)*

*(Continued)*

victory before they stepped on the field. That sound represented their brand. It was marketing perfection.

This is what you must do. It is not just about positive thoughts. It is positive action. Planning and preparation are the keys to knowing the battle at hand and determining your approach. Learn from your experiences and adapt. Your Guerrilla Resume becomes your bright red uniform and flying flags. It allows you to stand out through the smoky haze and chaos on the job battlefield. Once all of those are ready, it is time to blow your bagpipes. It will reflect who you are and what your brand is. It could be the coffee cup caper, Las Vegas postcard, the fortune cookie, or some creative idea you have. British troops in the 1700s knew the secret that David Perry has been teaching you in this book. The combining of all these tactics creates the force multiplier effect that establishes your position.

Blow your bagpipes and announce to everyone on the job battlefield: "I am on the way, and I have already won!"

---

Wayne Eells is a business accelerator who uses his *5-Star Backcast Methodology*™ to deliver strong, predictable long-term growth. More information is available at www.linkedin.com/in/wayneeells.

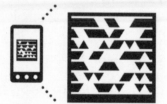

**Get the free mobile app at**
## http://gettag.mobi

*Part*

# I

# Your Guerrilla Mind-Set

# Chapter 2

# Personal Branding Guerrilla Style

## Shape Up Your Brand with Attitude

If Christopher Columbus had turned back, no one would have blamed him. Of course, no one would have remembered him, either.

—UNKNOWN AUTHOR

Embrace this fact: It is rarely the best qualified candidates who win the most coveted positions. Instead, it is most often the person who "packages" his experience best to meet the needs of employers.

The bad news is that it all comes down to how you look on paper and the attitude you bring to your job search. The good news is you have 100% control over both.

I'll discuss branding Guerrilla style in this chapter and then your attitude in Chapter 3: Attitude Check.

## ■ FREE—YOUR MILLION DOLLAR PERSONAL BRAND STRATEGY!

As Sun Tzu said 2,500 years ago, "Many calculations lead to victory and few calculations to defeat."

Before you begin job hunting, you need to craft a personal brand and marketing strategy that will guide your efforts. This plan includes the details about whom you will approach, how you will approach them, and what weapons you will need to use. (Refer to the job search flow chart in Chapter 1.)

As a professional recruiter, I know firsthand that all employers have a band or salary range they like to work within for every position. Once the most suitable candidate is found, it is my job to negotiate a deal that is acceptable for both parties. In nearly all cases, the difference between the median of a salary band and the upper end is $20,000—and I am not talking about executive-level candidates here. I am referring to individual contributors and midlevel managers where a salary band can run from $30,000 to $70,000 per year.

Your brand and marketing strategy will determine not only whether you get an interview but also where you fit in that band. If you market your skills as a commodity, you'll be lucky to land the job and you will be paid at the bottom end. However, if you market and present yourself as a "you-can't-do-without-me" solution to the employer, you will start near the top or over their salary band. Over the course of your lifetime earnings, this can easily amount to an extra $800,000 to $1 million in salary. Now you see why you need a personal branding strategy. Next, I show you how to create it.

## ■ HOW TO MAKE YOUR BRAND REFLECT THE SKILLS EMPLOYERS BUY

There are hundreds of books that explain how to sell yourself in an interview, but you need to get the interview first. To do that, you need to understand what employers are seeking in a candidate.

Being great at your job is not enough anymore. Employers have to know you are one of the best and that if they hire you for this job you really want it—not just kind of want it—really want it. As technology continues to shrink trade barriers and offshore competition increases, North American employers will have more options, and there are likely to be many other candidates whose qualifications look like yours.

The last recession raised the bar for job hunters. Indeed, many companies will opt to make no decision rather than risk making a poor hire. In fact, you likely won't even get an interview unless you are seen (branded) as someone who is in the top of your field. Actually, now that I think about it, you probably won't even see one-tenth of the jobs you might like to unless your name comes up in a keyword search. (We show you how to do that in Chapters 8 and 9—please stay with me until then. Do not skip ahead.)

You need to position yourself in a different way. You need to emphasize those qualities that will let you leapfrog over other competitors and showcase the skills and experience employers are looking for. This is very straightforward. The following qualities will land you at the front of the hiring line:

➤ Leadership skills

➤ Communication skills

➤ Bias toward action

➤ Passion

➤ Cultural compatibility

## ➤ Leadership Skills

At every level of an organization, employers hire leaders who can galvanize talented people toward ambitious goals and motivate them to succeed. Employers today don't need another team player. Many employers have learned the hard way that team players are often afraid to voice their opinions. Who wants another hanger-on? Every company in the United States is battling the clock to stay in business, increase market share, and meet the demands of its shareholders. In this environment, you must convince an employer that you will have a positive influence on its ability to win and that you are an integral part of its solution. If you can't communicate your personal commitment and drive through your words and actions in the interview, you won't be the company's first choice. Be a team leader instead.

## ➤ Communication Skills

Your ability to communicate a clear vision for your group must be far above average. Unclear writing and lumbering speaking skills rarely indicate sharp thinking, whereas clarity and concise expression are favorable signs. Slang expressions may work well on the factory floor but they will not impress customers or your prospective boss. Employers hire articulate candidates before all others. No one has the time to interpret what they think you said. More and more, companies are requesting that candidates prepare and deliver presentations. This is especially true in sales and marketing roles, but it also extends down to line positions on the shop floor.

## ➤ A Bias toward Action

Because companies are hiring fewer but better qualified people, they are pushing decision-making authority down the chain of command.

Today, a manager may need to make a decision that a few years ago might have been approved by a management committee. So no matter what level of employment you are seeking, do not be afraid to ask the hard questions and make tough decisions. You must demonstrate your ability to take action with limited or imperfect information. (You are actually going to demonstrate this in every interview.)

➤ **Passion**

Clients often ask me to find someone with "fire in their belly." That is employer-speak for passion. Employers know that many employees coast through life preferring to be safe rather than sorry in their careers. I have had the great fortune to work with brilliant technical people who are also passionate about what they do and want to leave their mark on the world. They challenge others to stretch and open their minds to new possibilities. Passionate workers envision what is possible, not just what is. They have a zest for life and a sense of urgency that infects everyone around them. Show an employer that you have that spark, and they may hire you over a more experienced candidate!

➤ **Cultural Compatibility**

In the 1930s, the cumulative codified knowledge base of the world doubled every 30 years. In the 1970s, the cumulative codified knowledge base of the world doubled every 7 years, and in 2010 it began to double every 11 hours! What you go to bed knowing at night will be outdated by daybreak.

Shelf life for knowledge is the same as that for a banana. To succeed today, a company's employees must share knowledge freely, a concept that is foreign to most organizations where people hoard knowledge to safeguard their jobs.

In an upcoming book, *Building Organizations That Leap Tall Buildings in a Single Bound* (Ottawa: Totem Hill), Ron Wiens, Ken Sudday, and I (David Perry) focus on how to build a corporate culture that produces a winning bottom line by focusing on the organization's Relationship Intelligence. We explain that the ability of employees to trust is a measure of the organization's Relationship Intelligence. Companies with high Relationship Intelligence will succeed because they can build new knowledge and therefore new products and wealth on a constant basis. In contrast, companies that have low Relationship Intelligence and hoard their knowledge will fail.

This is exactly why you, as a job hunter, cannot risk being viewed as "political" or as "playing games." Everyone knows that managers who play politics have a devastating impact on their organization regardless of their personal performance. The winning companies are the ones whose players play for the good of the whole. They know how to fight and disagree with each other but they do so not for personal gain but for corporate gain. The paradox is that managers who play this way end up with the fattest personal bottom line.

That is just the beginning of what is expected. Particular qualities and attributes dominate each hiring level, and you need to be aware of the different interests that govern each. We go into greater detail in the chapter on interviewing, where we discuss face-to-face interviews.

## ■  "YOU INC."—YOUR PERSONAL BRAND

More than ever before in our history, huge value is being leveraged from smart ideas and the winning technology and business models they create. In the years to come, employers will try harder than they ever have to attract and retain smart, bold, entrepreneurial over-achievers. In the new world of work, value is not salary driven—not for the employer, not for you. With millions of dollars at stake, an employer's search for an employee will be value focused, not salary driven.

As a job hunter, you need to comprehend that the production of value is the most important criterion for an employer. Articulating your value is your key to successful job hunting; it separates you from other job hunters. Worth does not flow from a job title. Knowing what's important to a company means looking beyond job descriptions and compensation tables, especially today when sudden changes and uncertainty are the norm.

You need to comprehend:

➤  What value a company is expecting from an employee's contribution?

➤  How do you communicate your value to an employer?

Especially for management and senior positions, companies are rarely looking to fill in a box on a standard employee recruitment form; they are looking for something nebulous and more important. They are searching for a person who can explode outward from an open-ended initiative-driven space and create value. Think Mark

Zuckerberg, founder of Facebook. (If you have seen the movie, you know what I am talking about.)

Qualities are difficult to find, measure, or test, and you don't find these qualities by searching for specific salary levels—the qualities that make up the new value table are money-resistant, as initially explained in *Career Guide for the High-Tech Professional: Where the Jobs Are Now and How to Land Them*, by David Perry (Franklin Lakes, NJ: Career Press, 2004).

The new value table (Table 2.1) goes beyond skill sets and resumes. In its simplest form, Table 2.1 represents the base elements of your personal brand. Building your brand—making a name for yourself—need not be expensive.

Table 2.1   The New Value Table

| An Employer's Value Requirements | Your Quality That Counts |
| --- | --- |
| Create new intellectual wealth for my company; add to my intellectual assets. | A consuming desire to make something new; to cut a new path rather than take a road. |
| High-energy enthusiasm for the job, regardless of the hours worked. | Work is a game—an integral, vibrant part of his or her life. |
| Not only is money not the most important issue—it's beside the point. | Internal pride to leave a "legacy signature" on their work, rather than strive for a paycheck. |
| Enduring performance. | An ability to stay and finish the race, because not finishing is inconceivable emotionally. |
| "Think around comers" to solve problems creatively. | Have an inner voice saying "There's always a way [to create a technology fix: make a deal]." |
| Bring up-to-date professionalism into every fray. | Contain a desire to grow professionally—to become the best person he or she can be: Invest in themselves. |
| Ever-increasing contribution. | The key to inner pleasure is recognized as making an individual contribution. |
| Identify and develop values for your company. | Instinctive grasp and exploitation of today's real value: the intangible capital of brand image, staff talent, and customer relationships. |
| Challenge the status quo. | Willingness and courage to speak the truth when you see a conflict. |

*Note:* In its simplest form, the New Value Table represents the base elements of your personal "Brand." Building your brand—making a name for yourself—need not be expensive.

# ■ CREATE YOUR BRAND GUERRILLA STYLE

Personal branding is not about projecting a false image. It is about understanding what is unique about you—your accomplishments, experience, attitude—and using that to differentiate yourself from other job hunters. Your brand is your edge.

Do you buy generic beer, clothes, cars? Do you buy any no-name large-ticket items at all? Not likely! If you are like most people, you buy a brand because of the security and peace of mind that come from the quality and reliability of a known brand. Employers do the exact same thing when they hire people.

Personal branding is critical for Guerrilla Marketers because:

➤ Employers are looking for results.

➤ Your results demonstrate your qualities, which satisfy an employer's value requirements.

➤ Employers won't buy generic employees (generic employees have their jobs outsourced).

➤ Employers will buy the intangible qualities implied by your brand (you are like Nike, too).

### ➤ How to Create Your Brand

Personal branding is about making yourself stand out so that people trust you and are interested in you. Guerrillas do this by leveraging their previous employers' brand (names, slogans, and logos) to create an identity that is memorable and desirable to the people they want to reach. In marketing speak it's called the "Halo Effect." Wikipedia describes it succinctly as follows:

The halo effect is a cognitive bias, whereby the perception of one trait (i.e., a characteristic of a person or object) is influenced by the perception of another trait (or several traits) of that person or object. An example would be judging a good-looking person as more intelligent.

For example, your cover letter; this means naming the projects you worked on or the clients you sold to (if you are an engineer or sales professional). Be specific. Be detailed. Sell the sizzle and the steak.

For your resume, it may mean placing the logos (with permission, of course) of the companies you worked for or products you developed on your resume for extra punch. Nothing will get an employer's attention faster than a well-known brand's logo, especially if it is a competitor or a coveted account.

| Table 2.2 Suggested Images for Your Personal Brand | | |
|---|---|---|
| Suggestion List | | |
| Position Sought | Reader's Interest | Suggested Graphics |
| Sales | Who have you sold to? Are there any major accounts you know they would like to have or would recognize as difficult to get that would make you look like a superstar? | Logos of the companies you have worked for or the major customers you have sold. Perhaps a product you sold if it's more recognizable than the company's logo. |
| Engineering | Who have you worked for? What major product where you part of designing? | Logos of your employers or customers. A logo or photo of the product you designed. |
| Marketing | What brands have you helped create? Where have you gotten press coverage for your products? What trade shows have you worked? | Logos of your employers. Logos of the newspapers or magazines you have had coverage in. Media quotes you were responsible for. |
| Finance | Have you done an IPO on NASDAQ? Have you secured funding from a major venture capital firm? | Logos of your employers or significant partners with whom you have negotiated. |
| Administration | How have you increased efficiencies? | Logos of your employers. |

So, what would make the person reading your resume take notice of you? Could it be your training at another company? Might it be the companies you have sold to? Were you responsible for a major product that the employer might recognize? There are likely thousands of images you could use.

Table 2.2 is a list of suggestions for you to use in choosing your images.

Let's get right into how to choose your most marketable skills and write about your accomplishments to reflect your brand. We will use the output you produce in this section with the clever design of your resume(s) in Chapter 6, Resume Writing and Cover Letter Boot Camp. As a Guerrilla you will be reusing this information for LinkedIn, Facebook, Twitter, and so on as well as for your voice mail messages. Of course, I know you will use this to guarantee consistency.

## GUERRILLA INTELLIGENCE

*Personal Branding*

### Chris Perry

More and more people are talking about the importance of personal branding, both in career searching and in career development. Effective personal branding not only makes you stand out from the crowd to employers and recruiters, it can also increase your job security by communicating your value as a leader and team player to your organization.

### What Is Personal Branding?

Personal branding is the process of identifying the unique and differentiating value that you can bring to an organization, team, and/or project and communicating it in a professionally memorable and consistent manner in all of your actions and outputs, both online and offline, to all current and prospective stakeholders in your career.

### The Lighthouse Personal Branding Model

The lighthouse is a great model for breaking down the personal branding process into its four key components or steps: the foundation, the beacon, the tower, and the beam.

*1. Foundation*

➤ **What is the foundation?** Your foundation comprises your unarguable strengths and/or experience in your chosen area.

➤ **How do you establish your foundation?** Write down your differentiating strengths (those you feel make you stand out from the rest) and ask your friends, family, and colleagues/managers to do the same for you. Identify the top three to five strengths that you feel will support the career direction you want to pursue.

*2. Beacon*

➤ **What is the beacon?** Your beacon is the memorable and consistent communication of those strengths and that experience.

*(continued)*

(*Continued*)

➤ **How do you light your beacon?** Now that you have identified your strengths, create/find a word or phrase that can become your personal brand and that represents these strengths. Develop a short pitch that can follow your brand, describing your strengths in more detail. Ensure that your word or phrase is versatile and can change with your direction.

3. *Tower*

➤ **What is the tower?** Simply put, your tower is your visibility, reach, and presentation, both online and offline, which support the beacon. This is really everything you do to passively build your personal brand. The higher you build your tower with your efforts, the more visible you will be to potential career stakeholders.

➤ **How do you build your tower?** Here are some ways to passively build your brand and credibility in front of your target audience:

➤ Create a LinkedIn profile and follow the suggested steps to complete your profile 100%, making sure you include your personal brand and pitch in your subtitle and summary sections.

➤ Create a Google account and profile for improved search engine optimization.

➤ Include your personal brand on your resume, cover letter, business cards, e-mail signature, voice mail message, and across your other social networks, such as Twitter and Facebook.

➤ Consider creating a personal web site/blog site where you can house all of your information, including experience, education, skills, honors, entrepreneurial efforts, and more.

➤ Start your own blog with a unique point of view on your industry/area of interest.

➤ Contribute value via book or product reviews, your tweets, your comments on other blog posts, your own blog articles or articles for print publications, your discussions in LinkedIn groups, and your advice via LinkedIn Answers or other forums.

➤ Found a company full-time or on the side with relevant and valuable products/services/resources for the industry.

➤ Publish and offer print and/or electronic publications.

➤ Get quoted in the media by joining HARO (Helpa Reporter.com) and contributing advice, experiences, and insights to writers and journalists seeking expert source.

*4. Beam (Path of Projection)*
➤ **What is the beam**? Your beam is your career direction and more active personal branding and career search strategy. It involves you gaining and projecting a strong understanding of where you want to go, what you want to pursue, and how you will pursue it.

➤ **How do you target your beam?** First, you need to determine what functional area, geography, and industries/companies you want to target. Then, you need to actively network your brand with potential career stakeholders. Here are some ways to start:

➤ Join associations or networking groups within your industry and try attending their events or others to meet new contacts and build your target network. Be sure to share your personal brand with those new contacts.

➤ Conduct informational interviews with target network contacts (whether or not you're seeking a job) and share your personal brand with them in your introductions.

➤ Find ways to bring fellow industry thought leaders together on a project or at an event.

➤ Find ways to contribute to the projects or events of fellow industry experts.

➤ Get recommended on LinkedIn and any other sites or networks where you or your offerings are available

*(continued)*

(*Continued*)

and/or collect and display testimonials from customers, clients, and partners.

*Personal Application*

I used this model to help develop my own personal brand during my career search. Having identified my differentiating strengths, or my foundation, to be my endless energy, out-of-the-box creativity, and relationship-building and problem-solving abilities, I looked for a word that could pull all of those strengths together into one memorable brand message. The word, or beacon, I chose was "generator" as I generate energy, creativity, relationships, and solutions to problems. I was pursuing a career in marketing and brand management, and therefore, I became a brand and marketing generator.

I passively built my tower by incorporating my brand directly into my online profiles, my resumes, and my entrepreneurial efforts. I then took a more active approach, targeting the beam by incorporating my personal brand in my interview responses, networking introductions, and informational interview outreach. It was this process that helped me successfully secure my current employment, and this model continues to help guide all of my professional and entrepreneurial ventures.

As you create, build, and improve upon your personal brand, keep the lighthouse in mind as a visual model and guide to personal branding success.

Chris Perry, M.B.A., is a Gen Y brand and marketing generator, an ambitious entrepreneur, a career search and personal branding expert and the founder of Career Rocketeer, Launchpad, and other online career services and networks, including MBA Highway, www.linkedin.com/in/chrisaperry.

---
**A WAR STORY**
---

### Jill Tanenbaum

My most recent hire sent me a beautiful hand-designed booklet that contained the best samples of her design work. She didn't just e-mail me a link or send a resume. The fact that she went over the top to design the booklet was impressive. In fact, her experience on its own wouldn't have gotten her the interview, much less the job. But the booklet did it!

---

Jill Tanenbaum, president, Jill Tanenbaum Graphic Design & Advertising (www. jtdesign.com)

---

## ■ EFFECTIVE BRANDING IS ABOUT SELLING WHAT MATTERS

 Download available

This section is designed to help you do two things that are essential to your brand:

1. Determine your marketable skills.
2. Find achievements that prove your claims.

The data you assemble here will help you write your Guerrilla Resume later (in Chapter 6). Do not skip this step! In fact, if you can't find the time to do these two steps, please stop reading now and ask for your money back—this book will be of no use to you.

Ready? Let's begin.

First, we will . . .

### ➤ Determine Your Marketable Skills

Your Guerrilla Resume will highlight your most valuable and attractive skills in such a way that employers are more likely to call you. So, what are your most marketable skills? Just answer these two questions and you'll find them:

---

### GUERRILLA MISSION

#### *Exercise #1: What do you do well?*

What do you do better and more easily than other people? Is it the work you're doing now? Something you studied in school? A hobby? Take out a pad of paper and write down your answers, no matter how unrelated they are to work. The goal is to get your creative juices flowing.

Let's take a fictitious job seeker, Sally, and write down what she does well: public speaking, sales, client service, managing projects, solving computer problems, managing others, speaking French.

---

---

### GUERRILLA MISSION

#### *Exercise #2: What do you enjoy doing?*

What skills do you most enjoy using on the job or in school right now? What would you do even if you weren't paid? Write your answers down.

Here are Sally's answers to this second question: public speaking, bicycling, client service, solving computer problems, baking cookies, managing others, speaking French, serving as a Girl Scout leader, hiking, writing.

Now, you'll see that Sally's answers to Exercise 2 produced a different set of skills from Exercise 1. That's okay. But you will notice several skills that appeared in both lists. That's better than okay—that is exactly what we're after!

When you write down a skill that you enjoy doing (Exercise 2), which you have also written down because you do it well (Exercise 1), underline it.

Let's go back and underline Sally's skills listed in response to Exercise 2 that were also answers in Exercise 1: public speaking, bicycling, client service, solving computer problems, baking cookies, managing others, speaking French, serving as a Girl Scout leader, hiking, writing.

For Sally, the skills she does well and enjoys doing are: public speaking, client service, solving computer problems, and speaking French.

Pretty simple, huh? By answering these two questions, Sally now knows more about herself than roughly 90% of job seekers who don't know what they do well or what they want to do.

Now, do this exercise yourself!

Write down your answers to questions 1 and 2 above, then underline those skills found in both lists. These are skills you do well and enjoy doing. You may come up with three, four, seven, or more skills.

You're almost done. Now, choose the two or three skills you think will be most attractive to the hiring authority reading your resume. These are your *most marketable skills*. They will form a base around which you build your profile and arsenal of marketing materials: your Guerrilla Resume and Guerrilla Cover Letter, as well as your LinkedIn, Facebook, Twitter, and other profiles. You will repurpose this information over and over again.

---

WARNING

This is the most important step in the process of writing your Guerrilla Resume. Do not go on without completing this exercise. Stop. Do it now. Write, right now!

Why? Because once you know what your most marketable skills are, you can highlight your most relevant experience, which will help you find the job that's best for you. It all flows in order, like painting your garage—first the prep work, then the painting.

Okay. We're ready for the second part of this two-step process.

---

# ■ FIND ACHIEVEMENTS THAT PROVE YOUR CLAIMS

Download
available

Now, what achievements/accomplishments prove the marketable skills you listed above? For each skill, write down at least three things you did that you're proud of, along with their specific results.

Use facts. Be specific. The more exact the better—figures, dates, percentages, and so on. What have you done to increase productivity, profits, efficiency, sales, and so on? Your achievements can be from paid or volunteer employment, school projects, or even hobbies. As long as they're relevant to the work you want to do, you may include them in your resume.

Here are some more examples to illustrate what you should and shouldn't list as achievements.

First, here's what *not* to write. These nonspecific achievements prove *nothing*:

Managed numerous projects to success.

➤ Provided sales and customer service to house accounts.

➤ Wrote reports and correspondence for busy executives.

Now, here's what to write. These specific achievements *prove* your skills:

➤ Managed 100% of 27 projects to successful completion in 2011, finishing an average of 10 days early on budgets ranging up to $256,850. Built and led teams of up to 34 staff.

➤ Increased sales $456,000 in one year by managing and penetrating 34 house accounts.

➤ Saved $52,000 after writing three employee manuals that stan-dardized operations. Also wrote more than 85 reports for team of 23 executives, meeting all deadlines.

See the difference?

It may help to interview yourself as a newspaper reporter would, and ask yourself a series of questions (Who? What? When? Where? Why? How?) about the things you've done that you're proudest of.

Example: Let's say that, in your last job, you overhauled an Oracle database. Most job seekers would stick this phrase in their resume: "Cleaned up Oracle database."

And then ... nothing would happen, because language like that tells readers nothing at all about your value on the job. The phone won't ring because employers won't be interested.

Instead, ask yourself questions about your achievements, like these:

➤ *Why* were you assigned to clean up the database?

➤ *How* did you do it?

➤ *When* did you do it?

➤ *Who* did you do it for?

➤ *What* happened as a result of your efforts?

Your answers will often lead to surprising results, which will serve as the basis for a very powerful Guerrilla Resume.

Example answers:

➤ *Why* did I clean up the database? One of our clients was ready to take their business elsewhere, because a database we built for them kept failing.

➤ *How* did I do it? By working 12-hour days for two weeks straight.

➤ *When* did I do it? In 2011.

➤ *Who* did I do it for? Our company's #1 client, which repre-sented $14 million in annual revenue.

➤ *What* happened as a result of my efforts? The client was happy and stayed with us.

Now, here's how you can rewrite this boring statement—Cleaned up Oracle database—to include the specific results of your actions:

"Helped retain $14-million account by working 12-hour days for two weeks to clean up Oracle database for firm's top client in 2011."

See the difference? A few sentences like these are all you need in your Guerrilla Resume to make the phone ring with interview requests from employers who are dying to meet you.

I think you'll agree that this is powerful stuff, right? It really is easy to uncover specific results in your work history by asking yourself these questions.

But let's give you more ways to skin that cat. Specifically, here are two more shortcuts to help you create a list of achievements for inclusion in your resume.

➤ **Shortcut 1**

Write down all the money you've saved or generated for employers in every job. What have you done to increase overall profits in your current and prior jobs? *Be specific*!

➤ Do not write: "Sold products and met quotas." Write: "Sold $516,750 in one year while exceeding all four quarterly quotas by an average of 21%."

➤ Do not write: "Produced substantial savings." Write: "Saved $45,890 in 45 days."

➤ **Shortcut 2**

You may find it difficult to quantify your work in terms of dollars. You may even find it impossible. If so, try to come at it from a different angle.

Write down everything you've done to increase efficiency or save time. Time is literally money to employers. Perhaps you wrote an employee training manual, or created a way to back up data faster each night, or devised a way to speed up shipping out on the loading dock. Anything and everything is fair game here.

The key is to figure out exactly how many hours you saved per week, then assign a dollar value to those hours. Then annualize that figure to get the highest, most impressive number. This requires you do one very important thing: You must *do the thinking* for the reader of your resume. It's your responsibility as the author of your resume to connect the dots for the reader. Make it easy for the reader to picture you as an excellent employee without thinking.

For example, say you created a process that saves 10 hours a week. How much does your employer pay someone to do what you just automated? If it's $30 an hour, add another 30% to cover insurance and other benefits, and you'll get a figure of $39 an hour. Multiply $39 by 10 hours per week and you've saved $390 per week—$20,280 per year.

So, you can write this eye-catching sentence in your resume: "Saved $20,280 annually by automating widget process."

Now, here's the fun part. When you save $20,000 here and $20,000 there, pretty soon you're talking real money. Include all these money totals in your Guerrilla Resume.

When you fill your Guerrilla Resume with specific achievements that are quantified in dollars, guess what? You turn yourself from just another job seeker, crying, "Give me a job!" to a walking, talking, blue-chip stock, who says: "Hire me at $50,000 and I can deliver a 400% return on your investment, because I've routinely saved $200,000 annually at my prior jobs."

## ■ YOU ARE CHANGING THE RULES

While ordinary job seekers are crying out, "Please give me a job!" your resume will convey a simpler, more appealing message: "Hiring me is like buying money at a discount." While other job seekers will come across as supplicants, begging for work, you will come across as a superhero minus the cape.

Put another way, you will put an immediate halt to the "apples versus apples" comparison that employers make when considering ordinary job seekers. It's now "apples versus oranges"—and you're the only orange. A big, fat, juicy one.

You're changing the rules of the game and slanting them in your favor. It's kind of like picking up a Monopoly board and tipping all the money, hotels, and houses into your lap.

Nice, eh? And it all starts when you stop thinking of yourself as an ordinary job seeker and start thinking of yourself as a living, breathing investment.

You establish your value to the company in terms of how you're going to impact their bottom line. That is truly how you negotiate. You don't just negotiate salary at the end when the offer is made. Establishing your value as an employee is a specific skill you develop and use throughout the interview process. You're laying the seeds for negotiation all along the way. That's how you have real success, by linking your skill to accomplishments, bottom-line value, and revenue to the company.

Here's a final tip on how to uncover the dollar value for good things you've done on the job. It's this: Don't be afraid to call up current and former coworkers to ask for help. You may not know how much money your top client brought in last year or what the budget was on the X-14 project you managed, but someone in the accounting or marketing department might. Leave no stone unturned in your search for accomplishments.

Let me reemphasize this critical point: When you do the thinking for the reader and include specific results in your Guerrilla Resume, good things will happen in your job search.

If you do nothing more than use the instructions in this chapter to come up with three solid, specific achievements for each job you've held, you will immediately improve your resume. You should start getting more calls from employers to interview. And you will have received full value for your purchase of this book.

But this is only the beginning. You're not just going to improve your resume. You're going to create an eye-popping Guerrilla Resume and cover letter that will produce rapid results in your job search in Chapter 6.

Okay, put the exercise and results away for now. We'll be using them soon enough, but first let's talk about what really matters most when you're job hunting—*attitude*!

---

### GUERRILLA INTELLIGENCE

*Social Media and the Guerrilla Job Hunter*

**Dennis Smith**

Why is our brand such an important part of our job-searching efforts? Because our personal brand creates a strong, consistent association between us and the perceived value we have to offer an employer.

And, like it or not, our brand precedes us in the interview process. That's right. Think of it this way: long before the wide-eyed hunter focuses his scope on the massive profile of the hairy beast, he hears the thumping sounds of the gorilla (note: gorilla, not Guerrilla) beating his chest in the jungle. The gorilla noise (and his reputation) precedes the inevitable meeting.

Similarly, you—like all job seekers—send signals to prospective employers. They precede you—by a jungle mile. However, the difference between the aimless job hunter and the Guerrilla job hunter (cheap cologne aside) is this: *a carefully crafted brand*. It whets the appetite of the potential employer, laying the foundation for a dynamic, chest-thumping interview supported by well-defined facts about goals smashed and lessons learned.

Besides a knock-your-socks-off Guerrilla Resume, there are few tools as compelling as social media to help the Guerrilla Job Hunter spread the word about his or her carefully crafted brand. Spanning 59 countries and 95,300 Internet users, recent research by Universal McCann found that almost 70% of Internet users are members of an online community (up from 52% three years ago) such as Linked In, YouTube, Facebook, or Foursquare. No longer confined to the realm of the college set, today's online social networks are an extremely powerful platform to connect with colleagues and industry professionals. In fact, according to Universal McCann's study, there are approximately 2 billion visits to social network sites every day. As someone once said, "If you are not online, you don't exist."

Chances are, then, long before you arrive for a personal interview, your hiring decision makers will look you up online. *Will they find you?* If so, what will they find? Are you sharing your knowledge in professional forums? Connecting with like-minded professionals who share your passions? Establishing yourself as the resident expert in your profession? Is your resume up to date? Does it match the profiles you highlight in your social networks? Who is in your network? And most important, does your online persona really reflect the brand you've been working so hard to create?

A lot of questions—all worth asking. Undoubtedly, this information works together to represent your online digital footprint. More important, it contributes to how a potential employer sees you. As a savvy Guerrilla Job Hunter, you understand this, and you can carefully position yourself to be "findable" online.

Need an easy place to start? Here are 10 social media activities that will help you—even if you are an Internet novice—join the online conversation and begin spreading the word about *you*.

*(continued)*

(*Continued*)

### Online Networks

1. Look for online networks that share your career focus, volunteer interests, geographical area, professional associations, or alma mater. Join them, offer to guest post on their blogs, participate in their forums, and share your expertise.

2. Get a LinkedIn account for your professional network. Then, create a group on LinkedIn focused on your profession (e.g., the "Wireless Hires" group, which I started in 2007, has almost 30,000 members). Invite the experts in your profession to join the group.

3. Get a Facebook account. Smart job hunters use the massive demographics of Facebook (more than 500 million active users) to their benefit. Ditto with Twitter (use it to follow the online conversations about your profession, your company, and you).

4. Check out podcasts and iTunes and listen to thought leaders, not just in your professional arena, but in other areas as well.

5. Get a StumbleUpon.com and/or Digg.com account for voting, and a del.icio.us account for social bookmarking.

### Blogs

6. Create a blog (e.g., iamMedical.com) or a microblog (e.g., Twitter) and begin interacting with and reaching out to your target audience.

7. Comment on other people's blogs. This is a great way for others get to know you, especially when your ideas are pertinent and meaningful.

8. Promote others—their blogs, articles, and ideas—on your site.

9. Don't let your blog go static. Keep it fresh with a daily mix (or at a minimum, three times a week) of information, opinion, interviews, and lists. Throw in an occasional self-recorded YouTube video and you'll cement your brand more quickly in the eyes of your audience.

**10.** Subscribe to Google's web-based feed reader to keep up with the blogs and news pertaining to your industry (reader.google.com).

Tim Sanders said, "In the twenty-first century, our success will be based on the people we know." Guerrilla Job Hunters get this, and because they understand that relationships serve as a predictor of our success, they include social media as a standard part of their job-search strategy.

Make no mistake—no other investment opportunity can compare with the global reach of the Internet in your efforts to evangelize the value of your brand. Social media will help you use the power of the network to gain opportunities and build relationships. In other words, it will help you get the attention—your brand in the crosshairs—of the people with whom you need to connect.

Dennis Smith's LinkedIn profile: www.linkedin.com/in/smithtx e-mail: smithtx@gmail.com Twitter: @DennisSmith blog: www.iamMedical.com.

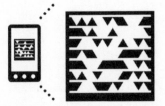

**Get the free mobile app at**
http://gettag.mobi

*Chapter* 3

# Attitude Check

## *Upfront and Personal*

Kites rise highest against the wind—not with it.

—Winston Churchill

The most important characteristic of the Guerrilla attitude is the *penchant for action.*

You may have noticed times are tough. Well, they're tough for businesses, too. Now, more than ever, employers need people who can create solutions to their problems and add value to the business. Today that means you must be able to be a revenue generator, whether that means saving your employer money or creating wealth.

On top of this, employers want to hire positive people as much as they need to hire people who are competent. Hiring managers often refer to it as "gut feel." It's an irrational emotional connection. If you have both a great attitude and the right experience, the employer's decision becomes obvious.

When hundreds of job hunters have similar skills, most employers I know, including yours truly, will hire an employee with a great attitude over a slightly more experienced one with an okay attitude. Why is that, and how do you show it?

## ■ THE IMPORTANCE OF A CAN-DO ATTITUDE

Employers face a future of constantly accelerating change where they must look aggressively for ways to expand, grow, and stay in business. They are hiring employees who will have a positive impact on the company's results. When employers interview they look for people who:

➤ Believe they can change the impossible into the possible.

➤ Do things better, smarter, and faster as a natural force in their life.

➤ Can find new ways to accomplish something without a map.

➤ Will relentlessly search until they find a way.

Hiring managers spot "can-do" people immediately. They're the ones who relish in describing the obstacles they faced and how they overcame them—in fine detail. Can-doers are also quick to admit they haven't been victorious every time, but they analyze each failure and take away valuable lessons from it. That's what employers are hoping for, and they'll make every effort to hire job hunters who can demonstrate that they have gone the extra mile, who are ready to shoulder a little more responsibility when needed, and who don't automatically expect to be rewarded for it.

Most employers have had the pleasant experience of interviewing a job seeker who had a certain nebulous quality they couldn't quite put their finger on. That experience encouraged them to hire a rookie with a bounce in her step and a desire to win. And every employer is bound and determined to find the next diamond in the rough—where the rough is the experience, not the attitude.

Employers hire people because they want to grow their business. If you approach your job search with a negative attitude that conveys you just want a paycheck, employers will pick it up quickly and react accordingly.

Guerrillas leap tall buildings . . . because their attitude proclaims "can-do," and they do not let the naysayers of the world get them down. Adam Lambert of American Idol fame has done quite well for himself since finishing in second place. Lambert continued to push forward to find the success he wanted.

You must decide right now to accept all setbacks as temporary. If you were good enough to be interviewed at a company, then you doubtless have what it takes to land a similar position with another. It is your attitude in reaction to an event that colors your success.

## GUERRILLA INTELLIGENCE

### Job Hunting and Dating
#### Dave Howlett, RHB

Looking for the perfect job is like searching for that perfect partner. Some of the best job and love matches are set-ups. So how on earth can you get people to say nice things about you when you aren't in the room? How can you be confident they'll smile and say, "Hey, I know someone who would be a great match!"

Recently I chatted with an executive assistant who works at a large wealth management firm. She told me she had been with the company three years. She confided that she had been referred by a friend who also worked there. I asked her if she had friends she would also refer into the company.

"Some of them," she replied.

"Why wouldn't you refer all of your friends?" I inquired.

She shrugged, "I guess some would embarrass me."

#### You Need to Make Others Look Good

Word-of-mouth and referrals happen when your friends know you aren't going to embarrass them. If you possess "an interesting personality" it's likely your friends won't bring up your name. Think about it; they can envision their friend (or boss) saying, "Who the heck referred this person?" The real issue is that your friends are too polite. They won't tell you your pants are one inch above your ankles and that your jokes are offensive. So take some Guerrilla control!

Memorize two questions and start asking them to everyone. "What is it I do well? If I could do one thing better, what would it be?" Keep a journal and look for trends. A client told me his greatest takeaway from one of my workshops was "Never turn down a breath mint." Remember, your friends have been interviewing you for years; they know exactly what you need to do to improve. You just need to get them to complain to your face.

(continued)

(*Continued*)

### Assume Everyone Is Intelligent

Ask any woman how she feels about going on a second date with a guy who went on and on about himself and then acted in a rude manner with the waiter. A managing director told me she talks with her front-office staff after interviewing a consultant/job seeker. She trusts her staff to inform her how someone acted around people he didn't think were worthy of his courtesy. That's indicative of how well the individual will fit into her company. Who do *you* consider beneath you?

### Have a Passion for What You Do

I have divorced friends who have a habit of making unkind comments about their ex and about marriage in general. "All women are after my money." "Men are such pigs." Then they ask me to keep an eye out for any dating opportunities. I am honestly reluctant to do this. Dumped from your last job? Worked for a psychotic boss? Feeling sorry for how your life has turned out? Find a good friend (or a counselor) to discuss your troubles. But *don't* use your next date or your next job interview to moan and vent.

### Get Over Yourself

Pastor Joe Palusak is an extraordinary guy I met seven years ago. Joe ministered to the needs of police and firefighters at the World Trade Center after 9/11. He shared with me a sentence that I have said aloud each week since then: "You would care less what other people thought about you if you knew how little time they spent thinking about you." Write this down and keep it on your desk.

In job seeking and date seeking, the days seem like weeks and the weeks seem like months. You start to think, "She didn't return my call because of something I did," or "They didn't like my resume and that's why they're not calling." Don't give up because one person or one company doesn't get back to you right away. Until I hear a client say, "No, we don't need you this year," I always assume they are busy doing other things and it's not about me.

You've got too much time on your hands. Get over yourself. Keep busy, keep the pipeline filled, volunteer at a school or immigrant-assistance program and put your experience and knowledge to work helping others. Join a Toastmaster group and meet amazing and motivated people (www.toastmasters.org). How would you answer this question on your next date or job interview? "So, you got divorced two years ago, what have you been doing since then?"

*One Last Thing*
Start asking couples how they met. Start asking employees how they got their job. You'll find a lot of similarities. Opportunities are around us every day. Treat job hunting like looking for a date. Make other people look good and they'll send leads your way. Then tuck your new business card inside your wedding invitation.

Dave Howlett is founder and managing director of www.realhumanbeing.org. RHB hosts seminars on networking, sales, and company culture. He can be reached at dhowlett@realhumanbeing.org.

## ■ THE THREE R's OF SUCCESSFUL JOB HUNTING

In grade school, we learned the three Rs—Reading, wRriting, and aRithmetic. Those were our most important lessons (okay, so I'm dating myself here). For job hunters, Research, Relevancy, and Resiliency will deliver an A+ interview.

### ➤ Research

As a job hunter, you need to research and determine:

➤ Which are your marketable skills?
➤ Which industries/companies should you target that use those skills?
➤ What are the specific needs of each company in your target market?
➤ Who is in a position to hire you in those companies?
➤ What is the best way to approach them?

Your research will determine the way you approach people. We talk more about research later in the book.

## ➤ Relevancy

Your offer (skills) must fit their needs. It has to solve the employer's issues, not yours. It is not about you. At the core, employers only want to know three things about you:

1. Can you make me money?
2. Can you save me money?
3. Can you increase our efficiencies?

As global competitiveness increases, employers will be looking for all three. Later in the book, we show you how to express your relevancy—value—to an employer.

## ➤ Resiliency

Resiliency is the ability to spring back from disappointment and keep moving forward. This is the quality that keeps Guerrillas focused on their goals and driving forward. Adopt a positive mind-set no matter what. Guerrillas always look for the positives even when people and events are clearly indicating they should not.

## ■ HOW TO STAY MOTIVATED

Plan your work and work your plan—most people do neither. Guerrillas do both.

Rejection is a fact of life when you are job hunting. It's hard not to take it personally because every rejection pushes all the wrong buttons—not once—but sometimes hundreds of times. (Try being a recruiter!) What is even worse than the rejection letters is dead silence—the lack of acknowledgment that you even exist.

Job hunting is not a lot of fun. You will be rejected and ignored and eventually the stress gets to everyone. You can lessen the sting and still maintain/develop that critical can-do attitude by taking the following four empowering steps.

## ➤ Step 1: Take Charge of Your Job Hunt

Only you know your strengths and weaknesses. Only you know what you really enjoy doing. Only you know where you want to work and why. Only you know how you can help a prospective employer. Only you can articulate your interests and strengths in a cover letter and resume. Don't let anyone else do your resume or your cover letter. You need to do it yourself. You can ask people to review it but it must come from you—even if you are receiving outplacement counseling. Come interview time, you need to mirror the person you have portrayed on paper or you will strike out. You can sell yourself better if you own every word on the page.

## ➤ Step 2: Adopt a Tough Mind-Set

Surround yourself with positive people. Get rid of anyone who sympathizes with your plight and is eager to commiserate. You do not need sympathy. You need support, and there is a huge difference. Supportive, helpful, optimistic family, friends, and reputable professionals remind you of your strengths and give needed encouragement and feedback. Sympathizers zap your energy and self-esteem. Staying inspired requires the input of inspiring people, so find a trusted confidante who can help you polish your presentation, provide moral support, and strategize.

## ➤ Step 3: Stay Focused

You need to feed your opportunity funnel in the same way that salespersons feed their sales funnel: so many leads, so many calls, so many interviews. Like a good salesperson, you need to track and record your efforts. You must keep a record to show yourself that you are making progress. If you can visually see progress, you will have an extra incentive to keep at it. If you've completed 10 calls today, then record it. If you have sent out a batch of networking letters, note that, too. I encourage my friends to chart their accomplishments on the wall as I do, because "seeing is believing." Note how many interviews you've scheduled, calls you've made, callbacks you've noted, and how much research you've completed. It is critical to be able to view your job-hunting funnel to ensure you have adequate leads to provide a steady supply of interviews.

## ➤ Step 4: Think Positive

As Henry Ford once said, "Whether you think you can or whether you think you can't, you're right." It is important for you to believe you'll succeed. You must convince yourself, through your own self-talk, that you are successful. Write out positive affirmations about your job-hunting skills such as the following:

- ➤ I interview well.
- ➤ I come across with confidence in interviews.
- ➤ I find the perfect positions that use and grow all my talents.

Keep your statements in the present, not the future tense. Read your list every day. Post it at eye level as a subliminal motivator. You can be your own worst enemy or your biggest fan. Give yourself credit for what you've completed and don't beat yourself up over what you haven't yet accomplished. Work at a steady pace with your end goal in mind. Your new job, and the burst of self-esteem that comes with it, will be worth all the effort.

> Most people give up just when they're about to achieve success. They quit on the one-yard line. They give up at the last minute of the game one foot from a winning touchdown.
>
> —ROSS PEROT

# ■ GUERRILLA TIPS FOR STAYING MOTIVATED

➤ Regard every "no" as a "not today" and a step closer to "yes." This book explains how to repackage and repitch yourself until the persuasion works.

➤ Monitor your self-talk. Only you have the power to change your attitude and your perspective. Keep a vigilant eye out for negative self-talk. Notice what you are saying to yourself as you move through your search. Your mental dialogue can boost your esteem or drag you down.

➤ Measure yourself by your own standards. Avoid comparing yourself with others. People aren't going to tell you things are tough in their lives. When you ask how they are doing, they usually will say, "Great. Never better," which will make you feel like crap. That's just their game face; they are not doing any better than you are. You are the only person you need to please. If you stick with your plan, you will achieve success.

➤ When someone suggests you try something new—do it. Guerrillas aren't afraid to try new things and fail. I recently had a woman tell me that none of my ideas would work, although she hadn't tried even one of the 50 suggestions I gave her—which might explain why she has been unemployed for two years.

➤ Stay healthy. Get enough sleep. Eat well and exercise. A brisk walk at noon will burn off the blues and ward off the flu. See your doctor if you are always sad. If it is wintertime, you may not be getting enough sunlight.

➤ Be social. Get out and see your friends and don't talk about your job hunt all the time, but do let people feed you leads and encourage you.

## A WAR STORY

### A Risk That Paid Off

*Rayanne Thorn*

Three years ago I saw the writing on the wall. My job as a corporate recruiter was at risk. The trickling fallout of the recession was taking its toll, seemingly one soul at a time. I surveyed the landscape of my gig and realized that, due to the changes that were taking place within my company and on Wall Street, I needed to prepare. I needed to prepare for the worst. I wasn't really sure how to do that. My own landscape included a marriage beyond resuscitation, a job that was becoming as endangered as a spotted owl, and escalating bills.

I decided to look for work, and once I secured a new position and got that first month under my belt, I gave my husband his pink slip. With one less income in the house, the third issue—bills—was not going to go away any time soon. I had begun to write about recruiting and gone back to school to get my business degree, so life was well-rounded between my daytime job and the numerous activities my gut was telling me in which to get involved. Number one activity? Social Media. I had been unable to get enough of it—interestingly enough, I still feel that way today. While I watched the tragedy of the new recession unfold, my online writing increased, and with much consternation from those around me, I decided that I needed to focus on New Media/Social Media. I needed to figure it out and use it. I knew I did—I was pulled to it like a moth to flame.

I took a huge chance in making the choice to write more and dive into an unproven area of business. The thing is, the risk paid off. Through my study and writing, new areas opened up to me. I left the software sales recruiting firm at which I had landed and went in-house: my house. I began to consult with small businesses about hiring practices and how to use social media to augment their online presence with the hope of increasing revenue as a result. I couldn't stay away from the computer. I started getting asked to speak at local business meetings and networking events. I developed Bonus Track and presented the idea to Jason Davis here at RecruitingBlogs. I worked consistently every day to build my own personal online presence. I created profiles on every network I could get my hands on. I attended networking events as close as two blocks from my home and as far away as 2,600 miles. My bank account was nonexistent and I was afraid, but I kept at it.

Why? Why would I keep plugging along, working so hard at something that didn't come close to paying my living expenses and supporting my family? Because it was work. It was hard work, and in my book, hard work always has a payoff. Always. The risk seemed greater every day. Every day, bills arrived at my door. Every day, I seemed to get further away from my goal. Then, about a year into my quest to survive and thrive, I met someone at a networking event who retained me to help him market his business—using social media. Then I contracted with someone else. Then someone else.... It was working, I was working, and I loved what I was doing. And it was hard work; it was constant work. I worked long hours and tried everything I could to scrounge a few dollars together to buy groceries. My children needed to be fed; I needed to be fed. I will be honest with you, it was extremely difficult. It was the hardest thing I have ever done. I wasn't sleeping because those hours were filled with worry.

As a result of my involvement and work at RecruitingBlogs, I started getting noticed and my requests for conversations were being granted. One such request was to speak to and have lunch with Kelly Robinson at Broadbean. By the end of our first conversation, Kelly offered me a job. A full-time job—not a contract position as I had first thought. That was in the summer of 2009. The risk, the macaroni and cheese, the endless hours spent online building relationships and expanding networks, the marketing and business plans written for clients and partners, the late nights spent writing and blogging, the losses, the changes—they were all worth it. Social media brought me significant ROI. The investment hurt, the ache in my stomach was hunger, and not just for food but for total sustenance.

It was a risk that paid off more than my credit cards—a nice side effect, by the way.

Having worked in many facets of recruiting, technology, and social media, Rayanne Thorn is well-versed in what makes the best recruiters tick. She is an avid writer and loves to unveil a business twist in all things. Contact her at www.linkedin.com/in/rayannethorn.

## ■ THE FOUR MOST COMMON CAUSES OF JOB SEARCH FAILURE AND HOW TO AVOID THEM

Do you have a job search plan? It is the little things that trip you up when you are job hunting. You know, the inconsequential details like knowing what job you want or expecting other people to do your job hunting for you. Here are the four biggest mistakes and how to avoid them.

### ➤ Mistake 1: Fuzzy Goals

To wage an effective job-hunting campaign, you need to know your marketable skills and where you can sell them. Starting a job search before you know the job you want and what you have to offer will end in frustration. Employers expect you to be able to tell them how you can contribute. They don't want to figure it out for themselves, and that is not in your best interests anyway. If you are going to expend the effort to find a new job, then take the time to do it right. Target your efforts toward a job you want—or you'll likely be job hunting again very soon.

*The Solution for Fuzzy Goals*
The answer to fuzzy goals is self-assessment.

> ➤ What skills do you most want to use? No point getting a job doing something you hate.
> ➤ Where do you want to work? You need to identify your top 10 employers.
> ➤ What can you do for them?

If you can't do this yourself, find a career counselor and invest in yourself. More important than telling you what salary you can command, career counselors will help you understand the following:

➤ Your likes and dislikes.
➤ Your unique marketable skills.
➤ The transferable skills that you enjoy using most.
➤ Your most prominent personality traits.
➤ The working conditions and types of people you most value.

To do this on your own, read: *Claiming Your Place at the Fire: Living the Second Half of Your Life on Purpose*, by Richard J. Leider and David A. Shapiro (San Francisco: Berrett-Koehler Publishers, 2004) and Steven Covey's *7 Habits of Highly of Effective People* (New York: Free Press, 2004).

The following web sites also have tools you can use to help discover your purpose:

➤ Mission statement builder tool at www.franklincovey.com/missionbuilder/index.html
➤ The Inventure Group at www.inventuregroup.com

➤ **Mistake 2: Procrastination**

I had a colleague 20 years ago who lived to reorganize his office. He had the most meticulous desk and working area I have ever seen. He would do anything to avoid making marketing calls. Daily he would regale his colleagues with the elaborate tracking systems he built to log how many people he interviewed. I felt totally inferior, as my office was a living, breathing disaster. It was only after I left to start out on my own that I discovered that during the time I billed $758,000, he billed $5,000. You need to be able to find your files, but don't let that block finding your dream job. There is a huge difference between activity and results—$753,000, if my math is correct.

*The Solution for Procrastination*
Admit you are terrified at the prospect of failure. Most people live in constant fear that someone else is going to find out that they are not really as good as they say they are, so you are in good company. It is all in your head—literally; fear of failure and fear of rejection cause many people to create the perfect resume or cover letter over

and over and over again—but never send it. You have to complete the process by putting the resume in the mail and following up by telephone. The sooner you start, the sooner you will finish. Recognize that activity still matters, as long as it is the right activities that move you closer to your goals. Here are a few truisms to keep in mind if you are procrastinating:

➤ You were hired for your last job without a perfect resume.

➤ If you increase the quality (targeting of employers) and the quantity (sending resumes and calling to book interviews), you will experience explosive results.

➤ Nearly 50 million people were hired last year in the United States amidst the worst recession in modern history. Well, guess what, that represents:

➤ 137,362 successful job hunters every day, 364 days a year

➤ 5,723 per hour

➤ 95.39 every minute

➤ 1.5 per second

That means that 364 days per year, while you are poring over the latest revisions to your resume, thousands of less qualified people are getting hired.

For years, I thought that there must be some magic words other recruiters were using to pull their deals together. I read dozens of books on sales techniques that all offered similar advice: If you enlarge your funnel, you will increase your results. Get at it now!

➤ **Mistake 3: Relying on Others Too Much**

Job hunting is a do-it-yourself activity. There is just no way around it. Unlike baseball, you can't substitute a pinch hitter, yet many people rely exclusively on personnel agencies and executive search firms. This "let-the-other-guy-do-it" approach puts the burden of responsibility on others who, in most cases, neither know you nor care about your future.

*The Solution for Relying on Others Too Much*
You need to develop your battle plan for approaching employers. You need to choose your target companies and coordinate your approach personally. You don't get to send in troops. You're it. You need to be on top of all the details of your job search, personally, every

minute. Nothing less than your total commitment to your own success will do.

Your campaign should include a cross section of weapons and tactics:

➤ Networking
➤ Targeted marketing
➤ Newspaper classifieds
➤ Job boards, Facebook, Twitter, LinkedIn
➤ Third-party recruiters

### ➤ Mistake 4: Lack of Preparation

There is nothing worse than a candidate who comes to an interview unprepared. Job hunters who haven't taken the time to research the company appear more interested in themselves than in the challenges of the job. I have seen many people disintegrate before my eyes when a client has asked a question as simple as, "So, besides what David has provided to you, what do you know about our company?"

*The Solution for Lack of Preparation*
Look at the hiring process from the other side of the desk—from the employer's perspective. Employers want to know that you've gone out and looked at their industry and understand where they're going. Research, research, research—and then match your experience to their needs. Ask yourself, "What do they need a new hire to provide for them?" Then practice answering typical questions like, "Why should we hire you?" with answers that show how your skills and experience will solve their problems.

As a Guerrilla job hunter, you now know what you need to avoid doing. The solutions involve common sense and are easy to implement, so don't procrastinate.

## ■ THE MOST POWERFUL WAY TO CHANGE YOUR RESULTS

When you recognize that the basic aim of every company is to stay in business, you can begin to position yourself as a solution to their need to create and serve the customers who keep them in business, instead of focusing on your need for a job. Most people understand this intellectually but fail to act on it because on the surface it seems too simple an explanation.

"Solution selling" is in vogue all across the United States for a very good reason—it works. In solution selling, you begin by understanding your customer's business and therefore the need for the solution your product provides. You know what the buyer needs because you have researched the company to discover its "pain points."

When salespeople focus on solution selling, they increase the value of their products and services because their product is not viewed as just another list of features like those of every competitor. As a job hunter, you increase your value exponentially when you focus on the employer's needs.

For example: Two equally qualified accountants apply for a job in the accounting department of a growing company. Job hunter A researches the company and discovers the company plans to do an initial public offering. In his cover letter and resume, A emphasizes his experience with publicly traded companies. Job hunter B, who is equally qualified, sends in a standard cover letter and resume.

Job hunter A gets the call, and in the interview discusses the company's needs against the backdrop of his experience. The results are predictable—job hunter A gets hired and job hunter B is never even considered.

Job hunting can actually be that simple, yet all too many job hunters, even those adept at marketing, focus on their needs and not the employer's. Think about what you have to offer the company in light of its ability to serve its customers and grow—when you understand how you can help solve the company's problems, your interview becomes a business discussion—and that's what you want.

## ■ MANAGING YOUR SCHEDULE AND PLANNING YOUR WORK

Looking at your job hunting as flextime or a mini-vacation is a mistake. If you want to succeed, you need to stay disciplined. I have met too many people who have said, "I'm going to take the summer off," only to be scrambling before winter comes. Good for you if you can do it, but while you are lounging by the pool, Guerrilla job hunters are taking opportunities away from you. My advice: take two weeks off after you land a job.

Your full-time job is now looking for a job. Begin your day between 5:00 and 6:00 A.M. At that time of the morning, you will be free from distractions, and many executives will be in their office waiting for your call (I'm kidding). They will be in the office trying to get a jump on their day's work, and you will be a nice distraction—after you learn how to talk to these people. It is also a mental conditioning exercise.

When you're job hunting, you need to maintain a regular day schedule. You must start your day at the same time every morning. You also need to finish on schedule and walk away at night or you'll quickly go nuts. My suggestion has always been to start at 5:00 A.M. working the phone and doing the related record keeping until 3:00 P.M. At 3:00 P.M. you start planning your activities for the next day and take any calls that come in from employers.

Balance your activity levels carefully. You need to plan your attack, and be immersed in the minutiae of your campaign on a daily basis. There is no point in firing off a thousand resumes and not following up on any of them—because the follow-up is what gets you the interview. Nor is it sensible to forsake uncovering new opportunities while you are interviewing, because you may not land any offers and then you will have to start all over again from ground zero.

Your day should be organized around calling employers to arrange interviews, networking, researching new opportunities, talking to head hunters, sending correspondence, and interviewing. To the best of your ability, you should establish a routine for your activities. You want to do high-stress things when your energy level is at its highest, and call employers when they are most receptive to a call.

If you wake up each day in a cold sweat, start your day by networking with your friends because they are more likely to be pleasant than will a complete stranger. If you have a heart of stone, you can begin calling employers first thing in the morning.

I have included an organizer as one of the free downloads on the GM4JH.com web site for planning and monitoring all the essential components of your job search. I suggest you take it to your local photocopy center and have it copied onto an 11- by 17-inch sheet of paper. Keep the organizer on your desk—it'll be obvious what needs to be done at all times:

➤ Make the calls to employers to set up interviews first thing in the morning (5:00 A.M. to 8:00 A.M.). Hiring managers will be easier to reach and are likely to be in a good mood because no one has had time to spoil their day yet. You are a solution to the problems they had yesterday—a welcome distraction. Trust me, when this is done correctly you will be appreciated and treated well.

➤ Next, move on to making networking calls to friends and associates to whom you've sent your resume. Put your effort where the results are going to appear first. You also want to make these calls early in the day because generally you won't have been rejected by many people yet and your voice will project enthusiasm (if you have already been rejected, it likely wasn't work related).

➤ Call recruiters next—after 10:00 A.M. Recruiters block out 8:00 A.M. to 10:00 A.M. for marketing calls. So, although you want to reach them early in the morning, do not interrupt those marketing calls . . . after all, they could be marketing you.

➤ Next, call those companies you identified yesterday as potentials. Use your voice mail scripts (more on this later in Chapter 12, Hand-to-Hand Combat: Winning the Face-to-Face Interview).

➤ Lastly, prepare for tomorrow today. Make a list of companies for tomorrow and start researching them on the web.

Now, some people think that getting an offer is the only indicator of success in job hunting, but I am going to tell you they are wrong—dead wrong. Job hunting is a process, with a beginning, middle, and end; if you nail the beginning and middle part early in the game, the end comes quickly.

## ■ THE GOLDEN SELLING HOUR(S)

If your calls are constantly being blocked by secretaries or receptionists, change your tactics. The best times to reach an executive are before 8:30 in the morning and after 5:30 P.M. Most are at their desk early in the morning and leave late. Support staff generally only work from 9:00 A.M. to 5:00 P.M. When in doubt, call the main number until you don't get a receptionist.

Personally, I coach my family and friends to get up at 5:00 A.M. and leave their well-scripted voice mails then. (More in Chapter 12, where I discuss the psychology of voice mail.)

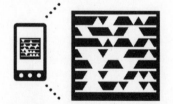

**Get the free mobile app at**
http://gettag.mobi

# Chapter 4

# Your Guerrilla Strategy

## *Think Like a General—Execute Like a Sergeant*

The general who wins a battle makes many calculations in his temple before the battle is fought. The general who loses a battle makes but few calculations beforehand. Thus, do many calculations lead to victory and few calculations to defeat: how much more no calculation at all! It is by attention to this point that I can foresee who is likely to win or lose.

—SUN TZU, *The Art of War*

Unlike the one-size-fits-all strategies in most job-hunting books, the balanced approach in *Guerrilla Marketing for Job Hunters 3.0* blends the best of networking, target marketing, cold-calling, and public relations into a cohesive framework for success. Strategy underpins every suggestion in this book. There is no silver bullet for job hunting. If there were, the publishing industry would not be grinding out new books because everyone would know exactly what to do.

Networking is not always the answer; neither are direct marketing and job boards. Instead, consider combining several tactics with the correct weapons to create a Force Multiplier Effect. It can lead to victory—your dream job. This section will show you how to plan your strategy, marshal your resources, and then execute it flawlessly.

## ■ THE HIDDEN JOB MARKET AND WHY IT IS HIDING

Okay, so it is a misnomer. The hidden job market isn't really hidden. It is just not in plain sight. It is called the hidden job market because of the way jobs are created and filled.

Most jobs are created in a company in one of three ways:

1. The company is growing.
2. Someone quits, dies, or is transferred, leaving a vacancy (attrition).
3. Someone is being replaced, and the employer does not want the employees to know about it.

When the company is growing, the owner, president, or someone else may know they need to make a new hire, but they haven't initiated any measures to find someone. They may not have had the time. They may not quite have the budget. They may not want to go through the hassle of advertising and interviewing. So while the need is real, the job itself remains hidden in the hiring manager's head.

When someone quits, managers will first consider eliminating the job. If that is not feasible, they will look inside their organization to see if there is an employee they can promote into the role. If they can't find anyone, they'll likely ask their coworkers for referrals. If that doesn't work, depending on the size of the company, they may run an ad through HR or hire a headhunter. They may even run it on a job board or in the newspaper as a "company confidential" box ad. Companies will contact a headhunter when secrecy is required because the recruiter can conduct a search without anyone ever knowing.

In all cases, the job remains hidden to the outside world for weeks if not months; hence the term hidden job market. The only successful way to access this market is to reach the hiring managers before they opt to go the advertising or HR route. The bulk of this book revolves around creative and effective ways to reach hiring managers who are just waiting to hear from you.

At the height of the recession in August 2010, a survey of employers indicated that despite all the economic doom and gloom, only 42% of companies surveyed had implemented hiring freezes. A Guerrilla would recognize that 58% of employers were still hiring. For a quick overview of the study from the Society for Human Resource Managers, Google: "Financial Challenges to the U.S. and Global Economy and Their Impact on Organizations."

# ■ CRACKING THE HIDDEN JOB MARKET

For most people, the Internet is a mess. It suffers from too much information and too little structure. Most people looking for a job online quickly get overwhelmed with the quantity of responses from a search engine. Headhunters use the following to find new job openings:

- ➤ Targeting of competitors
- ➤ Referrals from associations
- ➤ Structured Internet searches

Here is how to reverse-engineer what recruiters do, so that you can target your next employer.

# ■ TARGETING COMPETITORS

The easiest place for a recruiter to sell your skills is to a direct competitor or at least someone who is in your industry. Go to www. hoovers.com. Enter in the name of the company and hit the "capsule" tab. This will give you a snapshot not only of the company but also of its competitors. You can play the competitor's competitors game all day at Hoover's and never finish. Go in looking for what you need and don't waste your time playing with the technology. This is a very rich resource. So is www.edgar-online.com.

# ■ ASSOCIATIONS

The next best way to research an industry is through its associations. The best site to find the association most related to your interests is the American Society of Association Executives: www.asaenet.org. All I can say about this site is wow! I recently visited it so I could e-mail a colleague in New York a place to start her search for an accounting job. I did a keyword search on "accounting" that brought back 244 hits. By refining it to just include those in the state of New York, I received 15 hits that ranged from American Association of Hispanic Certified Public Accountants to the Society of Insurance Accountants. Clicking on Society of Insurance Accountants gave me their address and phone number. The ASAE site runs the gamut from "accounting" to "youth organizations" and represents more than 300 industries. It is a great place to start.

## ■ STRUCTURED INTERNET SEARCHES MADE EASY

By far the best way to discover new opportunities is by doing structured search engine queries. And it is fairly easy to do. Here is how to do targeted research to find companies and the people who can hire you.

━━━━━━━━━━━━━━━ A WAR STORY ━━━━━━━━━━━━━━━

### Bill Humbert

A college recruit graduated from an architecture program and wanted to work for Marriott designing hotels and hotel rooms. Prior to graduation, she contacted the architecture group at Marriott. They interviewed and liked her but did not have any openings. She asked if it was okay to keep in touch. Every couple of weeks, she would send a design for a room, a balcony, a lobby, a hall area, a convention area. Finally, after six months of constant contact (and probably to get her to stop sending designs they did not need), Marriott hired her.

_____

Bill Humbert, The Humbert Group (www.recruiterguy.com)

## ■ DEVELOP A TARGET LIST OF COMPANIES

Here is an example using Google.com to search for work in advertising in New York:

➤ When you do targeted research, generally you concentrate on an industry or a geographic preference (in this case, New York City). Use whatever city you like.

Google™  Advanced Search

| Find results | with **all** of the words | advertising |
| | with the **exact phrase** | new york |
| | with **at least one** of the words | directory conference |
| | **without** the words | |

Figure 4.1  Google advanced search.

➤  We need to find the names of all the advertising companies in New York. There are easy ways to do this using the Internet. Go to www.google.com and type the following words in the advanced option in Google: advertising, new york, directory, conference. You are instructing Google to search for a directory of advertising firms in New York or a conference on advertising held in New York. We want this for leads to companies.

Your text needs to be filled in as shown in Figure 4.1. The results returned when you hit the search button will be similar to those shown in Figure 4.2.

You can see that at the time I did this search, the first result was for a conference held in New York for the advertising industry. The next two hits are both for directories of advertising companies in New York, complete with web addresses, phone numbers, profiles, and more.

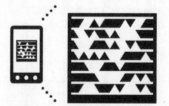

**Get the free mobile app at**
http://gettag.mobi

## ■ FIND PEOPLE WHO CAN HIRE YOU

Once you have a target list of companies, you need to find out the names of the people who can actually hire you. Go to each company's

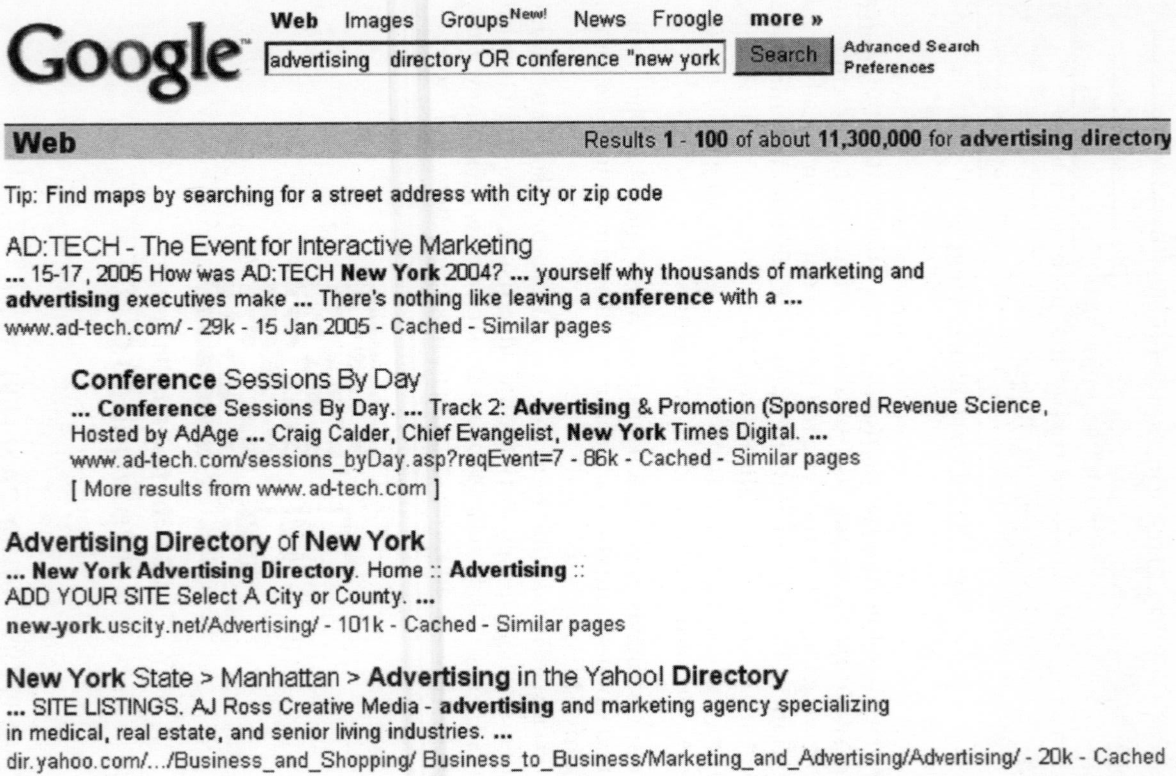

Google™

Web   Images   Groups^New!   News   Froogle   more »

[ advertising directory OR conference "new york" ]   Search

Advanced Search
Preferences

**Web**                                    Results 1 - 100 of about 11,300,000 for advertising directory

Tip: Find maps by searching for a street address with city or zip code

AD:TECH - The Event for Interactive Marketing
... 15-17, 2005 How was AD:TECH New York 2004? ... yourself why thousands of marketing and
advertising executives make ... There's nothing like leaving a conference with a ...
www.ad-tech.com/ - 29k - 15 Jan 2005 - Cached - Similar pages

Conference Sessions By Day
... Conference Sessions By Day. ... Track 2: Advertising & Promotion (Sponsored Revenue Science,
Hosted by AdAge ... Craig Calder, Chief Evangelist, New York Times Digital. ...
www.ad-tech.com/sessions_byDay.asp?reqEvent=7 - 86k - Cached - Similar pages
[ More results from www.ad-tech.com ]

Advertising Directory of New York
... New York Advertising Directory. Home :: Advertising ::
ADD YOUR SITE Select A City or County. ...
new-york.uscity.net/Advertising/ - 101k - Cached - Similar pages

New York State > Manhattan > Advertising in the Yahoo! Directory
... SITE LISTINGS. AJ Ross Creative Media - advertising and marketing agency specializing
in medical, real estate, and senior living industries. ...
dir.yahoo.com/.../Business_and_Shopping/Business_to_Business/Marketing_and_Advertising/Advertising/ - 20k - Cached

Figure 4.2   Google target directories.

web site and gather names. If you are lucky, every web site will provide the complete identification of all their senior executives, including names and sometimes e-mail, too. Web information should be up-to-the-minute accurate, but if you have any doubts, make a phone call to confirm it.

Once you have the name of the individual who is one rung up the ladder from the job you want, you need to process the name through Google again. This time you put the first and last name in the first box and the company name in the third box. This will produce a list of press releases and news articles in which the individual is mentioned, as well as conferences he or she has attended. Read an article or two and clip something memorable so that when you send a letter, you will be able to say, "I read your article in . . . about . . . which prompted me to write." Very powerful.

---

### GUERRILLA TIPS

If you get too many search results, here are ways to narrow your search.

➤ If it is outside the geographic area you are interested in, try putting in area codes instead of cities to localize the results. Area codes are a more exact means of honing in on a city.

➤ New York City consists of several boroughs, so if you do a 212 area code you will not pick them all up; you will need to search on 718, 917, and 347 to cover the whole city. If you were to just do a city search for New York you would probably miss 75% of all the jobs.

If you used Google, to find a construction job in New York, your computer screen would look like the one shown in Figure 4.3.

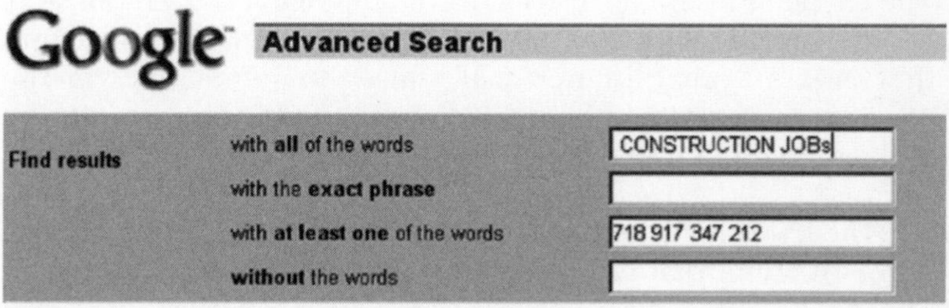

Figure 4.3   Google advanced search for construction jobs in New York.

## ■ OTHER SOURCES OF INFORMATION

Other sources of information on who can hire you can be obtained by referring to annual reports, 10-Ks, and proxies. You can look up the phone numbers in Standard & Poor's or another large general directory, or call toll-free information (800-555-1212.). Annual reports provide valuable organizational information, division and subsidiary data, locations, names, titles, revenues, numbers of employees, discussions about strategy and growth plans, and sometimes even photos of employees.

10-K reports are required by law to disclose names and titles of senior management, each executive's number of years with the company and a career summary, and his or her age. Age is relevant because shareholders have a right to know when key managers might be approaching retirement, which could materially affect the performance of the company. 10-Ks often provide plant locations and define a company's lines of business. They must also state if anything could adversely affect the company's performance or stock price, such as a major lawsuit or pending environmental expenses.

Proxy statements are required to disclose the compensation paid to the four highest paid executives. Proxies also provide detailed background information on the board of directors. You can obtain free hard copies of the annual report, 10-K, and proxy statement by calling the company. Most companies post these reports on their web sites.

### GUERRILLA INTELLIGENCE

*How to Find the Best Jobs from the Hidden Job Market*

**Simon Stapleton**

The best jobs aren't advertised in the newspaper or on the Web. Much like real estate, the best of the bunch are snapped up before they ever hit advertisements. If you scour job ad sites or the back pages of a paper, then you're really looking at the jobs the top people don't want. You're not in the domain of mediocrity, are you?

The truth is that the best jobs are created or shaped to capitalize on talent that has emerged from the labor pool (i.e., *you*). These jobs didn't exist before a potential employer knew you existed. Because top jobs are created for unique people.

The art of searching the hidden job market is to have high-impact self-marketing, providing proof and authority of your claims, making connections within organizations, working on your relationships, and then tapping these connections to seek job opportunities. How?

It starts with first knowing which organizations and departments you want to work in. So draw up your list.

Then you need to create an in-your-face, hard-to-resist profile. This is your primary sales tool. It's unthinkable nowadays to consider anything but a social profile using Web 2.0 technologies such as the ubiquitous LinkedIn, which is the best of the bunch for this kind of search as it's primarily for business use. Build up your profile to capture your personal and career achievements, and you should especially emphasize your uniqueness.

The next step is to market to your potential employers by building relationships and joining groups associated with their organization. Introduce yourself and ask others what it is like working in their organization. Demonstrate curiosity in the organization's brand, culture, and values. Enter discussions and answer questions posed by its workers to the best of your ability. Avoid going for the jugular and asking for work—that will come! Spend time building up your relationships and adjust your profile accordingly.

Once you've built quality relationships, it's time to decide which connections could become potential sponsors in each organization. These folks will introduce you to managers in the departments you're targeting. Spend time working on these people and engage in conversations on subjects of mutual interest until you've hooked them in. You'll know when this has happened, as they will begin to ask you questions about your current employment situation and about your future; you now have a sponsor. Remember, keep your profile adjusted appropriately.

Then, go all out on using these sponsors to push into your target department by asking for introductions to the hiring managers in it using LinkedIn. Be charming, be direct, but don't be pushy.

Once you've been introduced, it's time to work the charm again and to build on these relationships that will bear the fruit of opportunity. Your profile, by this stage, should be well stocked

*(continued)*

---

(*Continued*)

with your unique skills and experience as well as credible points of reference and a history of engagement with employees in your target organizations; your self-marketing has the highest impact at this stage. Maintaining these relationships, and those with sponsors, is worth every second. At some point, an opening will arise or be created for you—and you'll be first in line. Like this whole method, the key is to be persistent but not pushy. This isn't an overnight process, so you will need to keep working at it, but believe me this will pay off.

Last thought: The tools are there online and free to use. But they become most effective when you have a process and structure to work with. By applying a bit of this know-how, you'll avoid the dross and get first sight of the very best jobs even before they exist.

---

Simon Stapleton is a leader and innovator in information technology, and he has made it his mission to help emerging IT leaders with their personal and career development. His blog is www.simonstapleton.com. He can be reached at simon@simonstapleton.com.

---

## ■ STRATEGIC TWISTS ON TRADITIONAL STRATEGIES

Most people use a couple of traditional strategies:

➤ Newspaper ads
➤ Job boards

Although you shouldn't ignore these avenues completely, you should think of them as passive ways to find a job because they don't require a lot of work. The following tips will put you ahead of your competitors and at least double your odds of success.

### ➤ Newspapers

The major daily newspapers are still a rich source of job openings and not just in the classified section. CareerBuilder.com is a product of Knight Ridder and the Tribune Company, which, combined, represent more than 130 newspapers. CareerBuilder is used by many employers because it has both local and national pull through the newspapers.

Most major papers have their own online classified section in which jobs are archived. My advice, after you apply for everything that you are qualified for, go back 30 to 60 days through the online archives, because many jobs are not filled the first time they are advertised. Next:

➤ Post your resume if the site allows and enroll for the online classifieds job alert program, which notifies you of matches with your background. Be careful with personal information because you never know who has access. Get a Hotmail account just for job hunting and don't list in your home or office phone number. I suggest you use a service like www.my1voice.com to get a dedicated free number.

➤ Always check the classifieds. Display ads, or the "Career Section" as it is commonly referred to, are very expensive—as much as 100 times more costly than the classified "word ads." Small- and medium-size companies use the classified section.

➤ Business journals are full of decision makers. To find the one in your city go to: www.bizjournalsdirectory.com or www.bizjournals.com.

➤ Review the "appointments" or "onward and upward" column for the names of recently promoted or appointed executives. Send them your resume with a note of congratulations.

➤ Find out where the recently hired people came from because their old company may now be in the middle of a search that is a perfect fit for you. (Check LinkedIn for their profile and the company's, too.)

Most important, read the business and city sections to see what is going on in your town. Which companies are growing or announcing new products? They may be prime candidates for your skills. Years ago when I first got into the headhunting business, I was trained like every other recruiter in how to troll for leads. I read the classifieds every day and called the companies to see if I could help. My pitch was, "I have candidates who exactly fit your requirements," along with a bunch of other lame openers, and then I tried to overcome their objections to paying me to replicate their efforts . . . with disappointing but predictable results.

I soon realized that by the time an employer advertised a position, it was too late to try to sell my services. I would be competing with their newspaper ad and dozens of other recruiters to fill that slot and, frankly, I wasn't that good of a salesperson. I needed an alternative—fast! Sometimes you have to be careful what you wish for.

Quite accidentally, I read an article about a new office building being built. Still wet behind the ears and not realizing I was supposed to wait until they called us, I phoned the general manager and asked him if we could have coffee and talk about his project. The next day we spent most of the morning talking about the hurdles he faced in getting a team of construction guys together in time to complete the project. I volunteered to help and left with my first job order in hand. I knew nothing about construction, so I started calling my friends to see if any of them knew anyone in the construction business who would have coffee with me.

I found a guy who tutored me in the intricacies of hiring a construction manager: what to look for and where to look. I finished that project and was quickly hired to do seven more. They put me on retainer, gave me a company credit card, and offered me access to the company jet. At 26 years old I was in heaven.

All-in-all, I hired 37 people in four cities and never ran a newspaper ad—not once! Yet, I found the lead in the newspaper. So read between the lines of the business section and don't hesitate to call the president of a company you read about; he or she may be facing the same challenge as my first client. To this day, I still find the bulk of my projects by reading the business section, and I have little competition from other recruiters who are still getting their leads the old-fashioned way.

### ➤ Job Boards

According to John Sumser, the CEO of HRExaminer.com, a firm that monitors the comings and goings in the electronic recruiting industry, there are approximately 55,000 different job boards. So, where do you start looking? First, there is no master list. Nor is there any way to register at more than one board at a time. To make matters even more interesting, Monster.com, which at the time of my writing was the largest job board, has approximately 75,000 customers. With more than 10 million businesses in the United States, that means the industry leader has less than a 1% market share (www.hrexaminer.com).

Job boards do not share information with each other, so you need to register with as many as you can find time for. Only those companies that pay a fee can post a job or review your resume. Some sites are so expensive they are only used by the Fortune 1000, so if you are looking for a job in a small business, you are better off using niche boards.

Register yourself at all the top job boards and you will cover 2% of the available jobs. The usual rule in marketing is that the top 20% of companies in an industry own 80% of the market. Not true here obviously. You can find niche job boards for your industry by going to the Google search engine at www.google.com and typing in the words: "job board" and your niche (e.g., "retail" "construction" "software") and hitting the search button. That command in Google will bring you a list of job boards specific to your industry. You can also find niche job boards by function (e.g., sales or accounting at www.theladders.com).

## GUERRILLA INTELLIGENCE

### How Best to Use Job Boards
**Steven Rothberg**

Job boards have been around almost since the dawn of the Internet and became popular in the mid-1990s with the birth of some of today's biggest and best job boards. They're wonderful tools for both job seekers and employers, yet like all tools they can be dangerous in the hands of someone who misuses them. The following tips will maximize your chances of finding a great new job as quickly as possible.

#### Come, Use, Go Away
Although I'm the president and founder of job board CollegeRecruiter.com and therefore have a vested interest in getting job seekers to use job boards, I also recognize that far too many job seekers spend far too much time on job boards. No one can use all or even most of them.

Just about every job seeker will be well served by using the two big general boards (CareerBuilder and Monster), two or three niche boards that target your occupational field or experience level, and two or three niche boards that target your geographic preferences.

*(continued)*

(*Continued*)

Once you find the general and niche sites that best fit your interests, go to each of them, register, apply to all of the advertised jobs for which you are qualified, set up job match agents (sometimes called alerts), and then go away and don't come back until you receive an e-mailed alert telling you a job has just been posted. You should spend at most one day getting set up on the job boards and then at most an hour a week after that.

### Keywords Matter When You Search
Virtually every job board allows candidates to search by a combination of keywords and geographic parameters. Are you actually looking for a retail sales position in Manhattan? Then search using the keywords "retail sales" and the geographic parameter "Manhattan." Your results will be of much higher quality, as most of the potential matches you'll see will actually be of interest to you.

### Keywords also Matter When You Apply
The trick is to get your resume noticed by the employer when they are reviewing resumes submitted for a job for which you are both qualified and interested. Rather than referring to your previous experience just as an "account executive," also include the word "sales" if that's what your function actually was. Rather than referring to yourself as a "registered nurse," also include the acronym "RN" as some employers will search one way and others the other way.

### Fraud Alert
Protect yourself by posting your resume anonymously on the job boards that offer that option so that employers and fraudsters who search the resume bank can't see your name, e-mail, or other contact information. Better yet, patronize the small number of major job boards like CollegeRecruiter.com that do not sell resume searching access to employers so as to better protect the candidates who are using the sites.

### Follow-Up
Keep track in your account of the jobs for which you've applied. Follow up with each and every employer. Give them four or

five business days to review your resume. Then e-mail or call using any contact information included in the job posting. If there is no such information in the ad, and there often isn't, then go to the employer's web site and use the Contact Us or other such page to contact the human resources office. All you want to know at this stage is if they received your resume and when they'll likely review it. Be polite but firm in getting that information. Any good employer should be able and willing to communicate that to you. If they tell you five business days, call or e-mail them back on the sixth business day to ask for an update and the timing of the next step. If they tell you that they'll be setting up interviews in 10 business days, then call or e-mail them back on the 11th day. Keep repeating the process until you've been hired or excluded from consideration.

Steven Rothberg is the president and founder of CollegeRecruiter.com at www.CollegeRecruiter.com, the leading job board for college students who are searching for internships and recent graduates who are hunting for entry-level jobs and other career opportunities.

## ■ PROMOTE YOURSELF

Many think answering newspaper ads and responding to job postings on the Internet constitute a solid job search strategy. Nothing could be further from reality. In fact, you are likely to get depressed and frustrated within days if you adopt this as your major strategy. Guerrilla job hunters know that publicity—or self-promotion—is the only tried-and-true means of landing your dream job. Now is not the time to be shy. As we demonstrate in upcoming chapters, an active job-hunting campaign involves making direct contact with employers and headhunters on a daily basis.

Newspaper ads and Internet job postings should not be ignored, but they are of limited value because everyone else is using them. Guerrillas venture upstream to get the prize fish. It requires a little more effort, but they find a fishing hole that no one else has discovered. Responding to newspapers is not a strategy; it is just another tactic.

In my experience, responding to newspaper ads gives you a 1 in 1,000 chance of landing a job.

It is not unusual for an Internet job posting to attract 400 to 5,000 resumes when the economy is booming. Like those odds? And who does the screening? It is often the HR department's most junior people because it is a clerical function. Do you want them assessing your credentials? Still like your odds? Remember, employers stopped advertising during the recession because of the flood of responses.

---

### GUERRILLA INTELLIGENCE

#### *Okay, Be a Pink Chicken but Be Organized*
#### Gerard le Roux

So, you can get all caught up in trying something different—like dressing up as a pink chicken if need be (it'll work for someone)—to get that next job.

But my advice to clients who are having some trouble in the job market—or are about to have—is sure, try something different, in fact, I highly recommend it. Go ahead, be a pink chicken. But first get organized. Be professional about it. Hey, be a business. A good one.

And business is not just about sales or closing the deal. That's the inevitable result of the right activity. Business is built on systems, processes, goals, routine, planning, analysis, improvement. Boring business stuff.

Is a job hunt any different? No.

*Like a Business—a Good One—a Job Hunter Needs Five Things*

1. Clear direction and a clear offering. What are you looking for? Choose a target (a market/employer). Focus. Make your offer. Go. Go. Go. If it doesn't work out, fine, choose another, adapt. But remember: If you position everywhere, you're not going anywhere.

2. A system. A plan of activity, a schedule balanced with all the business elements from planning and goal setting to sales meetings (job interviews) and follow-ups. And innovation (think pink chicken stunt).

3. A goal. And importantly, *not* a goal related to an outcome you have no control over (crazy people hire crazy people sometimes) but rather related to your own activity. The right activity always gets results in time.

4. Persistence. Again, the right activity—perhaps including a dress-like-a-pink-chicken Guerrilla tactic—will get results. Don't dip that toe in. Dive in. My clients often say weakly, "I've tried that"—yeah, like once! No, dive in; drown until you can swim! You're worth it. Your kids think so.

5. An attitude of improvement. When the competition heats up, a lousy business throws up its hands and blames the economy, the market, the time of year. Great businesses say: "How can we improve? What can we do better? How can we add value? How can we better understand and meet our customers' needs?" And then they make those changes. Fast.

But it's easy to talk. Being a job hunter is a tough business to be in. And, sometimes, desperately so. But the way out, the way most certain to land a good, fast result is built on a routine of right activity.

So, be a pink chicken. But don't make that your only job search strategy. Be organized. Think and work like a business.

---

Gerard le Roux is the job hunter's "freedom fighter." His pioneering job search methods are published in the national media; he is author of several books on career and job search topics including *Job Search FAST TRACK—DYNAMITE for Job Hunters* and his online job search e-course has attracted more than 10,000 students. Visit www.jobsearching.co.za.

## ■ MAKE TECHNOLOGY WORK FOR YOU—NOT AGAINST YOU

The last five years have seen an explosion in technology that makes your job so much easier. Today, you can get more information faster than ever before. Job aggregators, job alerts, news alerts—they are all readily available. Uncover potential job leads at the job aggregators, which are spider engines that go to all of the job boards. Some to try are: www.simplyhired.com, www.indeed.com, and www.jobster.com.

The new kid on the block, Nat's Jobs at www.NatsJobs.com, also has a job tracker built into it that is easy to use—this way, you'll never lose a lead again or forget to follow up on a resume you sent out *and* it's free!

If you haven't already done so, subscribe to these aggregators and sign up now. It's free. To research newly available jobs from company web sites, try www.hound.com.

---

### GUERRILLA TIPS

➤ Look for positions that are one or two levels above yours; they can give you clues to what is happening at a particular company and may hint at other positions that will soon be open. When a company is looking for a new vice president of marketing, you can almost guarantee the new hire will realign the team he or she inherits. The same holds true for sales and engineering.

➤ Register at local job boards because most employers advertise and source candidates locally first.

➤ Use job boards as a source of leads.

➤ If you do not want to be bothered at home by recruiters, you should list an e-mail address as your main point of contact, preferably one you can cancel when you find a job.

---

## ■ LOGISTICS—BUILDING YOUR WAR ROOM

Next to knowing what kind of job you want, there is nothing more important than being organized. You will need to compile research, track your job leads, schedule calls, follow up your interview activities, and send correspondence. While this may not sound like much, it is a lot to keep track of, and if you misplace or lose information, it could cost you your dream job.

Here is what I suggest. First, find a space in your home where you can be out of everybody else's way—an area that you can get other family members to agree is yours and yours alone. Having said that, I must add that the lack of space is no excuse for failure.

When I started looking for my second job, I was working full-time 50 to 70 hours per week. My workspace was the dining room table in my dinky little apartment—until my best friend needed a place to stay. After he showed up, I put a filing cabinet in the trunk of my car with all my documents and resumes and a suitcase with two suits, four shirts, and two matching ties. I landed 14 interviews and 13 offers in a four-week period.

### Free Job-Hunting Tools to Download or Subscribe To

*Google Local.* Do you hate to commute? Want to relocate? If where you work is as important as whom you work for, you can limit your job search to a specific location. Google can help. At local.google.com you can search for employers and businesses in a specific area. Simply type in a business name or industry as well as your city (the more specific the better). Example: "advertising agencies near Detroit, MI." Take this string complete with the " " and put it into Google local. Always leave in the word "near" but play around with keywords and the city or address.

*Google Docs.* Ever need to change something in your resume at the last minute or wish you could show a recruiter or prospective employer your portfolio? Google to the rescue again—this time with Google Docs (www.google.ca/intl/en/options/). Make yourself two separate accounts, one where you can keep your private documents and another on which you allow employers or recruiters to view relevant material such as references, resume, transcripts, and sample projects. You might even walk someone through your portfolio during the interview if they'll allow you.

*Google Alerts.* Even more impressive for my money are Google Alerts, a service available at www.google.com/alerts. Essentially, these are updates delivered by e-mail once a day based on information you tell Google to watch for. Use it like the job board agents to establish daily feeds of the information you need. It's a fundamental tool in every Guerrilla camp, and it's free.

*News Alerts.* You can subscribe to a vast number of free services that will bring information straight to your desktop. Nearly every newspaper available on the Web has a News Alert function.

Subscribe to those you need to cover your interests. Here are a few that report on industry changes:

➤ Google News (news.google.com)

➤ Yahoo! News (news.yahoo.com)

➤ Alta Vista News (www.altavista.com/news)

➤ All the Web News (www.alltheweb.com)

➤ MSN News (msnbc.msn.com)

*Voice Mail.* Want to influence the perceptions of prospective employers? Then you don't want to miss "that opportunity" when it comes calling. With my1voice.com you won't. My1voice is a virtual phone service that works with the phone you already own. You can forward and screen calls, plus you can select a local phone number for any city you want, even if you aren't located there yet—this is a great option for people who need or want to relocate. It's also the best option for people who are employed and want to keep looking for a new job because it lets you take control of what calls you get, when and where you get them, and you can even have them delivered to your e-mail account. You can try my1voice free for 30 days.

*Lead Tracker.* One of the biggest issues you're going to face is keeping track of your leads. Responding and following up promptly is a challenge, but it must be done. SalesNexus.com is a customer relationship management tool that allows you to manage your job search from the cloud. The service is free for 30 days, so I suggest you use it when you're ready to launch. There are many features that you will find very useful like e-mail campaigns, for example.

## ■ STALKING FOR JOBS—LEGALLY

Remember the engineers in Detroit? I asked them if they knew how many jobs there were for automotive engineers in Detroit; they assured me there were none. As you can see in Figure 4.4, they were wrong. You can use this free service to search just like we did: www.twitjobsearch.com/.

And I also used Twitter Grader to see if there were any headhunters in Detroit tweeting about jobs, and of course there are: http://twittergrader.com/go/search. See Figure 4.5. Again, this is free to use and Twitter Grader is just one of a dozen tools from Hub Spot that allow you to search social network sites, even Facebook. Use it to locate jobs and power brokers who can help you. Tweeters want to be found—so it's not really stalking.

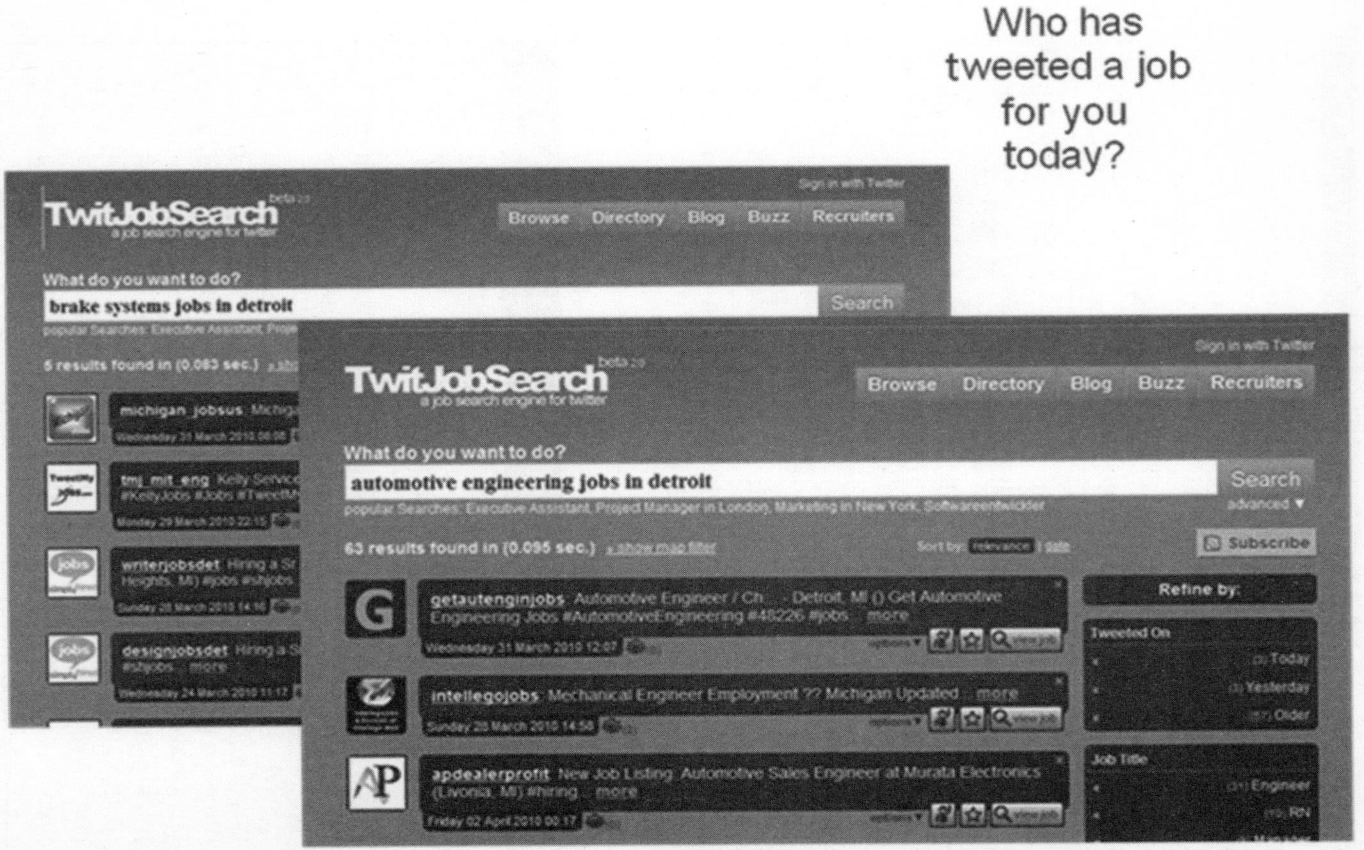

Who has
tweeted a job
for you
today?

Figure 4.4   TwitJobSearch returns open positions for "automotive engineering jobs in Detroit."

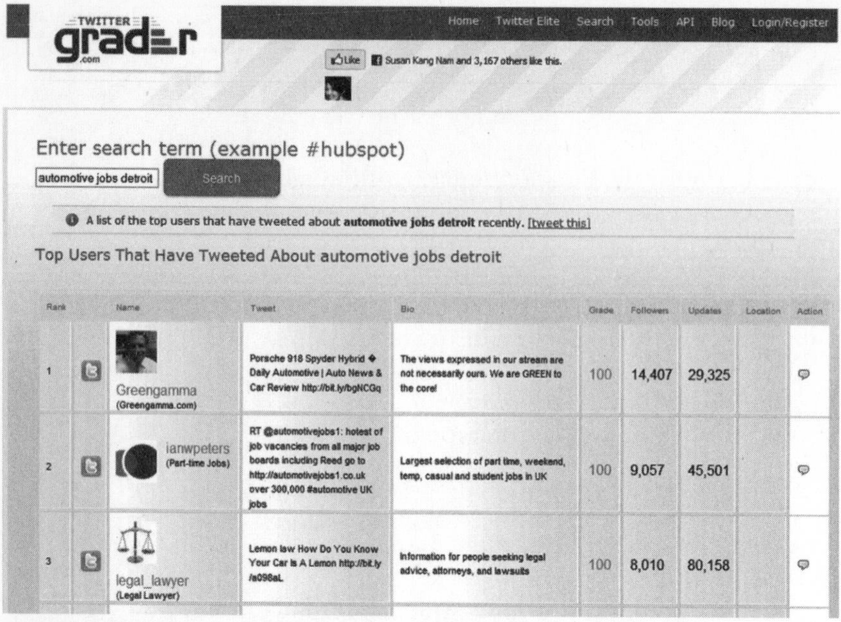

Figure 4.5   Twitter Grader.com lets you search on tweets for a particular topic.

## GUERRILLA INTELLIGENCE

### The "Shotgun Blast" Approach

#### Dave Mendoza

A weak personal branding strategy, an ineffective e-mail protocol, and a lack of online due diligence will often adversely affect the quantity and quality of job leads and interviews.

The most common mistake of job seekers is the "shotgun blast" approach. Too often job seekers e-mail, mail, or call anyone and everywhere without a strategy other than hoping the law of averages will inevitably be in their favor. In an online world, however, recruiters can sense desperation or lack of care in the approach of job seekers, and that can easily call their competence into question. For instance, if a sales candidate only wants to work in Chicago, but e-mails a recruiter in Denver who only works in semiconductor engineering, it becomes readily apparent the job seeker failed to take the time to perform minimal due diligence. Likewise, an ambiguous e-mail subject header such as "Does it make sense to chat?" without any context within the correspondence, without a resume attached, and no explanation for why the job seeker assumed relevance in the relationship, suggests minimal regard for a recruiter's time. Recruiters are keenly aware that the most adept job seekers are as capable as they are of utilizing online resources for efficient introductions. When job seekers ignore online etiquette or avoid the more efficient means of introduction, they showcase their vulnerabilities and present themselves at a disadvantage in the ever-important first impression.

*It's Not What You Know, It's Who Knows You*
The phrase, "It's not what you know, it's who you know," is one we learn early in life. We are most keenly aware of it when we submit our college applications and as we enter the workforce. Today, however, the emphasis of one's effort in effective networking is commonly misplaced. Social and professional networking used to be defined largely by power calls to foster candidate generation. Today, the emphasis is broader and often two-pronged; the effective phone call references the online connection as an introduction. Meaningful and sustainable networking emphasizes "knowledge transfer"—what you learn—in your associations and likewise a benefit by association. The personal brands of job seekers are optimized when they develop an online presence that signifies particular areas of expertise within their respective skill discipline and within a certain industry. How job seekers position themselves within this realm is critical to attracting employers via online search tools that can sort by industry, company, discipline, and organizations. The successful job seeker is always cognizant of the refined and relevant mantra, "Who knows you."

---

Dave Mendoza is an award-winning blogger, global speaker, and sourcing consultant. A corporate partner to RecruitingBlogs.com, he is one of the top 20 networkers worldwide on LinkedIn (www.LinkedIn.com/in/davemendoza, www.sixdegreesfromdave.com).

Part

II

# Weapons That Make You a Guerrilla

# Chapter 5

# Your Research Plan

## Research: The Guerrilla's Competitive Edge

There is no passion to be found playing small—in settling for a life that is less than the one you are capable of living.

—NELSON MANDELA

Research is a Guerrilla's competitive edge. It is an integral part of your job search. A company's web site and corporate marketing materials are designed to promote the best possible image; by learning a few clever research skills, you will be able to uncover and assess information that ordinary job-hunters won't have. This information will help you make informed career choices.

Most job-hunters think that reading a company's web site is all the research they need to do before an interview—but they are wrong. Guerrillas know that it is only a start. In fact, it is not even where most Guerrillas will start. When an interview is imminent, Guerrillas will visit the web site and those of their chief competitors. Then they Google the company for:

➤ Resumes of former employees
➤ LinkedIn, Facebook, and Twitter accounts
➤ Articles
➤ Blogs—personal and corporate
➤ Company newsletters

➤ Industry newsletters
➤ News clips
➤ Speeches or keynote presentations
➤ Membership in associations

The research skills discussed in this chapter will enable you to fully research any industry or company anytime, anywhere, and will show you how to direct-source jobs like a headhunter. These two skills will give you the inside track. You will be able to fill your opportunity pipeline full of jobs that other job-hunters will never know exist.

## ■ YOUR RESEARCH BUDGET

Time, not money, buys the best research. Most of the information you need is available free through your local library or online. There certainly is a lot of information that you can buy, but usually these reports are summaries of information you can find yourself with a little digging if you know where to look. You won't learn these techniques anywhere else.

The basis for all good research starts with understanding what you need to know. You want to understand the intricacies of the industries that interest you and how to best position yourself—not just into your new job—but into a succession of jobs that you can parlay into a five-star career. To accomplish this, do your research in three steps:

1. Identify which industries you want to, or are qualified to, work in.
2. Locate which companies in those industries are of interest.
3. Evaluate who has the authority in those companies to hire you.

## ■ I. RESEARCHING AN INDUSTRY

To select an industry to research, you need to know which industries employ people with the skills you are marketing. Skills assessment can be tricky if you don't have access to a career counselor or career coach. Don't fret; the fastest most effective way to determine which industries use your skills is to visit America's Career InfoNet online at www.acinet.org (also now known as www.CareerOneStop.org).

Go to their home page. On the home page, there are four major sections: Occupation information, Industry Information, State information, and Career Tools. I want you to click on one of two sections depending on where you are starting your search: (1) if you are a new grad or you want to change careers, select the section labeled "Career Tools" and then scroll to the bottom of the menu box and select "Skills Profiler" or (2) if you already know which industries you want to explore, select "Industry Information."

## ➤ Skills Profiler

If you need to get a better understanding of the industries that use your skills because you are just starting your career or want to switch careers, start with the Skills Profiler. It has a menu-driven assessment tool called "Skills Explorer" that will tell you, in about five minutes, which occupations and industries employ your skills. This is the most comprehensive tool of its kind on the Internet, and it is free. Not only will this easy-to-use tool tell you which industries use your skills, but when used in conjunction with the Industry Information tools that are available on the site, it will identify opportunities in your city or town that match your skills. Even if you already have a strong sense of what you want to do and where you want to do it, don't pass up the opportunity to consider all your possibilities.

## ➤ Industry Information

Download
available

The Industry Information section includes a menu-driven tool that allows you to look inside an industry and see which sectors employ those skills. Here are five questions you should be asking yourself as you start to explore industries. Some, but not all, of these questions are raised and answered in the available reports:

1. What are the general trends in the industry—by sector?
2. Where are the hot spots—those areas where growth will remain steady for several years?
   a. This can be represented by a group of products or services, or

**b.** By a specific geographic area.

For example, construction may be slowing down in one section of the country and getting ready to boom in another, or residential construction may have peaked and commercial construction is rising. It is important to drill down to find details if you want to make an informed decision.

**3.** Which skills are in demand?

**a.** Now and in the future

**b.** By discipline: sales, marketing, finance, engineering, trades

**4.** What is the demographic profile of the workforce? (These studies or reports are most often referred to as Labor Market Information [LMI] studies.) You want to be able to assess whether there might be a continuing demand for your skills, and a good indicator of this may be the median age of the workforce. If the median age is, say 55, then there will be people retiring soon and this might increase demand for the profession.

**5.** Is the industry prone to outsourcing or off-shoring?

Look into which businesses are starting up and getting funding from banks and venture capital firms, and look at which companies the mutual fund companies are investing in. The easiest way to do this for the mutual fund companies is to find the web sites of some of the mutual fund companies that are reported on weekly in your local daily newspaper.

Looking for start-ups? Then you have to check out:

➤ startups.alltop.com/ run by none other than Guy Kawasaki—Apple's first Marketing Guru and the author of many of the most useful books on management today.

➤ The Money Tree Survey, run by PricewaterhouseCoopers (www.pwcmoneytree.com/moneytree/index.jsp)

➤ PE Week Wire (www.pewnews.com/)

If you can't find what you are looking for, you need to contact the industry associations. When you find the national association, visit its web site and see what free resources are available to help in your job search. This could include:

➤ Labor market information studies

➤ Membership lists

➤ Industry reports

➤ A job board

Also see if there is a local chapter that may have networking events. Some associations even have official Discussion Forums. Review all the industry information with a keen eye to what the industry leaders feel the challenges are for the future. For an up-to-the-moment view, read industry trade magazines. They are listed at the Special-issues.com web site: www.specialissues.com/lol.

## ■ 2. LOCATING COMPANIES OF INTEREST

Once you have identified an industry, you need to research companies. Your research could be very local—or it may be broad and include all the companies in the industry because, frankly, you will move anywhere for the right opportunity. Your first mission is to locate national directories that include lists of the companies. A Guerrilla would start at CEO Express online at www.ceoexpress.com. CEO Express has links to nearly every source of information you need to get yourself started: news, stock quotes, and IPO filings, all in one place.

➤ **Privately Held Companies**

These are the hardest to research cheaply because the companies don't have a strict requirement to report to anyone but their limited shareholders. If they have anything to hide, like pending litigation or poor financials, you really have to dig. Here's where to start:

➤ Dun & Bradstreet (www.dnb.com/) are masters of information, much of it à la carte or free.

➤ Hoover's (www.hoovers.com).

➤ D&B Million Dollar Database (www.dnbmdd.com/mddi) has information on approximately 1,600,000 U.S. and Canadian leading public and private businesses.

➤ Forbes 500 Largest Private Companies (www.forbes.com/businesstech) is always one of my favorites, but it is only useful for the largest companies.

➤ *BusinessWeek* works well, too (www.businessweek.com).

➤ Thomas Register (www.thomasnet.com) provides information on most manufacturers.

### ➤ Publicly Held Companies

Public companies are easier to research, especially with the increased reporting requirements that have been dictated by Sarbanes-Oxley Compliance. However, it still requires work. Here are your best sources of information:

➤ Dun & Bradstreet (www.dnb.com/us); always start here.

➤ Edgar Online People (www.edgar-online.com/) searches Securities and Exchange filings by a person's name or displays all people associated with a specific company name. Very useful.

➤ Million Dollar Database (www.dnbmdd.com/mddi) provides information on approximately 1,600,000 U.S. and Canadian leading public and private businesses.

➤ Lexis Nexis (www.lexisnexis.com) has legal, news, public records, and business information.

➤ Corporate Information (www.corporateinformation.com/) is a free site that requires registration.

➤ Financial Web (www.finweb.com/) lists stocks, SEC filings.

➤ Fortune 500 (500 largest U.S. companies).

➤ Wall Street Research Net (stocks.Internetnews.com) has the most comprehensive company news, EPS estimates, links to home pages, and so on.

*Hardcore news sites you should monitor include:*

www.cnbc.com

www.money.com

finance.yahoo.com

www.marketwatch.com

www.foxbusiness.com

Next, visit those company web sites. If they are not available in this day and age, that will mean they are very, very small. The easiest way to research small businesses that don't have a web presence is your local Chamber of Commerce or the archives of the local newspaper.

----------A WAR STORY----------

*Lauryn Franzoni*

A methodical strategy paid off for this ExecuNet member who was very active in her local human resources groups. She contacted the national headquarters for the names of local chapter presidents, and mounted a campaign of contacting each one every two months. Her persistence paid off when she received an offer.

_____

Lauryn Franzoni, managing director of ExecuNet (www.execunet.com).

# ■ COMPETITIVE INTELLIGENCE

Download
available

Here are the questions you should ask yourself about each company you are interested in as you are gathering background information.

# ■ COMPANY GROWTH

➤ Is the company in growth mode? Why or why not?

➤ What external factors affect its growth?

➤ Where is this company in the cycle? At the end or just the beginning?

➤ Who are its Tier I and Tier II competitors?

➤ Is there turnover in senior management? Has it been forced by the board or did people reach retirement age? Was a successor being groomed in the wings?

## ➤ Financial

➤ What do the numbers say? How are the company's balance sheet, income statement, earnings per share, dividend(s)? what do they indicate about the company's health?

➤ What is the debt-to-equity ratio? Remember, cash is king.

➤ How is the stock price doing? Why is it moving?

➤ How is the stock doing against its competitors? Against the market as a whole?

➤ Are there other companies where you should be interviewing?

➤ What do the analysts think?

## ➤ Strategy

➤ What were last year's short-term and long-term strategies/ objectives? Were they met?

## ➤ Market Share

➤ Are they dominant players? Why? How big is the market? What percentage of the market do they own? What is the next market?

➤ Does the company have any new products/services/patents?

➤ Is the company strong or weak domestically versus overseas? Where does the company make most of its profit?

➤ What do each of the regions and products/divisions contribute to the whole?

## ➤ Technology Issues

➤ Can cost efficiencies be driven through modernization?

➤ How does the Internet affect the company? If it is a threat, does the company have a strategy to address it?

➤ **Legal and Regulatory Issues**

> ➤ Are there any pending bills or regulations that might have a significant impact?

> ➤ Are there any patent infringements?

➤ **People**

> ➤ What do people say about the company publicly?

> ➤ Is the company being sued or has it been sued by former employees?

➤ **Fit**

You don't want to waste your time and effort on companies that are not going to be a good fit. Guerrilla, use this information to get a picture of the organization. Do you think the company/organization has a future? Why or why not? What factors impede? It is critical that you understand this information thoroughly before you approach the company. Armed with this background information, you will be able to answer with confidence these typical interview questions:

> ➤ What do you know about our company?

> ➤ What are your thoughts on the challenges facing our industry and how can you help us?

> ➤ What would you do in your first 90 days if we hired you as a _____?

Imagine how surprised the interviewer will be when you can articulate what the company's issues are—how your experience fits with their needs and what you would do first. You'll blow them away. On the other hand, if you haven't done your homework before you go in for an interview, you're dead on arrival.

## ■ LIBRARIANS ARE YOUR ALLIES

If you're having trouble finding lists of companies or information on specific companies, call your local library and talk to the research librarian. Treat these people like gold. Put them on your Christmas list. Bring them boxes of candy. Buy them flowers on their birthdays. They have forgotten more about how to retrieve information than you will ever know. They are the Sherlock Holmes of reference information. So make friends, ask lots of questions, and take notes, but only after you have at least tried to find some of the information on your own.

# ■ 3. HOW TO FIND THE HIRING MANAGERS

Now that you have a list of 10 to 20 companies, you need to find the people who can actually hire you.

## ➤ Alternative 1

Guerrillas know the most direct way is often the easiest. Use your telephone. I always call first and ask who is responsible for "X." "X" is the title of the executive I want to speak with. Seven out of 10 times this will work. If it doesn't, call back at lunchtime and ask the noon hour receptionist; generally, they are not as guarded about the information they give out.

## ➤ Alternative 2

Go to each company's web site. If you are lucky, it will identify all their senior executives. Web information should be up-to-the-moment, but phone and verify.

## ➤ Alternative 3

Google your way in. If you are having difficulty finding the name, go to Google's advanced search box. Type in the company name in the first box and the title of the person you think your future boss reports to in the third box. Try doing this with the company "Google" in the first box, "vice president" in the third, and "free" in the fourth box "without the words" (see Figure 5.1).

If you run the search, you will find a list of Google's executives at: www.google.com/corporate/execs.html. This is a simple way to find information fast.

Once you have the name, run a search on the individual through Google. This time you put the first and last name in the first box and the company name in the third box. This will produce a list of conferences the person has attended, speeches, press releases, news articles, clubs the executive belongs to, and so on.

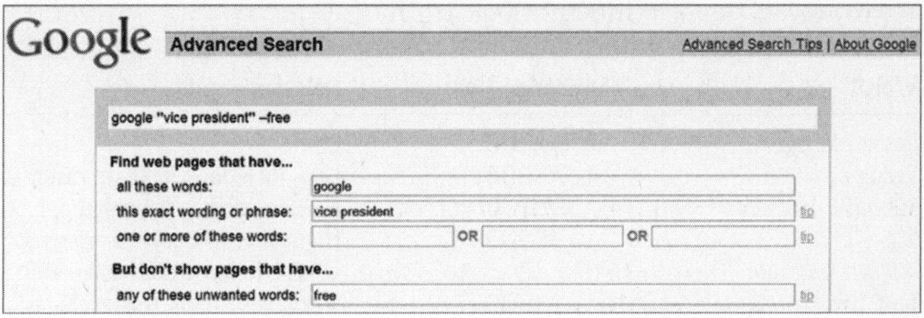

Figure 5.1 "Without the words."

# ■ A GUERRILLA RESEARCH ALTERNATIVE

What if you don't have time to do a full search because you need a job now or at least by tomorrow afternoon? Is there a faster way? Yes!

Here's a super-fast way to find nearly all the companies in your area that can use your skills:

➤ Decide what job you are going to look for. In our example, we are going to look for retail management jobs in New York City.

➤ Choose key words that are specific to the type of job you are looking for. In Figure 5.2, we use Retail and Manager. You can use a job title if you wish, in which case you need to encapsulate the term in quotation marks: "retail manager."

➤ Add these four words: "job," "resume," "submit," and "free" as illustrated in Figure 5.2.

As constructed, this search string instructs Google to return web sites that have retail manager jobs but are not ads for resume-submitting businesses.

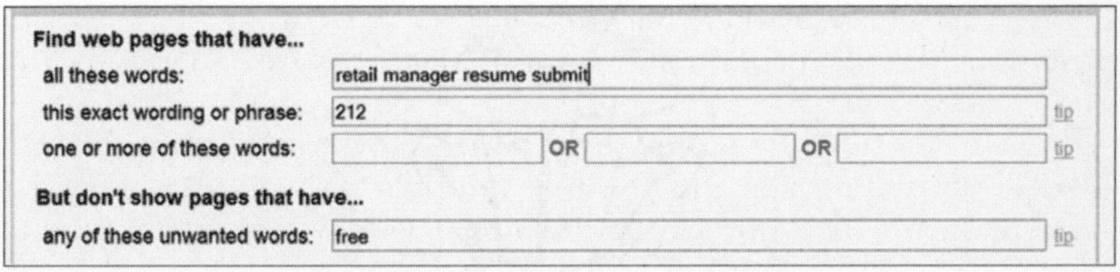

Figure 5.2 Advanced Google search.

Table 5.1   Search Term Results

| Words | Number of Hits | Relevance to Us |
|---|---|---|
| Retail Manager | 11,700,000 | Low |
| Resume | 1,670,000 | Low, includes candidate resumes |
| Submit | 302,000 | Low, includes job boards |
| 212 | 45,900 | High, it restricts responses to just the area code 212 |
| Not "free" | 1,300 | Very, very high, this excludes all the resume submittal sites and shows just the jobs available in area code 212 for New York. |

In the "without the words" option, we type the word "free." Why specifically ban the word free? Because the word free is not used on corporate web sites nor is it used in job descriptions. It is, however, used to sell resume-submitting services, and we don't want to waste time wading through those sites to find the real jobs.

You can see the number of hits that are returned by adding the words one at a time (see Table 5.1).

There are still too many hits, so we add the area code 212, which in turn reduces the hits to local retail manager jobs in the 212 area code only. This is a good list to start with.

*Note:* Your results may vary because Google changes minute by minute.

---

GUERRILLA MISSION

Now you try it. Fire up your PC and connect to the Internet. Go to www.google.com. Click the Advanced Search link and you should see a screen like the one shown in Figure 5.2. Replace the two words "retail" and "manager" with two words that are specific to your job search. Next replace the 212 area code with your area code or the area code of the city you want to research. Click the "Google search" button and start reading. This research is fast and accurate. It won't uncover every opportunity, but it will enable you to find many more offerings than you would see using just the job boards or newspapers—and you will do it much faster, too.

---

## ■ FINDING LISTS OF PROSPECTS

Using the Internet is not the only way to gather information. Here are some easy ways to find lists of prospects for your job-hunting campaign.

### ➤ Chambers of Commerce

Nearly every city and town in the United States has a Chamber of Commerce whose sole job is to promote commerce. If you call their office, I guarantee you they will give you a list of their members. It may also appear on their web site. Chamber of Commerce members tend to be among the most civic minded in your community and are quite accessible. Finding them on Google is simple: Just type in "Chamber of Commerce" with the name of your town or city and Google will find it for you.

### ➤ Industry Associations

If you are looking for information on a specific industry, business associations can be helpful. As noted, the American Society of Association Executives is a good place to start: www.asaenet.org.

Figure 5.3 Google search by industry.

> ### Industry Newsletters and Professional Journals

The targeted readership for these publications means that you can often pick up leads from the authors of the articles by calling them. These authors tend to be industry experts who know everyone.

> ### Web Sites for Conferences, Conventions, or Trade Shows

To find events that are specific to your chosen industry, do a web search for an industry name and terms such as conference, trade show, or convention.

Figure 5.3 shows the screen for a Google search for [conference or tradeshow or convention] and the industry, which for this example is medical.

Google's results reveal two large shows. Clicking on the links will bring you the site and a wealth of information (see Figure 5.4).

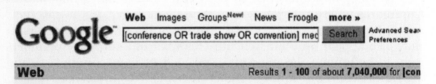

Figure 5.4 Google search industry links.

## GUERRILLA WISDOM

*Service Corp of Retired Executives (SCORE)*
### Mark Haluska

SCORE is comprised of both retired and working business executives. These people know decision makers! In many cases, they still work together, go golfing, belong to the same clubs, and mix at socials. So, they personally have a first-degree contact with decision makers, many of which are current or past close colleagues.

Most people think of SCORE as a resource (which it in reality is) when you want to get advice to start up a new business venture. But with a little tact, a true Guerrilla would turn that inside out to obtain solid leads.

Contact SCORE; ask to speak with an executive who (and this is important) has worked or (most preferably) is working in your profession/industry. They will assume you need business advice. Pleasantly greet them, preferably on the phone, and tell them you have a problem and thought they would be someone who could help. Then tell the counselor what you really need and do it in this order: tell them what you do, then quickly (in no more than one minute) hit them with quantifiable and truly impressive facts that you've outlined on your Guerrilla resume. Next, ask how your experience sounds to them.

Then, go for the gusto and ask as to how you can obtain the specific decision makers' names and contact information (not HR, unless you are in HR) at a given company or companies who could use your expertise to help them solve a pressing problem(s).

This "back door" approach will probably take the counselor by surprise, but that is okay. They have volunteered to join SCORE because they want to help people. SCORE is a free resource that all Guerrillas should attempt to use. This tactic can fast-track you into a decision maker's office, and your competition won't even think about it until they've read this book. I highly recommend you go to www.score.org/index.html first,

*(continued)*

(*Continued*)

but afterward to find a SCORE representative near you, go to www.score.org/findscore/index.html.

Contributed by Mark J. Haluska, founder and Executive Director, Real Time NetWork, www.rtnetwork.net LinkedIn address: www.LinkedIn.com/in/MarkJ.Haluska

## GUERRILLA TIPS

An immediate way to find hot leads is to ask your friends, family, or business associates who have recently landed a job in the industry if you can see their lists of prospects. The research will be current and likely pretty detailed, too. They may even know of openings that were not suitable for them but might be ideal for you.

Here are a few other sources:

- ➤ Career centers and job clubs
- ➤ College and university career placement centers
- ➤ Internet career sites
- ➤ Job fairs and career days
- ➤ Local and federal government personnel offices
- ➤ Yellow pages
- ➤ Your area business journal (www.bizjournals.com)

# ■ STUFF THE CIA WOULD RATHER YOU DIDN'T KNOW

The length of this book does not allow me to do a detailed exposé on the really advanced means for unearthing information. A lot of cloak-and-dagger work goes on behind the scenes of many search assignments. Your quest to find your dream job is unlikely to require that kind of search. Explaining those advanced strategies and tools is beyond the scope of this book and would require two or three hundred additional pages, but I won't leave you hanging either.

The United States has two gurus on the application of competitive intelligence to recruiting and job-hunting: Shally Steckerl and Dave Carpe. These two professionals are the absolute best when it comes to using the Internet. I highly recommend you visit their web sites if you want more information or a deeper understanding of how to use search engines and the Internet to maximize your job search.

➤  Shally Steckerl's site Arbita [http://aces.arbita.net/] has more than 100 screens full of tips and techniques for finding your way around. A "Google GuruGuide" and a "Tool-Bag CD" are available on Shally's site.

➤  Dave Carpe is a virtual magician whose cornucopia of tools and tricks will take you deep into the world of competitive intelligence. The only way to find Dave is to Google "Confessions of a Call Girl . . . or How to Give Good Phone." Or sneak on to www.davidcarpe.com/

---

### GUERRILLA TIPS

➤  Use free resources first: Yellow Pages, Internet, and the library.

➤  The more specific you can be about what you are looking for, the more relevant will be your results.

➤  Use free government services—you have already paid for them.

➤  Determine which companies are doing business in your field.

➤  Narrow your choices geographically if appropriate—look locally first.

➤  Read the annual report first and then compare it with last year's.

➤ Start with the company web site.

➤ Run a Google search.

➤ Review appropriate blogs.

➤ Google former employees.

➤ Always weigh information with a critical eye.

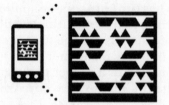

**Get the free mobile app at**
http://gettag.mobi

# Chapter 6

# Resume Writing and Cover Letter Boot Camp

## *Overhaul Your Personal Marketing Materials*

In order to be irreplaceable one must always be different.

—COCO CHANEL

Despite advances in technology, job hunters have predictable habits. Most look for a job the same way they always have. They write a resume. Ask their friends. Respond to newspaper ads. Click and apply through job boards. And wait. And wait. And wait . . . for something—anything to happen. Not too terribly twenty-first century of them.

Guerrilla, your resume is a marketing tool. It must compel its reader to pick up the phone and call you. Job hunters who write conventional resumes can count on the competition to be fierce. Let me show you a more successful approach.

But first . . .

## ■ WHY YOUR RESUME MAY BE OVERLOOKED

My wife will periodically call me at the office and ask me to pass by the supermarket on my way home to pick up bread and milk. Like most men, I enter the supermarket on autopilot with my list in hand and head straight for the items I need. The nice displays and weekly specials are a blur as I pass by. The way I shop for groceries is not unlike how your resume gets screened when you apply for a job. Generally, the people who do the first pass on a stack of resumes are working off a list someone handed them with the instructions to "whittle down this pile by looking for these skills." So, that's all they scan for.

There isn't really a lot of thinking involved beyond that list. If you have the right stuff your resume goes into one pile; if not, well you're out. If the checklist says "Oracle" and your resume says "database," you're out—even though most people know that Oracle is a database. What about reading between the lines? There's no time, and generally little incentive, ability, or interest, from the people who do the initial scan.

Candidates often stuff their resumes with laundry lists of the functions and responsibilities they've had in past jobs in a desperate attempt to cover all their bases. This approach rarely pays off, however, because the amount of information you would have to put into a general all-purpose resume is so enormous that you'd need to write a book, which, of course, no one would read.

Length is not an issue. Content is. People will read any length of resume *if* the content is of interest to them, and that's the secret. Ideally, a resume should contain no more and no less than the exact information an employer is looking for. After all, every employer expects that you are so interested in their company that you have written a resume just for them. Realistic? No. Reality? Yes, I'm afraid so.

Never assume that just because you had a particular responsibility, performed a particular function, or accomplished miracles that required superhuman effort, the person reading your resume can automatically link that to the challenges faced by their company. The onus is on you to guide them to the conclusion you want them to draw. You have to motivate them to pick up the phone and schedule an interview with you.

The content of your resume has to be relevant to your reader. It must address their specific needs clearly—instantly. It's a laser-guided missile not a dumb bomb. If your resume is in response to an advertised opening, it reflects the exact needs profiled in the ad. If it's sent to a targeted group of companies, it demonstrates how you can make them money, save them money, and increase their efficiencies. If it's a networking resume, it addresses the type of problem your contact's peers are likely to be facing. It's never vague or wishy-washy. It's always direct and specific.

Don't let the one-size-fits-all mentality spill over into your cover letters, either. Many job hunters respond to the specifics of an ad in their cover letter and then cross their fingers and hope the reader connects the dots. In reality, though, cover letters are rarely read with interest because most are so vague or poorly written that they add little value. It's likely the opening line is the only one that has been customized and that the rest of it is as generic as the accompanying resume. People who spend even a minimum of time scanning resumes can spot these fakes quickly—with typical results.

Most people have many great accomplishments they can leverage for their next career move. Yet for many of these same people their resumes are bland replicas of the generic all-purpose resume in vogue these days—a document that merely mimics what a resume writer thought was important. In reality, only you understand what you've accomplished that would be of interest to a potential employer.

Ask yourself. No—better yet—cut your name off the top of your resume and give it to a couple of your best friends. Tell them it's the resume of one of your mutual contacts and ask them if they can guess who it is. If they can't tell it's you or, worse, if they think it's someone else, you have a problem—the description of your accomplishments and your jobs are too generic. If it makes you look like a hundred other applicants who are also "project managers," "teachers," "accountants," or whatever, how do you expect an employer to select you for an interview? Yes, you could get lucky, but luck is so unpredictable.

So, your first objective is to make sure your resume is read. One of the biggest mistakes candidates make is assuming that just because they send a resume to a prospective employer or recruiter, it will be read. 'Tain't so!

Guerrillas know this. They understand that people are motivated by their own selfish interests. They know they need to guide, cajole, and dare interviewers with a snapshot of what they can bring to the table: a hint of the results they can achieve.

## ■ ALL RESUMES ARE NOT CREATED EQUAL

If you want to be seen, you have to have a competitive resume to stand out. It's rarely the most qualified who land interviews; it's normally the ones who are the most impressive on paper. The best resumes "speak" to employers, providing quick insight into their owners' personality and drive to succeed.

A resume can serve you in a variety of ways, but it is primarily used to make the following types of contacts with prospective employers:

➤ Respond to a job opening.

➤ Create unsolicited demand for your skills.

➤ Cut and paste to fill out an online application.

➤ Supplement—not replace—a company's standard job application.

➤ Before interviews to rehearse.

➤ During interviews to draw the interviewer's attention to a particular accomplishment.

➤ After an interview to tailor a thank-you letter.

➤ As an aid for your references so they'll remember what you did, especially if you were one of many on a team.

➤ During telephone interviews as a reminder because, after all, the interviewer has a copy.

➤ To prompt a recipient for the purposes of networking.

**Get the free mobile app at**
## http://gettag.mobi

A Guerrilla Resume is a multidimensional, multipurpose tool. It is:

➤ Your introduction to a prospective employer.

➤ The first impression recruiters will have of you.

➤ The key to positioning your seniority.

➤ A bargaining chip for your salary negotiations.

In other words, it is a significant document in the advancement of your career.

## ■ HAIL THE GUERRILLA RESUME

### ➤ Standard Guerrilla Resume—Overview

A Standard Guerrilla Resume is a cross between a chronological resume and a functional resume . . . on steroids.

Like a functional resume, it highlights your best skills and achievements. Like a chronological resume, it presents your experience and education in order, from most recent to earliest.

You can use a Standard Guerrilla Resume if you:

- ➤ Are just leaving school and lack experience.
- ➤ Have extensive experience.

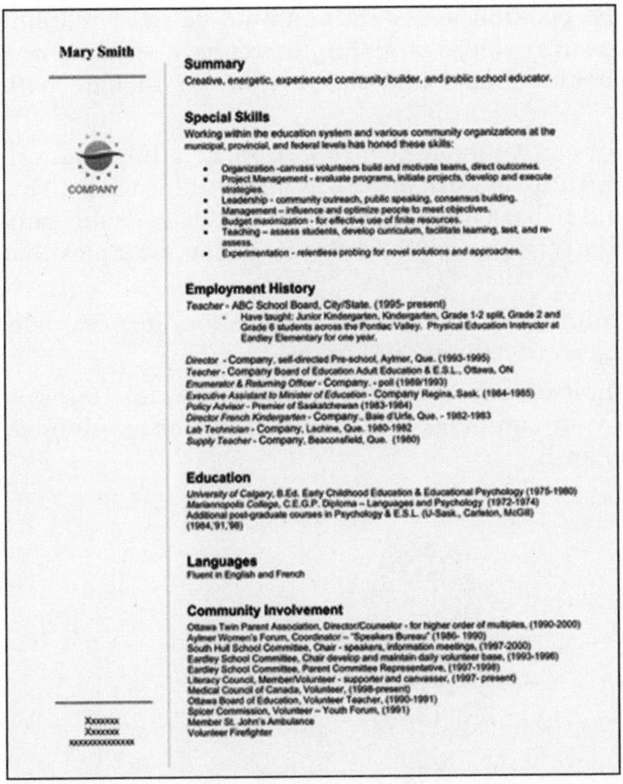

Mary Smith

COMPANY

Xxxxxx
Xxxxxx
xxxxxxxxxxxx

**Summary**

Creative, energetic, experienced community builder, and public school educator.

**Special Skills**

Working within the education system and various community organizations at the municipal, provincial, and federal levels has honed these skills:

- Organization -canvass volunteers build and motivate teams, direct outcomes.
- Project Management - evaluate programs, initiate projects, develop and execute strategies.
- Leadership - community outreach, public speaking, consensus building.
- Management – influence and optimize people to meet objectives.
- Budget maximization - for effective use of finite resources.
- Teaching – assess students, develop curriculum, facilitate learning, test, and re-assess.
- Experimentation - relentless probing for novel solutions and approaches.

**Employment History**

*Teacher* - ABC School Board, City/State. (1995- present)
- Have taught: Junior Kindergarten, Kindergarten, Grade 1-2 split, Grade 2 and Grade 6 students across the Pontiac Valley. Physical Education instructor at Eardley Elementary for one year.

*Director* - Company, self-directed Pre-school, Aylmer, Que. (1990-1995)
*Teacher* - Company Board of Education Adult Education & E.S.L., Ottawa, ON
*Enumerator & Returning Officer* - Company. - poll (1989/1993)
*Executive Assistant to Minister of Education* - Company Regina, Sask. (1984-1985)
*Policy Advisor* - Premier of Saskatchewan (1983-1984)
*Director French Kindergarten* - Company., Baie d'Urfe, Que. - 1982-1983
*Lab Technician* - Company, Lachine, Que. 1980-1982
*Supply Teacher* - Company, Beaconsfield, Que. (1980)

**Education**

*University of Calgary*, B.Ed. Early Childhood Education & Educational Psychology (1975-1980)
*Mariannopolis College*, C.E.G.P. Diploma – Languages and Psychology (1972-1974)
Additional post-graduate courses in Psychology & E.S.L. (U-Sask., Carleton, McGill) (1984,'91,'98)

**Languages**

Fluent in English and French

**Community Involvement**

Ottawa Twin Parent Association, Director/Counselor - for higher order of multiples. (1990-2000)
Aylmer Women's Forum, Coordinator – "Speakers Bureau" (1986- 1990)
South Hull School Committee, Chair - speakers, information meetings, (1997-2000)
Eardley School Committee, Chair develop and maintain daily volunteer base, (1993-1996)
Eardley School Committee, Parent Committee Representative, (1997-1998)
Literacy Council, Member/Volunteer - supporter and canvasser, (1997- present)
Medical Council of Canada, Volunteer, (1998-present)
Ottawa Board of Education, Volunteer Teacher, (1990-1991)
Spicer Commission, Volunteer – Youth Forum, (1991)
Member St. John's Ambulance
Volunteer Firefighter

Download available

Figure 6.1 Standard Guerrilla Resume.

➤ Are making a career change.

➤ Need to explain time away from work due to illness or other matters.

In short, the Standard Guerrilla Resume will work for most people in most situations.

This resume has all the information that experienced employment professionals are looking for in a candidate. To wit, every Standard Guerrilla Resume includes the following five components:

1. Objective or summary at the top, focused on either one job title or a narrow skill set.

2. Select accomplishments and/or special skills section. Think of this as an executive summary of the best, most relevant four or five bullet points about you, that map to the requirements for the position you want or would be most relevant to the employer(s) you're targeting. If you have a strong mix of specific achievements and skills, you can include both sections.

3. Experience or employment history section, detailing your relevant paid and unpaid work history as well as internships. This section should go back only about 10 to 15 years in detail; summarize earlier work, as we'll show you in the examples that follow.

4. Education/training section, where you list your degrees, relevant training, certifications, and so on.

5. Additional information section, as needed at the end. Here you can include your computer skills, relevant hobbies, volunteer work, and so forth.

## A WAR STORY

*Steve Duncan*

I remember when I first saw David's extreme resume example, and I thought it was pretty cool. I had some endorsements on LinkedIn.com, which I quoted in the margin, added accomplishments and skills, and got it together over a few days. I remember at the time that it seemed like such a bold way to do a resume. I was just sure the first time I sent it to anyone I'd get clobbered. My earlier efforts at nontraditional resume styles resulted in surly calls demanding a rewrite. I just didn't get the point. I'd rewrite it, resend it, and never hear anything again.

I sent my extreme resume to the first opportunity, and immediately got a call. The person was very interested in me, but then asked if I could send a "real" resume. At first I was frustrated. After all, isn't a resume supposed to be the silver bullet? First date, courtship, and marriage proposal all in one document? Nope. Part of David's advice was that the only purpose of a resume is to *get a call*. And it did. It took me a while to understand this and really leverage it.

"Real resume?" I learned to ask, innocently. "What do you mean?" The ensuing conversation was a great chance to learn what was important to the caller and was always decisive and effective, even if the opportunity wasn't a good fit. It helped me better understand what I was really looking for, and it also helped me tweak the resume a bit to better represent myself. Usually the person would ask about something that was already on the resume. "Where's your work history?" they'd ask. I'd point it out to them, and they'd soften. It's about getting enough foot in the door so you can start a conversation and really communicate.

I used my extreme resume to get my current position, and the HR director made no bones about telling me she loved it. Others, including headhunters, have said the same. I've had a few who apologetically asked for it in word format, or in strict chronological format, to satisfy the computer-based resume systems. That's okay, I don't mind because by then it's done the job—the rest is just satisfying the bureaucracy.

I've also had a few who just didn't get it. I've learned to not chase after them because if they don't understand the resume, then I'm not going to be a good fit. It's good to remember that the goal isn't just a position, it's the *right* position.

---

Compliments of Steve Duncan at www.LinkedIn.com/in/steveduncan.

➤ **The Extreme Guerrilla Resume—Overview**

Done correctly, an Extreme Guerrilla Resume will get you an interview almost every time. It's that powerful.

The Extreme version takes the Standard Guerrilla Resume to a whole new level. Like a triple espresso or a Ferrari Testarossa, it's not for everyone.

This version has all the parts of a Standard Guerrilla Resume, plus one or more of the following (the more of these you include, the more powerful your finished product will be):

1. Proof section (*mandatory*). This column goes on the left side of the resume, below your name. Here you can insert logos of past/current employers or clients, to take advantage of the "halo" effect of prestigious company names. Also, you can include quotes from people familiar with your work; these function like mini-testimonials and are *extremely* powerful.

2. "Grabber" statement at the top (*optional*). This can be a dictionary definition ("rainmaker" or "catalyst," for example) or a brief quote from someone familiar with your work. The grabber functions as a hook to literally grab a reader's attention.

3. Career driver section (*optional*). This aggressively worded statement comes right before your experience section. Here is where you tell employers—in no uncertain terms—how much better you will make their lives after you are hired.

Use an Extreme Guerrilla Resume when you:

➤ Face enormous competition for a limited number of jobs and need to crush your competition.

➤ Want to test the waters before launching a comprehensive job hunt.

➤ Want to create a job in a company that has no openings.

*Caution:* If you use an Extreme Guerrilla Resume, be prepared to back it up with facts and figures in the interview. You will be asked! So be sure to document your claims meticulously ahead of time.

■ **THE STANDARD GUERRILLA RESUME EXPLAINED**

In Chapter 2 on branding, you assembled the necessary facts, figures, and results; it's time to start putting them all together. It's time to start writing.

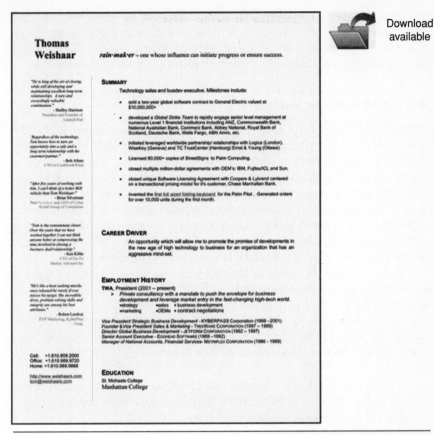

Figure 6.2  Extreme Guerrilla Resume.

Create a Standard Guerrilla Resume. Even if you plan to do an Extreme version later, you'll still need to include the parts found in this chapter.

To recap, your Standard Guerrilla Resume is made up of the following five components:

1. Objective or Summary.
2. Select Accomplishments and/or Special Skills section.
3. Experience.
4. Education/Training section.
5. Additional Information section, as needed, at the end.

And, it bears repeating that your Guerrilla Resume, whether it's a Standard or Extreme version, will be one page in length—no more. You may be asked to bring a longer, two-page resume, but don't worry, just do a two-page Guerrilla Resume aimed directly at their needs.

## ➤ 1. Objective or Summary

The first and most important part of your Guerrilla Resume is the Objective or Summary statement at the beginning. It should be focused on either one job title or one narrow skill set.

A narrow focus is essential, because you don't have 10 or 15 seconds for your resume to impress readers, as you may have thought. You have only about three seconds to impress today's harried, hurried, frenetic, time-starved reader. That is, employers must find something compelling in the first three seconds of reading your resume for them to want to keep reading. Otherwise, it goes in the trash.

So let's make the most of this all-important real estate at the top of your Guerrilla Resume—the part they'll see in those first three seconds—by leading with an eye-catching opening.

If you don't know the title of the job you're applying for, you should at least know what skills you can use. So, start your resume with one of two headings: Objective or Summary.

An objective with a job title is a great way to start your resume. It shows that you know exactly what job the employer is trying to fill. Here are some examples:

OBJECTIVE
Restaurant Management where more than 10 years of food service and management experience will contribute to efficient operations.

OBJECTIVE
Network Administrator where three years of successful experience and training will add value.

OBJECTIVE
Pharmaceutical Sales Rep where eight years of training and experience in health care and sales will add to profitability.

Notice the language and format here. By starting off with the title of the job you know the employer is trying to fill, it's like calling them by their first name. It shows you know something about their company and their situation. It creates immediate rapport with your reader and gives you an immediate advantage. It's so simple, yet, so powerful.

Plus, not only does this wording of this Objective tell the hiring manager exactly what job you want to fill, it also makes clear that you want to add or contribute something that will make their lives easier. Again, this is simple, subtle, and . . . effective!

But what if you don't know the exact job title the employer wants to fill? (Well, you should, from your research of the company and its job postings. So don't give up that easily.)

But let's say you don't have one specific job in mind. Then what?

Start your Guerrilla Resume with a Summary. This will focus the reader on the skills you've used while giving you a bit more flexibility to apply for different jobs. Bonus: You can include a second "killer" sentence that compels the reader to keep going.

Examples:

SUMMARY
Seeking a position where network engineering/administration and software development skills and experience will add value. Accustomed to long hours in pursuit of company goals.

SUMMARY
Experienced quality management professional with 10+ years of proven results. Turned around quality and operations for two business units, increasing efficiency 100% (2005–2006).

SUMMARY
Accomplished customer relations management professional with five years of award-winning experience. Quadrupled client satisfaction ratings from 1.0 to 4.0 average (2003–present).

Again, note the language here, especially those killer second sentences.

The way I see it, why wait to fire off your big guns? You already have the reader's attention, so why not include a compelling fact about you in this first section? Doing so will force them to read the next section of your Guerrilla Resume. And the next section. Line by line you build and stoke the fires of their desire to meet you. Then, they call you.

Whether to use an objective or a summary can be a sticking point for some people. Some folks even leave them off the resume, because they want to be considered for all jobs.

### No, No, No—Never Do This
A focused resume is a powerful resume. A resume that tries to be all things to all people ends up being nothing at all. You can always write a second or third resume to give you more options.

Spend as much time on this section as necessary to create a powerful opening for your Guerrilla Resume. Your objective or summary should be two or three lines long at most.

Your goal is to start your resume with a focus on the employer and his or her needs. Tell the reader what you can do for them. Then, force them to read further.

➤ **2. Select Accomplishments and/or Special Skills**

Think of this second part of your Guerrilla Resume as an executive summary of the best, most relevant bullet points about you. It should be so powerful and relevant that employers should not need to read any further to determine that you are the right person for the job.

In fact, according to many hiring managers I've talked to over the past 20 years, this section summarizing your key qualifications is the most important part of your resume. Employers who have to read hundreds of resumes are looking for shortcuts—and this section gives them one.

To make this section effective, it's vital that you target your reader. You need to understand who your reader is because different people read resumes looking for different things.

➤ Hiring managers look for skill sets first, then how flexible you are, and finally evidence of your ability to learn on the job.

➤ Recruiters look for "hot" marketable skills because they want to make money marketing you. If your skill set is not in high demand, they won't call unless you are an exact fit for a job order they have.

➤ HR folks look for an exact skill fit with a job first, then your stability, then your personality type.

How long should this section be? About three to five bullet points in length—not much more. Too long is too bad—if you need a dozen bullet points to summarize your experience, you're not really summarizing, are you? And it's always an odd number—three or five are best. (Why? Go ask an advertising copywriter.)

What title should you give this section—Select Accomplishments or Special Skills?

In general, people who produce revenue, such as sales or marketing folks, will have an easier time talking about accomplishments. Other folks, such as people in IT, customer service, accounting, and so on, have skills to highlight.

There are exceptions, of course, so feel free to break this rule. In fact, if you have a strong mix of specific achievements and skills, you can include *both* a Select Accomplishments and a Special Skills section in your Guerrilla Resume.

*Three Rules to Help Focus Your Accomplishments*

1. The accomplishment must be important to someone, ideally the organization you are targeting or its customers.
2. The result should have had a favorable impact, that is, enhanced your employer's bottom line or increased its visibility or viability and ideally both.
3. The accomplishment must specifically illustrate your competence as it relates to the position for which you are applying, highlighting your skills, experience, and personal qualities.

Now let's take a look at your current resume from an employer's perspective.

Here are examples of both kinds of sections:

*SPECIAL SKILLS*

➤ **Operating Systems**: Windows NT/XP/Vista, UNIX on Sun SPARC and MS-DOS.

➤ **Programming Languages**: C, C++, HTML, and Java.

➤ **Software**: Microsoft FrontPage, Image Composer, and Word; Lotus 1-2-3 and mSQL.

*SPECIAL SKILLS*

➤ **Execution**—regularly delivering to fixed time schedules against all odds.

➤ **Experimentation**—relentless probing for new R&D and product approaches.

➤ **Management**—optimizing people and finances to meet objectives with customers.

*SELECT ACCOMPLISHMENTS*

➤ Developed a Global Strike Team to rapidly engage customers in the FP1000.

➤ Delivered triple-digit growth numbers five times since 2000.

➤ Ignited sales for a U.S. multinational, closing $6 million in year one.

*SELECT ACCOMPLISHMENTS*

➤ Sold a two-year global software contract to XYZ Company valued at over $10,000,000.

➤ Developed a Global Strike Team to engage senior level management at 17 Level 1 financial institutions, including Client A, Client B, and Client C.

➤ Initiated leveraged worldwide partnerships/relationships with Client (London), Client (Geneva), Client (Hamburg), and Client (OPQ) in 2006.

*Attention Recent Graduates:* If you don't have much work experience, be sure to make the most of any university and part-time jobs you've held. For example, you can include a bullet point or two that summarizes the best of your experience, no matter what you did—so long as you make those accomplishments relevant to the job you seek. You can then go into details later, in the Experience section.

Have a look at the Select Accomplishments section below, from a resume that won a job for one new grad. It combines university and off-campus work experience.

*SELECT ACCOMPLISHMENTS*

➤ **Helped improve company performance** by surveying customers, then analyzing results with coworkers. Used data and staff discussions to increase service levels (Applebee's).

➤ **Experienced writer.** Led research project to study how expectations determine outcomes. Required superior skills in communication and analysis. Surveyed more than 230 students, then conducted telephone follow-up to interpret data (University of NY).

➤ **Proven training skills.** Experience orienting, supervising, and clarifying goals for up to 25 employees (Applebee's).

➤ **3. Experience Section**

You can also call this Employment History, if you'd like. Again, the name you choose is not as important as the details that follow.

The purpose of this third section of your Guerrilla Resume is to show employers what you have been doing since school. They will have already been intrigued by your opening Objective/Summary and the Skills/Accomplishments section that follows, so by the time they get to this Experience section, their mind will largely be made up.

Here you should follow a consistent, easy-to-read format. You can present a description of each job you've held in one of two ways, depending on what information is more relevant. Choose only one of the following formats and use it consistently. Don't alternate between the two, as you'll simply confuse the reader.

If your past job titles are more relevant to the job you seek next, lead with them, like this:

➤ **LAN/WAN Administrator**: U.S. Marine Corps, Camp Lejeune, NC (1993–1999).

However, if you've worked for impressive companies and want to lead with those names, you can do so like this:

➤ **IBM**, Vice President of Research and Development, San Jose, CA (2006–2007).

For each job you've had, include your title, company name, city, state, and the years you worked there. There's really no need to include the months, as this takes up valuable space and may highlight any gaps in your employment.

*Attention Recent Graduates*: If you lack experience since graduation, you can include a brief explanation of what you've been doing since then. You can also include any jobs you had while in school in your Experience section as long as you make them relevant by stressing desirable working traits that can't be taught, such as reliability, attention to detail, work ethic, and so on.

Have a look at the example wording below, from a resume that won a job for one new graduate.

EXPERIENCE

Following graduation, began extensive online research of information technology job market and leading firms. Also created Web pages; samples available upon request (2006–present).

➤ Detail Specialist: University Car Wash, Huntsville, AL (2004–2005).

➤ Provided detailing services and superior customer service. Employed while full-time student.

➤ Followed up with commercial and individual customers to ensure high levels of satisfaction.

➤ Proactively sought out new tasks to make best use of available time.

➤ Maintained good working relationship with all five managers and 17 colleagues.

While there are exceptions to these rules, this format gives you a lot of flexibility to describe your experience in an effective manner.

*Final note on wording*: You will notice that the Experience section of a Guerrilla Resume is limited to listing your job titles, company names, places of employment, and dates. Nothing more. And this is done for a reason—your Guerrilla Resume is designed to make the phone ring, not tell your whole life story. You can do this in the job interview.

In the advertising industry they call this a "teaser"—it gets you the initial invitation to interview. You can expand on your work history once you are face-to-face with the interviewer.

(Another way to think of this is that your Guerrilla Resume works like a classified ad. The job of a classified ad is not to tell every detail about the car or old refrigerator you're trying to sell—you just want to grab the attention of an interested party and get them to call you on the phone.)

In fact, you may be asked to bring a longer resume and provide more information about what you did on each job. This is a good thing. In Chapter 8, we will show you what to add to your resume and how to do it, if you are asked to do so by a hiring manager or someone in the HR department.

➤ **4. Education/Training**

Every employer is looking for this section, so you must include one.

> *Important*: If your degree is more relevant to the job you seek than your recent experience, put this section ahead of your experience. Otherwise, it should come later in the resume.

> Follow this format when describing your education:

> EDUCATION
> **Master of Arts: Communications**, University of Florida (2004).
> **Bachelor of Arts: Art History**, San Diego State University (2002).

> Now, what if you don't have a degree or an extensive formal education?

> Well, here's an insider secret. You can call this section Education/Training and list all the relevant courses, certificates, and training you've received after high school. This is a great way to give more substance to an otherwise-skimpy Education section. It shows initiative and employers like that—a lot!

Your combination section could look like this:

EDUCATION/TRAINING

**Professional training** includes courses in sales, problem-solving, leadership, management, quality, market research, and presentation skills (2005–present).

**Associate of Arts Degree**, City College, Chicago, IL (2004).

If you went to college but didn't graduate, you can describe your course of study, adding to it anything else you did that was notable, such as working full time or a GPA above 3.0, like this:

EDUCATION

**BS:** Finance course work, Ohio State University, Columbus, OH (two years). GPA: 3.2.

Worked full-time throughout to self-finance 100% of education.

Finally, if you're currently in school for something, include your expected year of graduation, like this:

EDUCATION

**MBA program**: Finance, Michigan State University (in progress; due in 2008).

## ➤ Additional Information

If space allows, you can include an Additional Information section to combine good things about you that don't fit in other parts of your Guerrilla Resume. If it's a hobby or volunteer position and you think it's relevant to the job you seek—and room allows—put it in.

Example: You can mention golf and marathon running if you want a sales job, since these interests portray you as active and energetic (plus, more sales deals get done on the golf course than anywhere else on earth ☺). But including such interests may not be relevant if you're applying for a position as a copy editor.

I recommend you put this catchall Additional Information section last, to finish the Guerrilla Resume with a bang. Follow this format, and list items from most relevant to least:

ADDITIONAL INFORMATION

**Languages**: Arabic, French, and English (fluent).

**Computer** skills include Windows, Excel, Word, PowerPoint, Oracle, HTML and search engine optimization (SEO).

**Interests** include marathon running, golf, softball, and international travel.

**Volunteer experience** includes Habitat for Humanity (2001–present), adult literacy tutoring (2002–present) and fundraising for diabetes (1999–present).

*Note*: I once got an e-mail from a reader, who wrote: "Why do your resumes have hobbies listed? I have interviewed many candidates for jobs in the past and at no time was I concerned if a person was a black belt in karate unless I was."

Everyone's entitled to their opinion. In this case, that opinion is wrong. If one hiring manager isn't interested in hobbies, that doesn't mean all hiring managers aren't. After all, if it's cloudy in Chicago, that doesn't mean it's also cloudy in New York.

Many hiring managers will start talking about your hobbies or interests as a way to break the ice and ease into the interview. They do this to put you at ease and, in some cases, to see if you have a life outside work, or if you're a workaholic who might be prone to burn out.

Because you're dealing with humans here and humans are unpredictable, you never know what part of your resume will make a hiring manager want to call you. So if you think your hobbies, interests, volunteer work, and so on are relevant and may give you an edge, include them.

In a hurry? Need to send a resume to an employer today? Refer to the resume examples in the downloadable Word file available at www.gm4jh.com. Pick one that appeals to you, customize it with your own information, and voilà! You have an instant Guerrilla Resume.

Download available

# ■ THE EXTREME GUERRILLA RESUME

Now that you've assembled a Standard Guerrilla Resume, you're ready to take it to a much higher level by creating an Extreme Guerrilla Resume.

*Remember!* This format is very aggressive. You should send it only to senior executives who can either hire you for an existing job or who can create a new position just for you.

Do *not* send an Extreme Guerrilla Resume to anyone in the HR (a.k.a. "Hiring Resistance") Department or anyone else but a person with the authority to hire you. Why?

HR types, administrative assistants, and other gatekeepers simply won't know what to do with this style of resume—it breaks too many rules. While every company claims to want to hire bold, courageous leaders (that's really just the president speaking), rank-and-file staff rarely want to hire people more skilled than themselves.

To recap, your Extreme Guerrilla Resume has all the components of the Standard Guerrilla Resume, *plus* one or more of the following (the more you include, the more powerful your finished product will be):

1. Proof section (*mandatory*)
2. Grabber statement at the top (*optional*)
3. Career driver section (*optional*)

Ready? Let's start with the ...

## ➤ 1. Proof Section (Mandatory)

This part runs down the left-hand side of your paper, below your name. It should be about one inch wide and it will include third-party information to "prove" you are a candidate every sane employer would want for its team.

What goes in here? The two best things you can include as proof are:

1. Logos of past/current employers or clients. Doing so let's you piggyback on the value of company brand names. It's called the halo effect and it sets your resume apart.

   Essentially, you're borrowing the credibility associated with that company. The opposite is also true, so be careful how quickly you claim Enron as a customer, for example. You know what the most-respected companies in your industry are, so try to find a valid reason to insert their logo on your resume. You can often download logos from company web sites—that's the easiest way to do it. Simply save them to your computer and insert them in your resume.

2. Quotes from people familiar with your work. These serve as mini-testimonials and are very powerful. You can get them from past/current managers, clients, suppliers, college professors, newspaper or magazine articles about you—anyone who's seen you doing what you want to do in your target job. You can also lift quotes from personnel/annual reviews or letters of reference. *Obvious warning:* Don't ask anyone for a quote who you don't want to know about your job search.

(Format tip: If you need help setting up your page so that you can include this proof section, refer to the Extreme Guerrilla Resume Master Template in the downloadable Word file available at www.gm4jh.com. Open the Master Template and simply paste your quotes and/or logos down the left side of the document.)

When it comes to quotes, you *must* have written versions of any material that you quote from to back up your claims. Never, ever include a quote that you cannot verify in an e-mail, performance review, letter of recommendation, or other written format.

Refer to the Extreme Guerrilla Resume example for Thomas Weishaar in this chapter (Figure 6.2), or the other examples available on the book's web site, www.GM4Jh.com, to see how these logos and quotes can be used as proof.

➤ **2. Grabber Statement (Optional)**

This section at the top of your resume is supposed to—yes, you guessed it—grab a reader's attention from the get-go and compel them to keep reading.

Your grabber can be a dictionary definition ("rainmaker" for a sales pro or "catalyst" for a manager, for example) or a brief testimonial from someone familiar with your work.

Example: Thomas Weishaar's grabber from his Extreme Guerrilla Resume in this chapter has this dictionary definition at the top:

*rain·mak·er*—one whose influence can initiate progress or ensure success.

Did this get attention? You better believe it. Was Thomas able to back up this rather bold claim? You better believe it. And you had better be able to back up any claims you make, too, whether it's here in your Grabber section or elsewhere.

Here's another example grabber statement, from a sales operations manager who used his Extreme Guerrilla Resume to get hired:

E*n*\**tel*"*e*\**chy*—becoming actual what was only potential.

And here's the grabber successfully used by a president/CEO:

*cat·a·lyst*—an agent that provokes or speeds significant change or action.

Keep in mind that, unlike the Proof section, this Grabber section is optional. If you can come up with something that suits you and that you're comfortable using, go for it. If not, leave it out. You won't lose points with the employer for leaving it out. You will lose if it's dorky.

➤ **3. Career Driver Section (Optional)**

This third and final Extreme Guerrilla Resume component is also optional.

Your Career Driver is an aggressively worded statement that comes right before your experience section. It's the part of your personality and skill set that literally drives your career forward.

Think of it like this: What one thing about you will make employers ecstatic about their decision to hire you? In other words, why should they hire you? The answer to that question is your Career Driver.

Here's an example:

Career Driver
Taking the surety of success, the passion to succeed, and the deft handling of economic drivers to build great organizations.

Here's another:

Career Driver
Inspiring and leading teams to develop breakthrough products, which solve customer demands and have real commercial value in the global market.

It's easier to show you how all these elements fit together than it is to describe it. So please take a moment now to view the sample Extreme Guerrilla Resumes you'll find on the book's web site.

After you've seen the examples, decide which formats and wording are most attractive to you. Then, consider including those in your own Extreme Guerrilla Resume.

And, as we explain in Chapter 8, be ready to bring a longer version of this resume to the job interview if asked. Some managers or HR types may ask to see more information to flesh out your Experience section, and this is a simple matter to provide, once you have the Extreme Resume framework in place. Please refer to the web site for examples of Extreme Guerrilla Resumes that won jobs.

In a hurry? Need to send a resume to an employer today? Refer to the resume examples in the downloadable Word file available through www.GM4JH.com. Pick one that appeals to you, customize it with your own information, and voilà! You have an instant Extreme Guerrilla Resume.

## ■ GRAPHICS THAT ADD PUNCH TO YOUR RESUME

Advertisers use their knowledge of human nature to evoke emotional responses from you like cool, sophisticated, comfortable, and secure—that's what prompts your buying decision. You don't buy a car because it's made of metal and glass. You buy it because of the way it makes you feel. The purpose of any graphic is to create a desire to have the product.

You can motivate a hiring manager to action through the clever use of three types of graphics.

1. Logos: The advertising industry knows all too well that a picture is worth a thousand words. Today we buy the value implied by our favorite brands, and employers do the same. Do you buy generic beer—clothes—cars? Not likely. Put your employer's logo on your resume if the company has a good reputation.

2. Symbols: Use ###, %%%, and $$$ to emphasize your accomplishments. One million dollars is less likely to be noticed than $1,000,000. Numbers and symbols jump off the page.

3. Charts: A graph adds visual appeal and is ideal for demonstrating any type of quantitative improvement.

---

### GUERRILLA TIP

➤ The purpose of graphics is to draw the reader's attention and lend credibility.

➤ They need to be in line with your accomplishments.

➤ Use logos and product pictures sparingly.

---

## GUERRILLA PROOFREADING CHECKLIST

Download available

Use this checklist to proofread each section of your resume. Check the box after completing each task, just like a pilot does before takeoff.

➤ *Contact information*
Verify that your name, address, ZIP code, and phone number are correct, as well as your LinkedIn address if you provided it.

➤ *E-mail address*
Use a personal e-mail on your resume, not one from work. Besides looking unprofessional (readers will assume you'll use company time to look for a job again after they hire you), it's dangerous to get e-mail at work about career opportunities. That's because employers often have the right to read any e-mail that comes to your work address. Furthermore, make sure your personal e-mail address is *not* something like hotstuff@aol.com or gameboy111@msn. If you need to get a new e-mail that looks professional, do so. And put some thought into it. Best yet, include your LinkedIn URL so readers can check out your online portfolio.

➤ *Facts and figures*
Check all years and numbers in the resume and cover letter. Do they add up? Are they consistent?

➤ *Clarity and content*
Read the resume aloud for awkward, missing, or extra words.

➤ *Spacing*
Make sure the space between each sentence and section is the same.

➤ *Spelling*
Use your word processor's spell checker and then read it yourself. Most misspelled words occur in the headings and in the names of software and companies.

*(continued)*

(*Continued*)

➤ *Punctuation*

Read the resume backwards, looking for missing or incorrect punctuation, such as commas, dashes between dates, apostrophes, and so on.

➤ *Layout*

Are the upper and lower margins even and pleasing to the eye? Is there white space throughout the document, or is the text too dense? Print the resume and show it to friends for their comments.

## A WAR STORY

*Mark J. Haluska*

In November 2008 I received a phone call from Anthony, who is at the director level in the fast food (QSR) industry. He asked if he could send me his resume. I said sure. The resume was like 99% of all the resumes I get. Boring!

It just so happened that the timing could not have been better because I just received a heads-up from an industry insider regarding a restaurant organization that is well funded and has an aggressive growth plan of becoming a $100 million company within the next two to three years. I was told they needed someone at the Director or VP level who could lead the operations side of the company.

As a favor to Anthony, but more realistically in my own $self$-serving interest, I asked him if I could help him create an Extreme Guerrilla Resume. He had no idea what that was, but he said, "Sure, you're the expert." Under my guidance, within two days we had the perfect marketing piece.

Now, I've never met, much less spoken to, the CFO or the COO of the company, but with a little networking and research I did obtain their e-mail addresses. Uninvited, I sent both the COO and the CFO Anthony's Extreme Guerrilla Resume. I removed his contact information to ensure the company had to call me if there was an interest.

Two days later a call came into my office from the CFO of that company. She introduced herself and asked, "How soon can we see this candidate?" I asked her what she liked about Anthony's credentials and she replied, "The company officers looked at his [Extreme Guerrilla] resume and were simply blown away!"

The first Guerrilla lesson here is that Anthony's original resume looked like everyone else's. Although he is impressive in every respect, his resume certainly did not reflect it and it certainly did not scream, "Hire me!" The second lesson is that Anthony was also doing what everyone else does. He was going to HR rather than directly to decisions makers. No wonder he had yet to get any interviews!

We broke all the so-called rules, and within one week of my first contact with Anthony he was invited to interview with this company that neither of us had ever spoken with. As I write this, talks are ongoing between Anthony and the company.

---

Contributed by Mark J. Haluska, founder and Executive Director, Real Time NetWork, www.rtnetwork.net, LinkedIn: www.LinkedIn.com/in/MarkJ.Haluska.

---

## ■ SELLING YOUR VALUE-ADDED ADVANTAGES

What's your personal 2-for-1 strategy? Why should an employer hire you over the next equally qualified person? You can bet that in the United States today there are thousands of people who have skills similar to yours.

Don't get me wrong. I'm sure you're well qualified, and I really am on your side, but you have to know that you'll have competition for every job you go after. Your competition will come in three forms: internal candidates, external candidates, and the status quo. You will need to convince interviewers that hiring you will get them to their desired future result better than any other option. Doing nothing is a very viable option, especially for people in middle management who are risk averse.

So, back to my question—why you?

As a job hunter, if you understand that you are likely to have competition for a coveted position, then you can leverage other skills to appear more qualified. You do this by selling your personal value-added qualities, and everybody has one or more.

The *American Heritage® Dictionary of the English Language* defines value-added as: adjective—"Of or relating to the estimated value that is added to a product or material at each stage of its manufacture or distribution." In short, it is something added to a product to increase its value. In this case, the product is you.

Your value-add is a skill, life experience, or attitude that, when added to your basic qualifications, gives you an advantage over the next candidate because you exceed the employer's expectations for the position. For example:

➤ Nurses who have had active combat training could have an edge over other candidates applying for an emergency room job at a hospital because they're already acclimatized to the environment.

➤ An engineer who has graduated from Toastmasters or a similar public-speaking program could have an edge because he or she can also be a spokesperson for the company.

The preceding job hunters added an unexpected but welcome dimension to their credentials because they highlighted their value-add in their cover letter and later in the interview. In essence, they shifted the interviewer's focus to areas they knew others were not likely to have.

On a more personal note, my wife was selected for a job as a drug and alcohol education supervisor by focusing her cover letter, resume, and interview around her military experience. The fact that she has a degree in psychology and ran several addiction centers qualified her for the job. But I'm convinced she was chosen because the selection committee knew she had the self-discipline to create the course material and the presence to deliver it.

Your value-add can come in the guise of:

- ➤ Complementary skills
- ➤ Alumni
- ➤ Great attitude
- ➤ Industry contacts
- ➤ Domain expertise

## ➤ Complementary Skills

For example, a nurse who becomes a doctor could leverage her bond with nursing staff when managing a medical team.

## ➤ Alumni

I can't count the number of people who have specifically asked me to recruit Wharton or Harvard grads because they would have experienced the discipline needed to graduate from those institutions.

Microsoft recruits engineers from the University of Waterloo because many employees are alumni. Want to know what happened to all those high achievers you went to school with? Surf over to www.classmates.com and start networking.

## ➤ Great Attitude

Employers understand that passionate employees outperform normal ones 10-to-1. Passion is a simple cost/benefit equation and qualities like drive, ambition, and vision tend to come as part of the package.

*Fresh from teachers' college and two thousand miles from home, my younger sister Monica decided to apply for a coveted position as a kindergarten teacher. She did her homework. She briefed me on the highlights of the six-hour interview, and I asked what questions they had asked her. She replied, "Well, not many really. I asked most of them. I started by saying I was not very experienced at interviewing so did they mind if I asked a few questions—and the time just flew. We talked about best practices, educational philosophy, and the work ahead of us." I roared with laughter. Monica's passion was evident by her preparation. Monica is the most passionate teacher I've ever met—it shows in the eyes of her parents and the hearts of her students.*

## ➤ Industry Contacts

Time is money, and if you can leverage your industry contacts to get up and running in a new job faster than the next candidate, all things being equal, you will be hired. Your contact list is very valuable. Are you leveraging it correctly?

## ➤ Domain Expertise

For a job hunter, domain expertise is knowledge and experience that has been acquired through a track record that represents a core competency in a specific technical area or marketplace (e.g., you could be a property manager who understands everything there is to know about HVAC systems, which in the building facilities industry makes you worth your weight in platinum).

Domain expertise is a hot commodity for headhunters. Someone in banking could be a success in insurance or financial services; sales professionals in the technology industry often have both domain experience and specific industry contacts, making them more valuable than the next candidate.

---

### GUERRILLA TIP

This new economy and relentless cost-cutting place great strains on the ability of managers to pick those few candidates who can provide them with the value they need to stay alive. Since top people knock on the door daily, you need to:

➤ Differentiate yourself by demonstrating you bring more to the job.

➤ Highlight your complementary experience in your cover letter.

➤ Exploit alumni points of reference.

➤ Leverage your domain expertise.

If you did something like the following, say it:

➤ Proposed and presented in-house training so that shippers would avoid mixing heavy and delicate items. Reduced product damage and customer complaints by 95%.

This shipping clerk is thinking, acting, and communicating like a manager and will be on top of any good hiring manager's resume file.

---

# ■ THE ONLY COVER LETTER YOU WILL EVER NEED

What does your cover letter tell employers about you? The one-size-fits-all form letter addressed to "Dear Sir/Madam," tells employers that you're too lazy to do a little digging to find out who should receive it and that you're not the type of person who is willing to go the extra mile when necessary. Think I am a little harsh? I'm not. If you remember nothing else, remember this—a cover letter with a proper salutation is essential—always.

A cover letter is a personal sales letter, and all good sales letters keep the reader's interests foremost. Correctly researched and written, your cover letter is your best opportunity to tap into an employer's hopes and fears. Your cover letter is your opportunity to go beyond the resume and its focus on the past and target what employers care most about—themselves.

Put yourself in the employer's shoes. Your resume may be one of several dozen or even several hundred they have to read. Most employers will quickly separate those that deserve a full read by reading the cover letter first. The cover letter is a screening device, but beyond that there are more important reasons employers like a cover letter:

➤ It tells them why you are interested in their company—remember, it's not about you, it's about them.

➤ It demonstrates to them whether you can write succinctly and express yourself—a vital skill for today's managers.

➤ It provides a snapshot of your accomplishments as they pertain to their needs, thereby answering their biggest question—can you fix my problem?

The goal of your cover letter is to convince that initial reader to select you for an interview. Your letter and resume may travel through many hands before they reach a hiring manager's desk, so put your best foot forward right from the start. This is your last opportunity to stand out from the crowd. Make sure you tell employers what's in it for them right up front. Make it clear and compelling that not interviewing you is an opportunity lost.

Initially, hiring managers don't know who you are, nor do they care for that matter; they have a problem to solve or an opportunity to exploit—and you are either the solution or you aren't. You can be the most competent person in your field, but if you can't connect your skills to their needs, you will go undiscovered. Make them believe that you can help them achieve their goals and they will interview you.

Following is an example of a Guerrilla Cover Letter for you to read.

## ■ EXAMPLE GUERRILLA COVER LETTER

(Numbered sections are dissected at the end.)

1. Dear Mr. Smith,

2. You have great technology and a great market opportunity. Now it's time to build a great company. That's why we should meet. I could tell you that I am an exceptional executive and leader, but why not let the facts speak for themselves?

3. Here are a few of the successes I have achieved before and can achieve again for you:

   ➤ ABC Corp.—From $0 to $40 million in five years. As Co-founder and then eventually President, I was instrumental in growing ABC Corp. from three employees to more than 350 in 10 locations, with revenues of more than $40 million.

   ➤ EFG Mega Corp.—From $0.69 per share to $7.10 in two years. I joined as Vice-President, North American Operations, just as seven consecutive quarters of losses had driven the share price down to $0.69. I delivered eight consecutive quarters of profit and increased earnings, helping take the stock to a high of $7.10 before the company was acquired.

   ➤ XYZ, Inc.—From start-up to strategic acquisition in four years. Starting as chairman and then as CEO, I successfully packaged and promoted XYZ Inc., resulting in the company's acquisition by Bigger Systems.

4. I think you get the idea: I have repeatedly outperformed in the face of start-up, turnaround, and growth challenges. I have done this in diverse markets and tough economic conditions, generating hundreds of millions of dollars in sales. I have developed a rare combination of experience, vision, and leadership—and that's exactly the combination your company needs to achieve its full potential.

5. I will call you Tuesday, June 10th at 8:30 A.M. to arrange a time for the two of us to talk. If this is not a convenient time please ask Ms. Jones to call me and suggest an alternative.
   Thank you,

6. Bob Smith
   www.bobsmith.com
   bobsmith@bobsmith.com
   212-555-1212

Now, here's that Guerrilla Cover Letter dissected, for you to analyze and emulate:

1. Salutation. Addressed to the hiring manager, by name. Do whatever it takes to get the name of the person with the authority to hire you.

2. Great grabber. He's got my attention.

3. The here's-what-I-can-do-for-you part. The three bullets here demonstrate that he can do a start-up well, a turnaround, and successfully position a company for sale. He has prioritized his most important points and done the thinking for the reader.

4. Here he implies that there is more and hints that you should read the resume.

5. Just in case you don't call him first, he tells you when he is going to call.

6. His contact information is readily available.

Is this letter too bold? No way. As an executive search professional, I would call straight away.

Keep this distinction in mind: If you talk about how you took a company from $0 to $40 million in five years at a neighborhood barbeque, you are bragging. But if you do it in your cover letter and resume, you are smart—and perfectly justified.

Employers respect take-charge, get-it-done, self-assured individuals. And this cover letter is all of that.

You can modify this Guerrilla Cover Letter for different uses, too, usually by slightly changing the first and last paragraphs.

For example, this paragraph:

*You have great technology and a great market opportunity. Now it's time to build a great company. That's why we should meet. I could tell you that I am an exceptional executive and leader, but why not let the facts speak for themselves?*

Can become:

*Does one of your clients [clients can be changed to colleagues for networking purposes] have great technology or a tremendous market and need to get traction quickly? If so, then perhaps you and I should meet. I could tell you that I am an exceptional executive and leader, but why not let the facts speak for themselves?*

I guarantee you this opener will elicit a return call from a recruiter or a colleague if they know of an opportunity.

Now, what if you're not an executive? What if you're a public speaker? There can't possibly be anyway to craft a cover letter that will make you stand out, right? Wrong! Kevin Donlin shows you how in the letter that follows.

J.L. Zoeckler
W243N2358 Saddle Brook Dr., #202
Pewaukee, WI 53072
Dear Mr. (name of the hiring manager),
Could your business use an extra $82,050? That's what I saved my organization last year as a professional public speaker and sales trainer.
Please consider the following:

➤ You will benefit from my persuasive public speaking and writing abilities, where I am able to inform, motivate, and close at a ratio that is 128% higher than other regional managers.

➤ I have a developed network and was able to raise $72,400 in donations by writing and presenting fundraising campaigns. My entrepreneurial efforts also saved a nonprofit agency over $54,000 in strategic leadership fees for the university student group that I lead.

➤ You will also gain from my ability to learn new tasks quickly. In a previous role, I learned how to tutor special education students, which added $388,880 in yearly revenue from our team.

I will call your office this Thursday morning at 8:30 to arrange a time for us to meet. If that is not convenient for you, please ask your assistant to call me at 414-759-1631 to arrange a better time for us to talk. Thank you very much for your time.
Sincerely,
J.L. Zoeckler
P.S. If you are not hiring now, please pass this letter on to someone who wants to save over $80,000 this year while closing 28% more clients, as I have done. Thank you.

## ■ THREE OTHER WAYS TO OPEN YOUR GUERRILLA COVER LETTER

Here are three other ways to open your Guerrilla Cover Letter, listed in order of effectiveness:

1. *Personal reference*: "Bill Smith from [ABC Corp.] suggested that I contact you because . . ."

This is one time that it is okay to drop a name, especially if the hiring manager thinks highly of Bill. Be sure to let Bill know that you're doing this, of course, and ask him for any insider information he may have about the hiring manager. This can help you make a great first impression if you get the call to interview.

2. *Refer to an article or speech*: "Your article on customer service in the February 27, 2007, *Business Journal* was excellent. As a matter of fact, I have used three of your techniques to increase revenues 65% in my five years managing client relations for National Widget Corporation. In addition, I have found two other methods to be helpful, including one that rescued a $3.4-million account.

"Perhaps we should meet? I could tell you that I am an exceptional executive and leader, but why not let the facts speak for themselves?"

I usually do this when I can't find a personal connection any other way. In the end, no one really cares about what you've read, but if you quickly segue into discussing how this news made you think that you can contribute to the organization, then you've got a strong opening.

Also, if the person mentioned in the article didn't write it, I try to connect with the writer first to get background info. I usually search Google or ZoomInfo.com. Either way it's surprising what you can discover. On several occasions, I've even called the author of an article when the person appeared in an interview in the business section of the newspaper. Reporters are great resources.

*Question or headline*: "How often have breakdowns in information technology cost your business time and money? I can help."

I love this approach and use it when all else fails, because it's still a strong opener. I adopted it from Tony Peranello's book, *Selling to VITO* (VITO stands for Very Important Top Officer). The book is a brilliant primer on booking appointments. It masterfully explains how to draw attention to your accomplishments in a manner that screams, *"You want to meet me!"*

As a Guerrilla, you know that you may only have a hiring manager's attention for a few seconds, so get to the point. Once you have a reader's attention, you must supply them with information that stokes their desire to read more and more until they have to call you.

Every sentence matters. Every paragraph must connect. Your thoughts must be crystal clear and written to benefit the reader—not you—so that when you ask for a meeting, he understands it's in his best interest.

## ■ HOW TO ASK FOR THE INTERVIEW IN YOUR LETTER

For years, I've told friends and colleagues to close their cover letters this way, and it's worked very well for them. Here's that sample closing again:

> *I will call you Tuesday, June 10 at 8:30 A.M. to arrange a time for the two of us to talk. If this is not a convenient time please ask Ms. Smith to call me and suggest an alternative.*

*Note*: You need to get the name of the hiring manager's assistant or the person who opens the manager's mail, then put that gatekeeper's name in the letter. The effect of this is extremely powerful. It tells the reader, "Hey, this person was motivated enough to find out who sets my schedule. If they're doing clever things like this now, before we've even met, I wonder what kind of creative solutions this person might deliver when they're on my team?"

How will the hiring manager respond to this "ask for the interview" tactic?

Like the Sex Pistols, asking for the interview in your cover letter might be loved, it might be hated, but it will *always* get a reaction. Specifically, the hiring manager who reads it might:

➤ Throw out your letter.

➤ Call you right away.

➤ Ask his assistant to call you and tell you when he's available.

➤ Make a note on his schedule and wait for your call at the appointed time.

More often than not, the hiring manager will call you right away or wait to see if you call at the appointed day and time. People who have used this closing in their letters have reported that the hiring managers have picked up the call on the first ring and said, "I was sitting here waiting to see if you would call." As you can see, it's vital that you follow through on this.

If the person isn't there when you call, leave a message stating, "Sorry I missed you. I will be waiting for your call back between [such-and-such hours] today." If this doesn't work, call the person's assistant and ask to schedule a call or meeting. If he is at all interested in you—and he should be, because you researched his needs ahead of time—he will call.

## GUERRILLA INTELLIGENCE

*One Unusual Way to End Your Guerrilla Cover Letter*

### Kevin Donlin

Here's a quirky, unusual, and, for true Guerrilla Job Hunters, excellent way to end your cover letter—include a P.S. at the end after your name and signature.

Let me explain.

Go open your junk mail right now (or fish it out of the trash). By "junk mail," I mean all those letters that try to sell you credit cards, magazine subscriptions, 10 CDs for a penny, and so on. Look at the bottom of each sales letter. What do you see? Ninety-eight out of 100 times, you'll find a P.S. at the end.

Why? Because over the last 100 years, direct-mail copywriters have found that a P.S. almost always gets read. So they put a compelling sales message where they know it will be seen—in the P.S. at the end of the letter.

You can do the same thing—and increase the number of calls you get from employers—by including a provocative P.S. at the end of your Guerrilla Cover Letter.

All you have to do is think of the one statement you absolutely, positively want hiring managers to read. Then stick it in your P.S.

Here are three examples to get you started:

1. P.S. If you do not have a current need, please pass my resume on to someone who wants to turn a $400,000 loss into $800,000 profit in two years, as I did for my current employer.

*(continued)*

(*Continued*)

2. P.S. Please call me at 612-555-0000 to find out why my supervisor recently said: "I have absolutely nothing but great things to say about Dan. His strengths are troubleshooting problems, taking care of situations in a timely manner, and always willing to go the extra mile. Dan is a great team player."

3. P.S. If you don't see a fit at this time, please pass my resume on to someone who needs to increase qualified deal flow by more than 300% and sales closing ratios by more than 25%, as I have repeatedly done.

Take advantage of the fact that people are trained to look for and read the P.S. in a letter. You will gain an immediate advantage over ordinary job seekers.

Kevin Donlin is Co-Director of Guerrilla Job Search International, Inc. and has assisted nearly 10,000 job hunters since 1996. He has written a job search column for the *Minneapolis Star Tribune* since 2000 and delivered nearly 100 seminars across North America. He's been interviewed by the *New York Times*, the *Wall Street Journal*, *Money* magazine, ABC TV (Detroit), NBC TV (Minneapolis), Fox News (Minneapolis), CBS Radio, *Entrepreneur* magazine, and many others.

# Chapter 7

# Guerrilla Networking

## A Radical Approach

Things come to those who wait, but only things left by those who hustle.

—ABRAHAM LINCOLN

At the core of every job search lies one individual who will determine your success. You alone are responsible for the failure or victory of your job-hunting mission. Let's face it, nobody cares more about you than you—not even your mother. Job hunting is all about you and what you do for yourself. You can count on other people but you're the one that counts. Too subtle?

## ■ THE NETWORKING MYTH

The world of work has changed dramatically over the past five years but did you know that most job hunters still depend on the same old tired ways to find a job? Ironic isn't it!

Traditional networking ultimately relies on having a fundamental belief in the kindness of strangers. At its core, it preaches that job hunters must have faith that they'll find a job through a friend of a friend of a friend. This is largely a myth.

Although I've heard that this strategy yielded great results in the past, it's not enough today. With the constantly changing marketplace, there is more competition for fewer leads. Traditional networking is much like casting your fate to the wind. It is too passive to rely on. Moreover, there are three flaws in traditional networking:

1. You need to have a network at hand when you find yourself out of work (by the way—being out of work is not the best time to start building one).

2. It requires you to be at least a little outgoing because you need to talk to strangers.

3. There's no way to guarantee the jobs people refer will be ones you'll be interested in, much less excel at.

Today, networking can either be the shortest route to your dream job or to a lengthy series of unsatisfying lunches—the difference lies in how you approach it. Let me show you how a Guerrilla networks.

## ■ HOW TO TARGET NETWORK LIKE A HEADHUNTER

Download available

*Note:* This particular section of the book is absolutely critical to the success of your job hunt. Mastering this (not hard at all) will allow you to reach into any organization or company you choose, regardless of whether you know anyone there. When you understand these concepts you will be ahead of 99% of all the other job hunters.

Headhunters network out of pure necessity. More often than not, they will have an assignment to deliver "X," whatever "X" may be that day, even when they've never recruited an "X" before. That doesn't stop them from completing the mission. There are tried-and-true methods for locating, identifying, and recruiting candidates. I pioneered the strategy and subsequent tactics you are about to learn 25 years ago.

You should focus all your networking energy at the tip of the spear; the companies you have already identified as being the Tier 1 buyers of you. Anything else is a waste of your time, energy, and money. We've been preaching target, target, target, for a reason—it works. Guerrillas target those companies where they know they can help solve a problem. The following four steps reverse engineer that process so you can find opportunities yourself.

### ➤  Step 1: Locate Your Target Companies

Determine which companies you want to work for, how you can add value, and why they should hire you. If you've followed the advice up to this point in the book, you've already done this work.

### ➤  Step 2: Identify Who Runs the Department

Find out who is in charge of the area you want to work in. This generally means identifying a vice president or general manager. For companies with fewer than 50 people, it may mean the owner or president. You can get this information by calling the company and asking, "Who's responsible for "X"? Or you can look on the firm's web site to find the person in that position. Several methods for doing this are outlined in Chapter 5. You can also use LinkedIn and if you don't already have a profile; worry not, because you're going to create one next. You can use ZoomInfo.com.

### ➤  Step 3: Research Referrals

#### 3. A. *Using Google for Leads*

Right about now, you're probably saying, "Great idea, Dave, but I want to do this right now. So where do I get the names of the people to call, bright boy?" Thanks for asking. Remember Google? Go to www.google.com and type in the name of the company you're interested in with the words "resume," "work experience," and "apply," exactly as shown in Figure 7.1.

For illustrative purposes, we're using PeopleSoft as the company.

This will bring back results that will include people who have worked for PeopleSoft in the past. The preceding example resulted

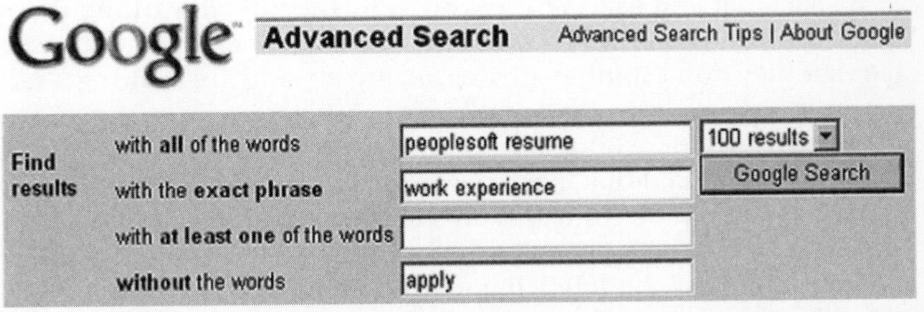

Figure 7.1   Google Advanced Search for company contacts.

in 127,000 hits at the time—your results will vary because Google changes by the minute.

Substitute the name of the company you want to research for the company in this example. Find a contact name among the returned links, get a phone number, and get ready to call that person—we tell you how next. Using Google in this way should provide a handful of leads to former employees—or, as I refer to them, "the newly departed."

There are, of course, other ways to do this. One of the largest databases of professionals in the United States is ZoomInfo (www.zoominfo.com). This search engine allows you to do a keyword search by title, company, location, and a host of other criteria. The free version of the product allows users to search for a specific person by name, with or without a company name. The lists include former employees. They are ideal because it's a universal truth that if approached correctly they will most often discuss previous employers quite openly. This is a tactic that successful headhunters use, and so should you. After the first couple of awkward calls it'll become as easy and matter-of-fact as pouring a cup of coffee. The good news is you can always hang up if you get nervous. Of course, there is an easier—if somewhat slower—way to do this.

### 3. B. How to Leverage the Newly Departed

So now that you know how to find people, how do you leverage this? You're going to call them on the telephone, and get information about:

➤ The person you are targeting at the companies you want to work for—your Top 10

➤ The department the person runs

➤ The company itself

Just pick up the phone and call them; use the Ice Breaker Question from 3.D., coming up soon.

Be sociable and ask these people how they liked working there. Watch for any hesitation before they answer. The pause may be a clue that they don't want to answer negatively and are framing a safe answer.

The reasons for asking most of the following questions should be obvious. Having said that, keep the following questions in mind even though it may not be immediately clear why you need to ask them. This exercise will help you prepare for an interview at a later date.

You should ask the following questions in the order they are presented here.

*About the Potential Boss*

1. Did you work directly for [insert name of potential boss]?
   - If the people you question did not work directly for the person, they may not be able to answer the questions 100% accurately, but their feedback may still be of value.
2. How long?
   - Longer is better.
3. What is [insert name] like?
   - What they mention first will be a dominant characteristic. You may need to push a bit to get the response.
4. What kind of person is [insert name]?
5. What kind of manager is he?
6. What does this manager look for in an employee?
   - How does your experience compare to that of the people they normally hire?
7. How is [insert name] positioned in the company?
   - This is a crucial question to confirm that you are targeting the right person.
8. Is [insert name] on the way up or down?
9. Does he have the ear of the president or owner?
   - You need to know whether this person has the capability to hire you and can get the president to sign off.
10. Is he political or a straight shooter?
11. What is his temperament?
12. Where does he get his good people from?
13. What type of people does he hire?
14. Is [insert name] forward thinking or reactive?
15. Is he aggressive or laid back?
16. How's his ability to pick winners?
    - You need to know now if this manager can easily recognize talent. This will dictate the amount of effort you may need to put into your approach.
17. Will [insert name] go to bat for his staff?
18. What was his biggest accomplishment?
19. Does he seek professional growth for himself? (If not, it will be difficult for you to grow on the job.)

*About the Department*

1. Is it growing or shrinking?
   — Either way, the information will influence which of your skills you emphasize.
2. Is the department under pressure from competitors?
   — How is it handling this?
3. What are the department's biggest issues?
   — Can you solve its problems?
4. Is the department respected by the rest of the company?
   — This determines whether it can get another hire in the budget.
5. Is the department seen as adding value to the company or is it viewed as just another cost center?
6. How's the department doing compared with other departments in the company?
7. What's the biggest thing the department needs to do to be successful?

*About the Company*

1. What new products or services are they looking to build or offer in the near future?
   — How can my experience apply?
2. How are they doing financially?
3. If there's one thing they need to do better than their competitors, what is it?
4. What do they do better than their competitors?
5. Who are their best customers?
6. Who would they like to have as customers?
7. What do their customers think of the company?
8. How's the turnover?
9. Can you think of anyone else I should talk to?
   — Get referrals, if you can, to people who currently work there to help cement your position even before you come in for the first interview.
10. Would you work there again?
11. Why did you leave?

- Asking this directly is a good idea, especially if the person has made negative comments about the individual, department, or company. A person who won't or can't return to a former job may have a beef with the company that makes any opinion of doubtful value.

12. Does the company have a clearly stated vision? Do people in the company know what it is?

### 3. C. Your All-Important Last Question

"If I decide to talk with them, can I say I was speaking with you?"

You ask that question for two reasons: First, if the questions you ask the former employee result in positive answers, that employee's name may help you later in securing a meeting with the hiring manager. Second, the former employee may phone his old boss and tell him about all the background due diligence you're doing on the company. That's a great thing.

### 3. D. Your Icebreaker Question

Download available

Here's your opening line—pick up the phone, dial the number, and say:

> *Hi, my name is_____ . I'm doing some research on XYZ Corporation, and I know that you used to work there because [explain how you found the person's name]. I'm thinking of applying for a job there. Can I ask you a couple of quick questions to see if it's worth my time and effort? I know this is an unusual way to do a job search but . . .*

Now be quiet and let the person answer yes or no. In my experience, 7 out of 10 times the person will answer, "Sure, what do you want to know?"

If he says "No," ask: "Do you know anyone who I can talk to about the company, because I'm really interested in finding out as much as I can before I approach them?"

Either you will get a referral with your second attempt, or the person may decide to answer your questions after all. Someone who had a good experience at the company will answer your questions without hesitation. If it was a bad experience, the person may tell you as well, but it's unlikely. If you don't get anywhere, move on to the next person on your list.

Expect results. With a few minor variations, this is exactly how headhunters network to find candidates.

Ask whatever you think is important for you to know before contacting the next person. You will be amazed by how much you will learn. Further you may be stunned by what people will disclose about former employers—if you just take the initiative to ask.

The competitive intelligence you gather is valuable. Now you can assess how your accomplishments fit with the employer's needs. After doing three to four of these interviews, you'll have the inside track. You will be able to assess which of your accomplishments might be of most interest to the employer.

When you approach the company, you will know far more than any other job hunter before you've even had your first interview. You might be able to decide if it's even worth working there. How powerful is that? That's how a Guerrilla job hunter networks.

➤ **Step 4: Refer Yourself**

Download
available

Instead of relying on someone to refer you, take the initiative and refer yourself. The rejection rate will be very low if you use the following script exactly as I have written it. There is powerful sales psychology at work here—too much to explain in this book—just do it. Trust my 25 years of experience.

Follow the following script. The text under each statement briefly explains why you are saying what you are saying and what the employer's response is likely to be.

Call the person you identified as running the department. Keep calling until you connect with the person.

You: My name is_____ . I've been researching your company and have talked to [name two of the people you spoke with if you have their permission] and they think that we should talk. Do you have time for coffee next week?

This opener is designed to build curiosity and establish your right to talk to this manager. Using the names of the people who have worked for the person in the past gives you credibility.

Employer: What's this about?

The tone of voice could be curious or annoyed because you still haven't said what you want. Stay with the script.

You: I've been examining the way you [market your product—sell to people—manage inventory—develop new products—(fill in the blank with the challenges you know they have that your experience can address)], and I have a few ideas I'd like to share with you. Do you have time for coffee next week?

The manager may think you're a consultant—which could be good or bad and there's no way to know in advance—or could sound grateful that the former employees were thoughtful enough to refer you because the department does have a big problem to solve. The person may invite you in right now or continue to cross-examine you.
Note: Make sure you're hitting the company's problem areas.

Employer: Are you trying to sell me something?

You may sound like a bit of a classic salesperson, but don't panic. Follow the script.

You: No. In the course of doing my market research on the [name the industry] industry, I've learned that your company might be a good fit for my [identify the skills you want to emphasize] but frankly you're the only one who knows that for sure. In the interests of time, I thought I would see if you had time for coffee so I can see if the types of results I achieved for [name the company] could be replicated for your company.

Now you're talking about how you solved a similar problem elsewhere and that will build your credibility and his interest in seeing you. But it still may not be enough.

Employer: Thanks, but we're not hiring anyone right now.

If you hear this, you need to verbally pull back to maintain control. Here are the two rebuttals you should use, one after the other if necessary.

➤ Rebuttal A

"That's good because I'm not saying I'm interested in working there—at least not yet—but we both know the time to identify talent is long before you need it—would you agree [you want him to say something at this point to keep him in the conversation]?

"[Name two more people you spoke with if you have their permission] said it might interest you to know how [throw out your biggest accomplishment at your current or last company that matches this company's need] for XYZ Corporation. Do you have 15 minutes for coffee next week?"

Often one accomplishment that addresses their problem will be enough to secure a meeting, but maybe not.

➤ Rebuttal B

"You know XYZ Corporation had the same concern—Here is what I did for them [throw out your next biggest accomplishment].

I have no idea if that's important to you or if you're the type of company I can do this for, but [name a few of the people you talked to] thought it might be of interest. Do you have 15 minutes for coffee next week?"

A second accomplishment that addresses their problem should be enough to secure a meeting, but again it may not be.

Employer: No, we're not hiring, but you can send me a resume.

Don't be fooled. The employer just wants you off the phone. Finish with this statement.

You: I don't have an up-to-date one. I'm not your typical [name your position]. I'm being smart about this. I've researched a few companies I want to know more about, and yours is one of them. After we meet, if you think my experience can benefit your company, then I'd be happy to do a formal resume and wait until you have an opening. Can we meet next week for coffee?

If you get the appointment, you need to pick the place and time and confirm it two days prior.

If the manager still doesn't bite, there's not much more you can do with the situation. Frankly, there's probably something wrong with the person and, in my experience, that may actually be the company's problem. So there's only one thing you can do—move up the chain of command to this person's boss. If you get the same reaction from the boss, move on to the next company.

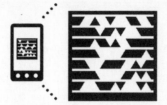

**Get the free mobile app at**
**http://gettag.mobi**

---

### GUERRILLA TIP

➤ Follow the script but practice until you don't sound like you're reading it. You need to sound relaxed and natural.

➤ Stand up when you are talking on the phone. It will take the pressure off your diaphragm, which makes you sound more self-assured.

➤ Practice on a dummy—approach companies where, for whatever reason, you specifically do not want to work. In the headhunting business, we call these throwaways; companies we try new marketing material on before approaching a real employment lead.

➤ Throwaways don't matter, so be as bold as you like. Practicing will build your Guerrilla confidence.

---

### GUERRILLA WISDOM

*Making the Best Use of Career Transition Services*

**Lee Wallace**

***Tip #1: Use the Career Transition Services Provided***
Get help with your job search skills. If the service is part of your severance, it doesn't cost you a cent. If you don't get these services as part of your package, you can look for a career coach or find community services that provide help at little or no cost to you.

*(continued)*

(*Continued*)

### Tip #2: Make the Best Use of the Program You Get

Sit down with one of the consultants and go over what is available in your program. Programs vary greatly, according to what your employer has paid. Choose from the menu those elements that best fit your needs. Even very short programs of one or two days have a lot of value.

### Tip #3: Create a Clear Personal Brand

Are you very clear about the value you can offer a possible employer? Before you rush off to network and send in applications, make sure you are ready. There is no point connecting with people if you are going to be ineffective in presenting yourself. Career transition consultants can help you be effective.

Your "elevator speech," your resume, and your answer to "Tell me about yourself" all have to convey your value—your brand—clearly and powerfully. Looking for work is not about telling people your work background. It's about demonstrating how you will be great in your next job. What you have done in the past has to be positioned as evidence for your claim. It's about marketing, not history.

### Tip #4: Brush Up on Your Job-Hunting Skills by Tapping into the Expertise of Several Consultants

Whether or not you have looked for work recently, you need to polish your job-hunting skills. Each trainer or coach will have tips that can be very valuable. Career transition companies employ a variety of consultants who usually have a wealth of Human Resources or coaching/counseling experience. To benefit from a variety of perspectives, try asking each consultant you meet for their top 10 tips for a successful job hunt.

### Tip #5: Make Use of the On-Line Resources Provided

There is a lot of good content provided on these companies' career transition web sites and there may be a job bank included. Sometimes you can get ongoing access to these resources after your time as an active client is over.

### Tip #6: Attend Any "Meet the Employer" Events that Are Organized by the Career Transition Company

Sometimes, companies that are hiring will meet with the clients of a career transition company. They know they will find very capable people there. At worst, you will get practice in talking about your value, tips about what employers are looking for, feedback on your resume, and practice with being interviewed. At best, you could get a job that is a great fit.

*Tip #7: Supplement What You Learn from Career Transition Companies with This Book*
I recommend it highly to my clients.

_____

Lee Wallace, is principal of Ascendo Consulting, "Helping you move, with confidence, from where you are to where you want to be." Reach him at http://ca.linkedin.com/pub/lee-wallace/2/80/30a or www.leewallace.ca

➤ **Micro-Target Using Facebook**

Want to microtarget an employer or a specific group of people? That's what we call a "smart bomb," and you can read about how Grant Turck used Facebook to target PR execs when he graduated (see Figure 7.2). You can also read how Richard Laermer and Kevin Dugan of Bad Pitch Blog fame drove up Grant's brand value in Chapter 11.

Facebook and other online sites are constantly changing. For this reason I want you to go to the book's main web site and download the piece on "Facebook and Other Online Networks." It will be the most up-to-date resource on the matter.

While I encourage you to have a current LinkedIn profile at all times, Facebook now owns the social side of social networking. At last tally there were well over one half billion people on Facebook. It is a critically important tool for finding people you can connect with—especially if those people aren't on LinkedIn. Just remember, while recruiters may look for people on Facebook, Twitter, and other social networks, they do so because they aren't already on LinkedIn. LinkedIn is the 800-pound Guerrilla. Recruiters look on LinkedIn first, so please focus on updating your LinkedIn profile before you spend time on Facebook—if you spend time on it at all. See Chapter 8, LinkedIn—the 800-Pound Gorilla.

There are hundreds of networking sites on the Internet. The easiest way to find one that may be useful for you is to enter this phrase into Google: "List of social networking web sites." It will bring you links to web sites that have indexed all the major social networking sites.

Figure 7.2   Grant Turck's Facebook ad.

The biggest challenge with social networks, of course, is that you're still relying on the kindness of others to send your request forward. Recruiters will simply pick up the phone and call. Of course, nothing stops you from finding the name of someone you want to talk to and then contacting that person directly and saying:

*"Hi [fill in the person's name], you and I are connected on [name of the social network] and I was wondering . . ."*

## ■ SELECT TWISTS ON TRADITIONAL NETWORKING

Okay, so maybe you want to network in person. If that's the case, here's how to find the venues you need and what to do when you get there.

➤ **Networking Venues**

Every town and city in the United States has a hot spot, a place where all the heavy hitters congregate. Find it and join. The easiest way to locate these business or professional alliances is to ask professional people such as your banker, insurance agent, or investment consultant what groups they belong to. The main job of bank managers is to solicit new business, and to do that they go where the influential people in town congregate. It will probably be a civic organization, golf club, or industry association. It really depends on where you live. If your banker has been replaced by an ATM, go to MeetUp.com instead and find a local venue.

Your contact network should always be growing, and the best way to expand it is to seek out new people and build relationships. It doesn't really matter whom you choose, so long as you like them, they like you, and you can help them. And when you get a job, let them know they helped with a quick note of thanks.

**A WAR STORY**

*Dave Opton*

One Classmates.com member, a Notre Dame alum, read in *Business-Week* that more CFOs attended his alma mater than any other university, so he obtained the list and wrote to them all. His "good old college try" netted him three interviews and one offer.

Another member leveraged his college connection when he learned his school was going to be in the NCAA tournament in Ann Arbor, Michigan. As a demonstration of school spirit, he decided to attend the event, but not before attending a professional association meeting. At the meeting, he learned of an Ann Arbor position that perfectly fit his credentials, so he scheduled an interview while he was

in town for the tournament. He became happily employed in a new
location as a result.

Dave Opton, president, ExecuNet (www.execunet.com).

*Alumni Networks*
If you're looking to make inroads with Fortune 1000 companies,
then use a keyword search in Google to see if they have corporate
alumni web sites. Many do, and it's the easiest way to find people. The
command for Google is "[name of the company]" and alumni (see
Figure 7.3).

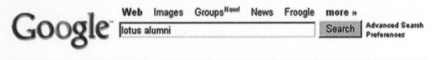

Figure 7.3   Google search for Lotus alumni.

If former employees have an alumni site, doing this will let you
find it. We were looking for Lotus Notes people recently and found
this site through that query: www.axle.org.

## GUERRILLA INTELLIGENCE

### The LinkedIn Manifesto
#### Jim Stroud

Unless you are new to the Internet—or are a novice to its
mysteries—you are no doubt familiar with social networks. For
the uninitiated, social networks are online communities where
people meet and share information with one another. There are
several such networks in operation (among them Twitter, Facebook, and MySpace), but the most popular with business users
is LinkedIn, of which I am an avid user. I have met quite a few
people using LinkedIn and can sing its praises. In the most perfect of scenarios, someone you meet in a social network will
connect you to one of their trusted contacts and business will
be consummated.

However, there is a downside to using social networks, and that is that many people who do not know how to network offline are no better at it in the online arena of social networks.

As a member of LinkedIn, my profile is open for public review. As I have been fortunate enough to work with certain well-known companies, I am often approached for leads into organizations I have been affiliated with. This results in a near avalanche of e-mails about which I offer no complaint. As I use LinkedIn as a recruiting vehicle (in addition to expanding my network), it is simply par for the course. My concern is the tone of the inquiries, which I will paraphrase as, "Gimme, gimme, gimme and give it to me now."

Initially, I thought such encounters would prove only a minor annoyance. Unfortunately, I find myself battling a growing disdain for those who do not grasp the concept of quid pro quo nor the dying art of courtship. If you are a fairly connected person with a "golden Rolodex" of leads, why should I expect you to introduce me to your more coveted contacts upon request? Furthermore, how much assistance should I expect you to give a perfect stranger whom you have only met virtually? Would it be illogical to assume that you are not so willing to risk your reputation with a trusted ally by arranging an introduction to someone you barely know? I would not think it illogical, but such seems to be the faith of several who have reached out via social networks. The end result? Hundreds (or is it thousands?) of requests go unanswered or flatly refused, leaving the disillusioned to claim the ineffectiveness of social networks. This also has a rebounding effect on those proficient in networking who wonder how much longer they will continue to suffer countless requests made by virtual hands outstretched for whatever they can glean from their solicitations.

"The most annoying requests are those made by people who have not read my profile but want to connect only for the sake of making a connection to their list or selling a product," said Steve Eisenberg, an e-Business professional and a faithful user of LinkedIn.

It is my good fortune, however, to report that there is a solution that benefits all concerned. I have crafted a guideline of conduct for social networks and would share it with you now, dear

(*continued*)

(*Continued*)

reader. I call it "The LinkedIn Manifesto" after my favorite social networking service. (Despite the actions of some, LinkedIn still remains on my short list of necessary web sites.) Please consider the following suggestions mandatory when you next decide to engage someone via a social network.

1. When approaching someone for the first time, do not ask for anything. Instead, offer a gift to encourage them to correspond with you. I would suggest that your offering be presented in one of three ways.

➤ *Offer an idea:* Consider the profile of the person you want to connect to and imagine a way to make his business life easier; then share it with him. For example, "I notice from your profile that you are a veterinarian with a focus on cats. I checked, and the domains CatDoctor.com and PurrfectPractitioner.com are not taken. Just a thought, but maybe you should consider snapping these up. If you would like to discuss veterinarian science or cats in general, drop me an e-mail."

➤ *Offer information:* Perhaps you could visit an online news source, browse stories, and share insight into an event that would prove of interest to your intended connection. For example, "I read in the paper that Company X is moving into VoIP and opening a center in Tacoma. Isn't that in your backyard? As a telecom professional, I hear about such things all the time and have no problem sharing the more interesting gossip. If interested, drop me an e-mail."

➤ *Offer introductions:* Exclusivity is always an attention grabber. For example, "I noticed from your profile that you own a firm that designs video games. My son works for Atari and when he is not developing games, he and his coworkers barricade my basement and play games until the beer runs out. My son is happily employed, but I cannot speak for his pals. If you like, I could introduce you to them. Just let me know."

2. Do not attempt to connect with people unless you plan on getting to know them. In other words, maintain

honorable intentions by inviting them to call you or meet with you for coffee at Starbucks. All too often, social networkers seek out what they can achieve at the moment, and this is counterintuitive to the nature of networking. Try hard to put a face with the name, learn about hobbies and future plans, and give the other person a chance to learn about you and find commonality. If at all possible, ferret out a nonbusiness activity that you can bond over (sports, TV shows, etc.). Successful, long-term business comes from trust and trust takes time to develop, yet it is always worth it.

3. Stay in touch with online contacts and advise them of your preferences should other social networkers approach them about contacting you. (For example, "my department is not hiring. However, if you come across someone from company X, I will gladly chat with them.") In the virtual world, it is easy to lose track of those you were once close to. Set a day on your calendar to speak to or visit with those connected to you and reacquaint yourself with them. Find new reasons to stay in touch and seek out ways that you can help enrich their lives professionally and socially. (It goes without saying that you should take note of your contacts' preferences as well.)

4. Jealously guard your list of contacts by being very selective about the invitations you accept. After all, we are all measured by the company we keep, and our associations testify to our character more loudly than our denials.

When declining a connection, attempt to offer help in some way. For example, "Thank you for requesting a connection to me on LinkedIn. May I ask why you chose to connect with me? In the event that I am unable to assist you, I am more than happy to refer you to another or offer any advice I can muster. Please advise."

In conclusion, the best advice I can give has already been given. In his book, *The Heart of Networking*, Ricky Steele, the consummate networker, said that "Networking is a thinking person's game." Strategy plays a huge part in networking offline and the same rules apply online.

*(continued)*

(*Continued*)

A social network is not a machine where you insert a quarter and instant business rolls out like a gumball. Rather, it is an opportunity, a chance to present yourself to those you may one day recruit. It is also a chance to be ignored. Social networks work well for those who know how to come bearing gifts, pursue long-term relationships, and value the contacts they have already developed. If you have considered joining a social network but do not have the time to cultivate the relationships that come from it, save your time, talent, and energy. Social networks don't work.

Jim Stroud has over a decade of recruiting, recruitment research, and competitive intelligence experience. He has consulted for such companies as Microsoft, Google, Siemens, MCI, and a host of start-up companies. As a prolific blogger, he has produced the award-winning HR blog The Recruiters Lounge; the recruiter training web site The Searchologist; and is the co-founder of The Hidden Job Report. For more information about Jim, please visit www.JimStroud.com.

Part

III

# Tactics That Make You a Guerrilla

# Chapter 8

# LinkedIn—the 800-Pound Gorilla

## *Your "Be Found" Epicenter*

Do not go where the path may lead, go instead where there is no path and leave a trail.

—Ralph Waldo Emerson

LinkedIn is the go-to social networking community for job hunters. Sure, you can use Facebook and Twitter to stay connected—and we deal with their strategic use in the next chapter—but LinkedIn is the only social network where you *must* have a professional presence. Guerrilla, LinkedIn is the epicenter of your job search universe online.

## ■ HOW TO TARGET REFERRALS USING SOCIAL NETWORKS

The key to networking is to find people you can network with. There are many online sites that facilitate networking. Most are based on the "six degrees of separation" principle that recognizes actor Kevin Bacon as the center of humanity. Each site has slight variations on how you build and grow your network; first, you join a site and create a personal profile. Your profile can include anything you want but generally it's your business profile that is of interest. Before you get too excited, let me tell you right now that the sites are designed to protect your privacy and that of the other members.

Second, you invite all your friends and business associates to join. Many sites have technology to facilitate inviting your entire Outlook database. When these people join, they are one degree away from you. Their network of contacts then would be two degrees away.

Your network will grow as quickly as you recruit members who recruit members. Your ability to e-network your way to a new job grows exponentially as your network develops.

# ■ WIRED AND HIRED

LinkedIn leads the field for those who want to network for success—in their pajamas even! LinkedIn has been my favorite networking site since 2004. It is simple to use, continuously updated with new features, and a basic account is free. You can upgrade to a premium account for less than a single night out on the town—not even a wild night at that.

LinkedIn works by first requiring that you set up your online profile and then invite your friends to join your network. After people join, they ask their friends and colleagues to join. For job hunters this is a treasure trove of leads.

There are several ways to use the site to find people you're looking for quickly. The site recommends doing a search on the company you want to be referred to and see whom you find. You then send a note to the person who is directly linked to the person whom you want to connect to. With our PeopleSoft example it would look like the Figure 8.1 networking example.

### ➤ The Results Show 13,653 Contacts

You can experiment with the technology to get more or fewer results. In my case, 13,653 people (via my network) is far too many to start to network with. I want fewer people but at a higher level in the organization. By putting in the title vice president, I narrow the number of contacts. In our example, this amounts to 1,263. I can narrow this further by location if I want to, so I add the zip code 10001 in New York. The 68 hits is a manageable number for me.

The basic idea is to then request, via the technology, that someone connect you to the person you want to network with. The technology is set up to facilitate the introductions electronically.

LinkedIn also lets people who are linked to you leave testimonials on how you were to work with. As a headhunter, I can view the testimonials, click to see if the testimonial writer is someone I should

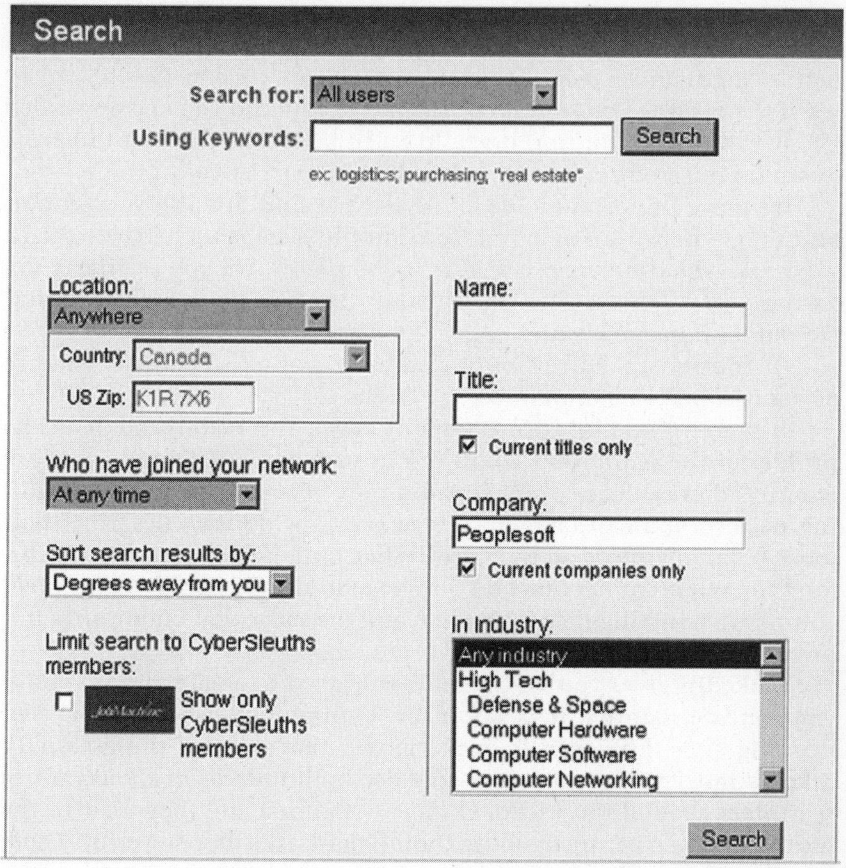

Figure 8.1  LinkedIn networking example.

believe, and then decide if I want to contact the person. Not having testimonials doesn't mean someone is a dud, but having 10 or more that are consistently good will make me want to connect with that person.

From a headhunter's standpoint, LinkedIn has it all. From a job hunter's standpoint, LinkedIn represents an opportunity of a lifetime to establish a powerful network and stake your claim on the Internet.

Here's a dirty little secret: Recruiters can and will use your LinkedIn profile as a screening tool. In fact, a recruiter may be looking at your profile even as you read this. (Need any other reason to join this network?) This is not how LinkedIn was intended to function when it was built, by the way, but this is how the site has developed.

Many employers and recruiters consider your LinkedIn profile your first interview. They'll read your profile, assess your previous employment and accomplishments—then call. Or not. They'll look to see if the resume you sent is consistent. If you said you accomplished "X" at your last employer, it would be in your best interest to have a quote saying so from your previous boss as part of your profile.

It's more important to be found than to find. It's also very important that, when you are found, your profile page is up to date. Once a week take the time to review it. Is it complete? Are you regularly updating it so it reflects who you are and what you are currently doing? Do not let it become stale.

Of course LinkedIn should also be your first stop when you are doing research on companies.

Just go to the LinkedIn Company Pages and read through all the profiles of the employees who work at your target company that are featured there. What companies did they come from? Is there a hiring pattern you can take advantage of? How do they describe their jobs? What keywords do they use? What LinkedIn groups do they belong to? What connections do you have to these people? This is real competitive intelligence, Guerrilla, and the more you know the better prepared you are.

LinkedIn gives you all the tools you need to create and maintain your online identity. It is not a toy. Unlike many other social networking sites, LinkedIn is for serious career-minded professionals. Like ZoomInfo, LinkedIn is used daily by hundreds of thousands of recruiters around the world. Often it's the first site they visit in the morning—even before opening their e-mails. It's that powerful. There are several great books on LinkedIn you can read for more insight; what I'm about to tell you will help you get your LinkedIn profile up quickly and supersize your network. One college student told me she went from zero to more than 14 million connections inside 48 hours just by doing this.

---

GUERRILLA MISSION

Stop reading! What you have just learned is so powerful that, before you do anything else, I want you to establish your LinkedIn profile and invite your network of friends and colleagues to join you—right now. I'm serious. Joining LinkedIn is free and not something you want to "get around to." It's very likely your next job won't be your last. You must do it now. Read the online tutorials and learn how to maximize your network.

---

# ■ LINKEDIN GUERRILLA CHECKLIST

Download
available

Finished? Here's a checklist to insure I don't have to hunt you down after we've connected.

If you want employers to find you, it's important that your LinkedIn profile details your credentials and qualifications. Which entails:

*Use SEO tactics.* Using keywords in your profile for search engine optimization (SEO) can make you easier to find. First, determine what words people looking for someone with your credentials might use in a search engine by going to SimplyHired.com first. Look for jobs that match your qualifications, and then write your profile in a way to include those words. If you understand what the employer is looking for and include those terms, they will find you when they are looking for someone with those qualifications. (Google Jim Stroud's e-book, *Resume Forensics,* for a guide to the key words recruiters use to find people.)

*Qualifications.* Be specific—if you have a Cisco Certification or an MBA, say so but don't stop there. Guerrilla, ask yourself if there are acronyms that are commonly used. If so, include them. For example, the Chartered Accountant designation can also be written as CA or C.A.; you need to account for people who will search using those keywords as well.

*Affiliations.* List the professional organizations that you have joined. These should include: college and/or employer alumni associations as well as any professional associations—yes, even Boy Scouts or Girl Scouts if you're a leader.

*Add a photo.* It's worth repeating, people like to do business with people they like and who are personable. Having a good picture on your LinkedIn profile will increase your likeability.

*Get recommendations.* The easiest way to get a recommendation is to give one. Why do Guerrillas write recommendations?

**A.** It's the right thing to do.

**B.** They believe in paying it forward.

**C.** They know that it makes it easier for recruiters to find them because recruiters check out peer, subordinate, and supervisor recommendations when they're trying to widen their pool of candidates.

**D.** All of the above.

Recommendations from people you have worked with carry a lot of weight and are strategic "digital breadcrumbs"—D is the correct answer.

---

### GUERRILLA INTELLIGENCE

*Get Linked to Conquer!^SM*

**Rob Mendez**

LinkedIn is all about what you want to be doing now and in the future. Unlike a resume, it is *not* about the past. Your profile should tell the story of "Here's what I can do for you, and here's the experience I have to back it up."

Needless to say, uploading your resume to LinkedIn is one of the worst things you can do. Why? Think of LinkedIn as your own infomercial whose main job is to get people to reach out and "order" your product (or resume). If you advertise with your product instead of your story, very few people will stick around to hunt for the information they're looking for because it's boring and doesn't stand out. However, if you advertise your Unique

Value Proposition (UVP) or Unique Sales Proposition (USP) in a professional yet interesting manner, people will *want* to contact you instead of you having to chase them. This is the way of the Guerrilla.

*Tip*: While uploading your resume to your LinkedIn profile is a bad idea, putting it on a free Box.net account and making that publicly available on your profile is a good idea. Not only does it give recruiters instant access to the information they're looking for, but it also helps weed out those with jobs that aren't a perfect fit. This means that the people who *do* reach out to you are usually more serious about you. Just remember—please don't leave your home address on there for privacy reasons.

*Here Are a Few Guidelines*

1. Always communicate first how you can help your audience, *then* let them know how they can help you.
2. Always strive to communicate your UVP or USP throughout your profile.
3. There's a difference between interesting and entertaining—LinkedIn should be interesting, Facebook is entertaining.
4. Make all of your profile sections public, but only put down what you feel comfortable having the world know about you.
5. You're on LinkedIn to be found, not traced—make it easy for people to reach out to you, not track down where you live.

Let's break down what makes a successful Guerrilla LinkedIn profile. I'm going to share with you my "Linked to Conquer" formula that has an average of three recruiters and/or hiring managers reaching out to me *every* week to see if I'm interested in applying for their jobs.

*Tip:* It would probably help if you looked at my LinkedIn profile while reading this section, so you can see how to apply this formula to your own profile. Visit http://linkedin.robmendez.com or search for me by name. And yes, I give you

(*continued*)

(*Continued*)

permission to copy anything from my profile you feel will help you (as long as it's true for you).

The header consists of your name, headline, photo, location, and industry. The *only* purpose of this section is to get people to click through and read your profile. If you were a headhunter looking for a project manager, you'd get thousands of results that say things like "project manager," "PMP," and so on. But if one of the results says: "Project Manager—Ask me how I saved a Fortune 500 company from losing $3,900,000," you would probably click on that profile. If you were looking for a real estate agent and saw a headline stating: "Real Estate Agent—I'll sell your home *guaranteed* in 30 days or give you $1,000 cash," you would probably click on that profile, too. Why? Because both profiles do three things:

1. Identify upfront what you're looking to do now or in the future.
2. Convey a UVP (or USP) using a dollar, percentage, and/or time frame.
3. Paint a picture (or tell a story) in the reader's mind.

Along with an effective headline, you want to have a professional-looking headshot. Light backgrounds are better than darker ones. Full body poses don't let your audience connect with you on a subconscious level because they can't see your face. Same goes for sunglasses, hats, recreational activities, and so on. If you're looking for your next superstar and find that person's profile, but the picture shows the individual laying in a hammock or drinking a beer, you might perceive him to be a goof-off, a drunk, or a number of other negative images. Unfortunately, perception is reality—but fortunately, you have complete control over how you create your perception.

Your name should be just that—your name. If you want to add a nickname or brand, put that in the former/maiden name field. For example, I brand myself as Rob instead of Robert, so that's what I put in that field. Sometimes, I'll change it to "On-the-Job Rob" if I'm promoting my consulting business instead of looking for employment. Special characters, phone numbers, and e-mail addresses are considered poor etiquette.

Now that you've gotten someone to click through to your profile, you need to make it easy for them to find you. You'll want to move your Personal Information section all the way to the top, just under the light blue box. I recommend getting a free Google Voice number, posting that as your phone number, and forwarding it to your cell phone for several reasons:

1. It adds a layer of privacy and protection.
2. If you change your cell phone or you can't afford to pay for one, you don't have to worry about losing important calls.
3. It's free.

In the address section, listing your city, state, and zip code is sufficient. You can also post a post office box or other mailbox service address, but I wouldn't recommend including your actual home address. Don't forget to add your networking e-mail address underneath your address—you're trying to make it easy for people to reach you.

*Tip:* Set up a free Gmail account, make it your primary LinkedIn e-mail address, and use that for your networking activities. You can add your personal e-mail as a secondary address so people can still find you. This will keep your personal inbox free from clutter, and Gmail integrates perfectly with Google Voice.

*Important:* Be sure to list your phone and e-mail address at the top of the summary and contact settings sections. LinkedIn will *not* show your personal information or contact settings unless a person is logged in, but it will display your complete summary section (this also applies to search engines like Google). Again, we're making it easy for people to reach us.

The next section you want under personal information is your summary. Remember, make two-thirds of this section about what you can do for others and the last one-third about how they can help you. Keep it short and sweet, but interesting—the *only* purpose of this section is to get people to take action (call or e-mail you, download your resume, or read the rest of your profile). If you bomb out here, they're on to the next profile. You'll want to speak their language (abbreviations are okay here). Make use of special characters, but double-check them

*(continued)*

*(Continued)*

after you save them as LinkedIn sometimes strips or changes special characters. And please, don't forget to spell-check.

In closing, test and test often. If something isn't working (say after a week or so), change it until you find something that does work for you. Make sure your resumes are in tip-top shape. There's nothing worse than getting someone excited about you through your profile and then telling them you'll send your resume in a few days after you finish tweaking it. Powerful recommendations should describe a problem, what you did, and the result of your actions. You can even use snippets of them in your Guerrilla resume and/or Guerrilla cover page.

By simply implementing the Linked to Conquer formula I've outlined here, you'll be 90% ahead of the competition. Congratulations on transforming yourself from a job seeker to a job hunter!

Rob Mendez is an expert Guerrilla who teaches people how to get hired using LinkedIn. Connect with him on LinkedIn at http://linkto.robmendez.com and through his web site at www.robmendez.com.

## ■ SUPER-SIZING YOUR ONLINE NETWORK

Guerrillas are not slaves to technology. They leverage it for their advantage. Here's what you should do right after you have created your LinkedIn profile:

1. Send a request to link to me at www.LinkedIn.com/in/davidperry. You'll get access to my second-level network of more than 1,412,000. They will become your third-level contacts instantly.

2. Get a personalized e-mail signature like mine (www.LinkedIn.com/in/davidperry). It's free and you'll have it for life, so no matter where you are five years from now your clients, friends, and favorite headhunters will be able to find you.

3. Download and install all of LinkedIn's productivity tools. LinkedIn has made it so easy to search, build your network,

and manage your contacts—all from the applications you use everyday like Outlook, Internet Explorer, and Firefox.

4. Download the Jobs Insider applet. This applet displays the personal connections you already have in your LinkedIn account, which are tied to the hiring managers and companies for any job listed online at Monster, CareerBuilder, HotJobs, Craigslist, Dice, Vault, and many more. It's a Trojan Horse (the good kind, like clever Odysseus's wooden horse in the battle for Troy).

5. If you have a blog, web site, Facebook, or MySpace account, which will add value to your job search, then link to it through the web sites section of your profile. Go to the widgets section and download—at a minimum—the Company Insider and Share on LinkedIn applications.

6. Go to www.toplinked.com/ and follow the instructions to link to the largest "connectors." These people, known as LinkedIn LIONS, are open networkers who will accept your invitation to connect with them without question. This will grow your contact base overnight. You can always uninvite people later, but why you would want to is beyond me. Open networkers are people who know the incredible value of connections. Here is a list of the best of the best in my opinion:

   a. TopLinked.com group (95,000-plus participants): www.linkedin.com/groupInvitation?gid=42031

   b. OpenNetworker.com group (35,000+ participants): www.linkedin.com/groupInvitation?gid=35555

   c. LION500.com group (35,000+ participants): www.linkedin.com/groupInvitation?gid=92107

7. Become a groupie. Go to the Companies tab at the top of your page. Select company search. Scroll to the bottom of the page and select browse all industries. Now select the industry(s) you want to search for a job in. Choose a company you want to work for. Find anyone in sales or marketing or the company's recruiter and look at their profile. Got it open? Now scroll down the page until you find the Groups and Associations section. Now, look at the groups this person belongs to. Remember the expression, "Birds of a feather flock together"? It's important in networking. If appropriate, join the group. Take off or make "private" the job search groups you belong to. It makes you look desperate—trust me on this. You also don't want your employer to see this if you have a job. At last count there were more than 2,600 different groups. Make sure you join the Guerrilla Job

Search group at www.LinkedIn.com/e/vgh/1189487/. Or, go to the groups link on your home page right now and join—there are extra resources available through that group. As well, you should look into these:

a. GroupsToJoin.com is the list of top industry and professional open networking groups: www.GroupsToJoin.com.

b. TopJobGroups.com is the list of top job and career groups on LinkedIn, organized by location, profession, and industry: www.TopJobGroups.com.

8. Show and tell. Just as when we asked you to prove your claims with your Guerrilla resume, you'll want to show people that you're the real deal. To do this, you need to ask your colleagues, customers, and others who know you professionally for recommendations. LinkedIn steps you through this on the site. Get recommendations that attest to your accomplishments first.

9. From the applications link on your home page choose which of the applications you'd like to install. Are you a sales or marketing person? How about uploading a PowerPoint that you use to sell your company's product/service (you may need permission from your employer). Are you an accountant who can make a spreadsheet sing and dance with beautiful tables? Upload an example. Remember, everyone says they're smart, creative, driven, and so forth. With LinkedIn you can also prove it.

10. Install the "polls" function. When you have 150 or more of your own first-level contacts, create a poll related to your job search. Send it to them. It's faster than a networking letter or the phone. You might also consider using it to launch your own version of an e-mail chain letter—but don't tell anyone I suggested that!

11. Electronically connect to your other social networking sites. Just as you can connect your blog or web site to LinkedIn, you should also link your Facebook, Twitter, and other social networking accounts to your LinkedIn profile. Many sites automate the process for you. For example, my Guerrilla Job Search blog hosted on TypePad automatically updates my Facebook, Twitter, LinkedIn, Amazon, and WordPress blog at www.GM4JH.com. This way I only need to enter my data once and it appears everywhere auto-magically.

12. Lastly go see what's new. Read LinkedIn's blog: http://blog.linkedin.com/.

## A WAR STORY

*Stephen Forsyth*

LinkedIn.com is one of the most useful networking sites for job seek-ers, in fact, it was the vehicle that gained me my position at CML Emergency Services. After submitting my CV to David Perry, I decided to research the company. I decided to use the "search by company" function on the "people" tab on LinkedIn.com. In the results, I rec-ognized Allan Zander's name, since we had studied engineering at University of Western Ontario together. Ironically enough, he was the hiring manager at CML and also had worked in the same group with me at Nortel. I sent a connection request to him through LinkedIn and a few days later he interviewed me and subsequently hired me. It was quite apparent that without LinkedIn, I would not have made the con-nection with Allan and may not have been selected for an interview. Since then, I have used LinkedIn to power my business network.

Stephen Forsyth's connection request to Allan Zander through LinkedIn.com:

Allan,

I recognize your name and it appears that we have crossed paths at Nortel and at Western Engineering, so I'm sure that we must have some common contacts and interests.

I am currently searching for opportunities in product management in the Ottawa area and came across your name on LinkedIn.

I am a senior manager with expertise in product manage-ment, strategic planning, relationship management, product development, and change management within the telecom-munications industry. I also recently completed the executive

MBA program at the University of Ottawa, and I have eight years experience at Nortel, including a two-year assignment in Germany.

I noticed that you are looking for some PLMs at CML Emergency Services, and I would appreciate it if we could connect to discuss opportunities.

Please contact me at your convenience.

Regards,

Steve

Stephen Forsyth is a consultant at Business Management Consulting. View his profile at www.LinkedIn.com/in/stephenforsyth.

## GUERRILLA INTELLIGENCE

*Unleashing the Real Power of LinkedIn*

### Skip Freeman

Want to find people, companies, and jobs fast? Read this closely.

Today, it isn't just *what* you know or even *who* you know that can help you find a new job—it is also *who knows you*. That means you have to elevate your "findability quotient," in other words, make sure that your name (and credentials) are known by as many decision makers as possible by building a powerful, dynamic network.

One of the very best—if not *the* very best—way for today's Guerrilla to quickly and easily build and maintain a powerful, dynamic network is provided by LinkedIn (www.linkedin.com). As this is being written, there are over 80 million people on LinkedIn. Let's take a look at how to use this site to find the people, companies, and opportunities you'll need to get hired fast.

### Finding People

With a free LinkedIn account, your access is limited to the names of your first- and second-degree connections. Access to your third-degree connections is limited unless you have a paid account. There are, however, two easy ways to get around this restriction and quickly identify professionals outside of your network:

1. Use the Groups function in LinkedIn.
2. Employ Google's X-ray Search with LinkedIn.

### Using LinkedIn's Groups Function to Find People

You can join up to 50 groups on LinkedIn. Once you have joined groups that are relevant to your area of focus, you have immediate access to the members of those groups, whether or not they are in your personal network.

**Step 1:** From your LinkedIn profile, select the Groups tab, then select Groups Directory and enter the desired keywords in the Search Groups section on the left. Click on the Join Group button to the right of the group to join (see Figure 8.2).

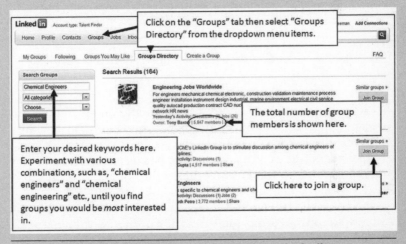

Figure 8.2   Finding groups to join on LinkedIn.

**Step 2:** Once you have joined the group (sometimes it requires the group owner's approval, which may take a day or two), click on the Members tab and search for people you can network and connect with.

*(continued)*

(*Continued*)

In the example in Figure 8.3, we are searching for professionals within the "Chemical Engineers" group who have "Georgia Pacific" in their profile.

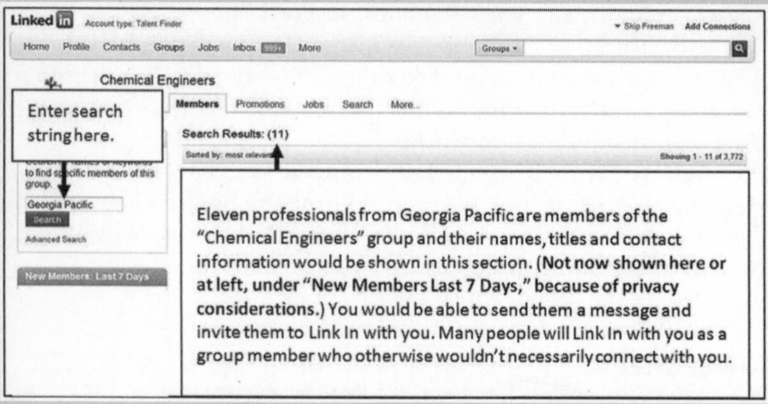

Figure 8.3    Finding members of a group to network with.

**Step 3:** A powerful way to learn the latest news about your areas of expertise, as well as to expand your network, is to join in on the discussions featured by the groups. Contribute to these group discussions as often as possible because, remember, when you bring value to the group, other group members will likely bring value to you.

Additionally, if you find someone in LinkedIn to whom you would like to send a message and they aren't in your network, look at the groups the individual belongs to and then join one of those groups. That way, you can send the person a message without purchasing a paid account. Once you have connected with the person, you can leave the group if you are nearing your limit of 50 groups.

To leave a group, simply click on "Groups" on the main menu bar, select "My Groups," then select "Actions" under any group and click on "Leave Group."

*Using Google's X-Ray Search to Find People Not in Your LinkedIn Network*

Google's X-Ray Search of LinkedIn is an extremely powerful tool that lets you search all public profiles within the *entire* LinkedIn database, regardless of whether the people are in your network. There are, however, two limitations: (1) If they have marked their profile "private," Google won't find them; (2) they will have had to put the key words you are searching for in their profile. For example, if you are looking for a "Georgia Tech" grad, the person has to have used "Georgia Tech" in building his or her profile. If the person used "Georgia Institute of Technology," then you won't find them unless you do a second search using those particular key words. (Boolean operators such as OR and NOT don't work as well in the X-Ray command, either, so stick with the AND operator, as you will see in the following example.)

**Step 1:** Go to www.google.com.

**Step 2:** Enter the following search string into Google:

**site:www.linkedin.com intitle:linkedin** ("Chemical engineer" AND "Georgia Tech" AND "Georgia Pacific").

-intitle:profile -intitle:updated -intitle:blog

-intitle:directory -intitle:jobs -intitle:groups

-intitle:events -intitle:answers

The portion of the search string in bold is required, as it forces Google only to look at people's profiles. If you don't put this into the Google search string *exactly* as shown, you will have returned to you results that have absolutely NOTHING to do with people (such as questions, answers to questions, information from discussion groups, polls, etc.).

The *italicized* portion of the search string represents variables, that is, they can be changed to reflect, specifically, what you are looking for in your search.

*Examples:*

➤ Using the search string shown, as of this writing, you will find two people who have public profiles, listed their title as "chemical engineer," and included "Georgia Pacific" and "Georgia Tech" in their LinkedIn profiles.

➤ If we change "Georgia Tech" to "Georgia Institute of Technology," you find three people.

*(continued)*

(*Continued*)

➤ If you want to find all Georgia Tech grads at Georgia Pacific, take out "chemical engineer" and use the following search string:

site:www.linkedin.com intitle:linkedin (*"Georgia* Tech" AND "Georgia *Pacific"*) -intitle:profile
-intitle:updated -intitle:blog -intitle:directory
-intitle:jobs -intitle:groups -intitle:events
-intitle:answers

With this search string we get 160 people.

➤ If we want to find all names at Georgia Pacific, in order to find hiring managers, people to network with, and so on, the string to use would simply be:

site:www.linkedin.com intitle:linkedin (*"Georgia Pacific"*) -intitle:profile -intitle:updated -intitle:blog
-intitle:directory -intitle:jobs -intitle:groups
-intitle:events -intitle:answers

This returns 10,700 people. Clearly one should be able to find good people to network with among that many people.

➤ Generally, however, that will be too many people to sort through and manage. Therefore, go back into the string and put in qualifying keywords to narrow your results. For example, to develop a potential list of hiring managers for sales positions at Georgia Pacific, use the following string:

site:www.linkedin.com intitle:linkedin (*manager AND sales AND "Georgia Pacific"*) -intitle:profile
-intitle:updated -intitle:blog -intitle:directory
-intitle:jobs -intitle:groups -intitle:events
-intitle:answers

This search reduces the number to 2,910 professionals.

The use of qualifiers within the parentheses will narrow or widen your search.

### Finding Companies

Within LinkedIn is another powerful research tool—company profiles. Profiles feature an overview of the company and who, within your network, is in that company. Additionally, you can use the X-Ray search described previously to find additional people within the company with whom you can effectively network.

*Components of a Company Profile within LinkedIn Include:*

➤ Company description.

➤ A list of LinkedIn users in your network who currently work at this company.

➤ New hires—LinkedIn users who have indicated in their profile that they have joined this company.

➤ Recent promotions and changes—LinkedIn users who have indicated in their profile that they recently changed positions at this company.

➤ Related companies (very powerful)—Companies that LinkedIn users worked for prior to joining this company or companies they are most connected to. Enables you to identify connections between companies.

➤ Key statistics—Examples include the schools most commonly attended by LinkedIn members in that company and other aggregated, nonpersonally identifiable data of LinkedIn users associated with this company.

In your career/job search, before you can connect with the right people, you have to find the relevant companies, so let's continue our study of LinkedIn by seeing how you can locate companies using this tool.

To begin your company search, start at the top of the home page on your LinkedIn account as shown in Figure 8.4.

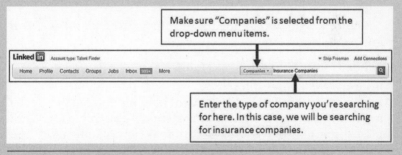

Figure 8.4    Begin your LinkedIn company search.

Figure 8.5 shows the 5,296 insurance companies included in this search, obviously, a largely unmanageable number.

*(continued)*

*(Continued)*

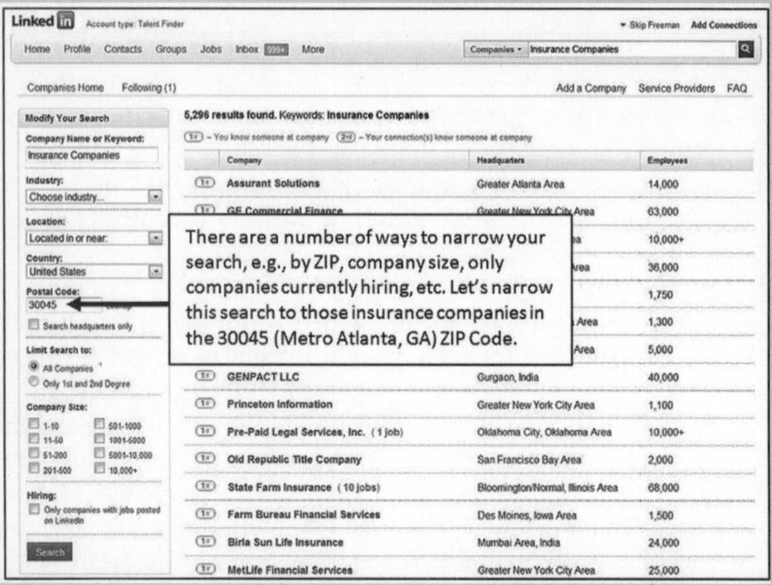

Figure 8.5    The search returned 5,296 insurance companies.

After narrowing our search to the 30045 ZIP code, we have a much more manageable list of companies—135—as shown in Figure 8.6.

Figure 8.7 displays a wealth of information about the company we selected, Assurant Solutions.

### Finding Career Opportunities (Jobs!)

#### The Semi-Hidden Job Market

Though we know that the majority of jobs are "hidden," LinkedIn provides you access to what could reasonably be called the "semi-hidden" job market. Yes, LinkedIn does have a Jobs tab where hiring companies have paid for the posting. Even though the quality of these jobs is often superior to what can be found on the job boards, they are still open jobs with the same competing forces as all posted jobs.

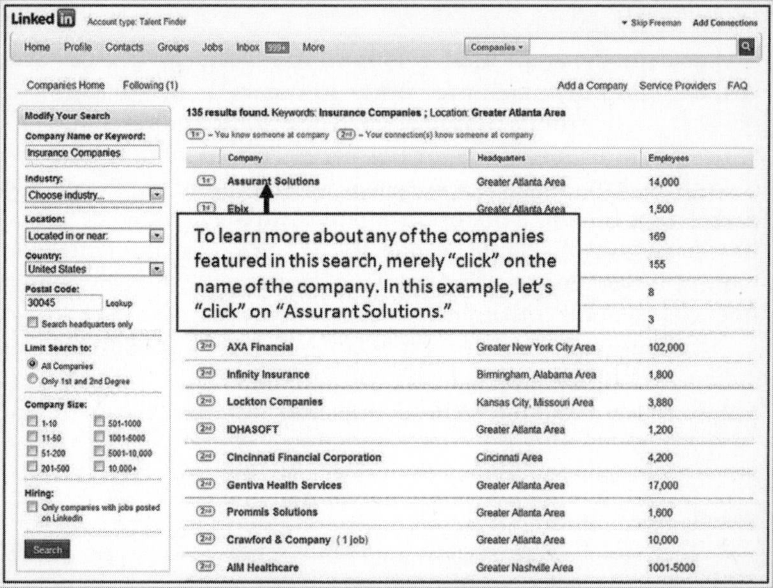

Figure 8.6   Using a ZIP code reduced the list to 135 companies.

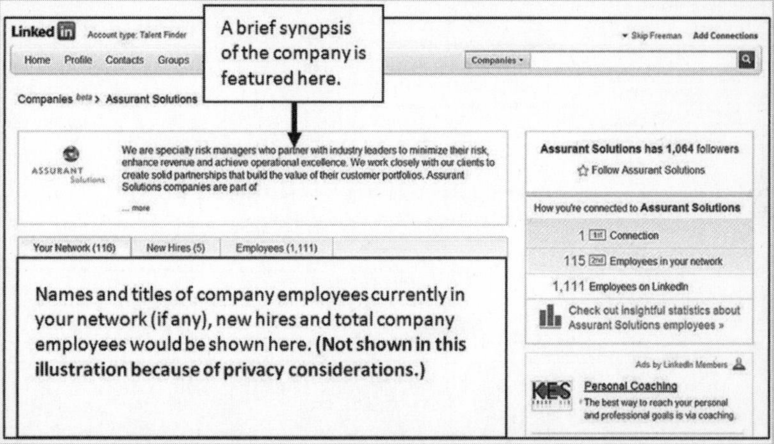

Figure 8.7   LinkedIn search for Assurant Solutions.

*(continued)*

(*Continued*)

Locating the semi-hidden jobs on LinkedIn can provide you with a slight advantage over other job seekers. It is within the jobs section of groups that savvy recruiters and hiring managers will post information regarding areas in which they may be looking to hire someone even before the opening becomes a formal requisition. This often enables hiring managers to test the waters and discern the quality of the talent pool prior to making a decision on the opening and the method by which they will go about filling it.

To ensure that you have access to the most up-to-date job tips and leads within a group, be sure to sign up for the "Daily Digest E-mail" when you join a group as shown in Figure 8.8.

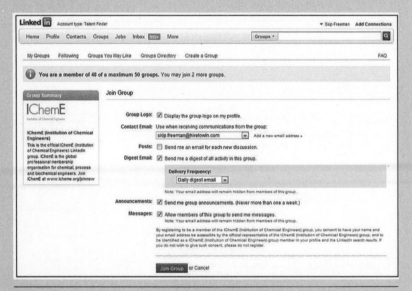

Figure 8.8   LinkedIn Daily Digest e-mail.

**JobsInsider**
In general, you will be much more effective in your job search if you are identifying and targeting companies and hiring managers and then powerfully conveying to them the value you can

deliver versus going after the posted jobs that most everyone else is going after.

However, there will be times when a posted opportunity is worthy of your consideration. The best way to separate yourself from the masses is still to identify the potential hiring manager(s) and connect with them directly, versus simply applying online, which, most likely, will only take you into the proverbial black hole.

LinkedIn has a powerful tool that can help you do just that, the JobsInsider toolbar shown in Figure 8.9. This toolbar is somewhat difficult to find on LinkedIn. The easiest way to get to it is by typing this URL into your Web browser: www.linkedin.com/static?key=jobsinsider_download.

When you find an opportunity of interest on Monster, CareerBuilder, HotJobs, Craigslist, SimplyHired, Dice, or Vault, the toolbar will show you the people in your LinkedIn network at that particular company. Using Guerrilla methods, you will be able to connect with them directly and increase your probability of success.

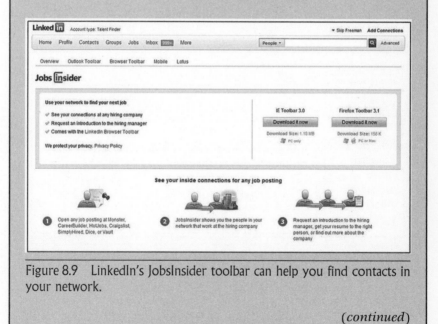

Figure 8.9   LinkedIn's JobsInsider toolbar can help you find contacts in your network.

(*continued*)

(*Continued*)

### *Recruiters*

LinkedIn is the primary resource for recruiters today. Remember, most recruiters are not generalists, but focus on a niche or professional specialty, such as engineers or salespeople. LinkedIn offers unparalleled access to recruiters. Because there are more candidates than jobs today, good recruiters are literally inundated daily with dozens and dozens of resumes and phone calls—to the point where they can't respond to all of them. Candidates who reach out to recruiters through LinkedIn are much more likely to break through the clutter and get recruiters' attention than are people who simply send in a resume and/or leave a voice mail.

Within a group that you have joined (and we will use Chemical Engineers as an illustration), enter the word "recruiters" in the search cell in the upper left. You will note, in Figure 8.10, that 203 recruiters specializing in chemical engineering placements are returned.

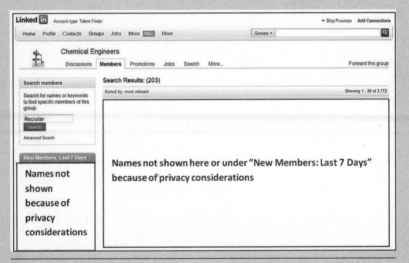

Figure 8.10  LinkedIn can help you target recruiters who specialize in a particular industry.

By employing the techniques, tips, and approaches outlined in this chapter you will be able to come up with a wealth of information that will significantly accelerate your Guerrilla job search. Not only that, unlike the vast majority of your fellow job seekers, you will be able to *target* your approach and reach the people and companies you need to reach, as well as find the job opportunities most appropriate for you and your skill set.

---

Skip Freeman is the founder and President of The HTW (Hire to Win) Group, an executive search firm focused on the industrial and manufacturing sectors. As a recruiter who has made over 300 placements in just 7 years, he teaches others how to be their own headhunter and powerfully market themselves in his hard-hitting book, *"Headhunter" Hiring Secrets: The Rules of the Hiring Game Have Changed Forever!* He can be reached via his web site: www.headhunterhiringsecrets.com.

## ■ GUERRILLA THE GORILLA

Now let's take a real strategic view of LinkedIn and what we can do with it. LinkedIn is not a toy. The person who has the most connections isn't the winner. Guerrillas understand how to leverage what they have times 100.

---

### GUERRILLA TIP

➤ Make a promise in your headline:
  ➤ "I save money for high-tech firms by _____."
  ➤ "I increase efficiency up to 32% by ____."
  ➤ Do not simply say "Unemployed and looking!"
➤ Prove claims (recommendations, numbers)
  ➤ Wherever possible, make sure your recommendations from other people:
  ➤ Describe what you did—what did you accomplish there?
  ➤ Quantify your accomplishments or good deeds in $$$ or ###.
➤ Show off expertise (link to blogs, PowerPoints)
  ➤ *Note*: It may be your first job interview, so be sure your dates of employment, references, accomplishments, and responsibilities that are in your LinkedIn profile line up with the ones on your Guerrilla resume.

➤ Goal: Turn virtual connections into real meetings.

➤ Leverage the brotherhood/sisterhood of LinkedIn. When you call people, tell them you're connected on LinkedIn—even if you are not connected directly. It will open an enormous number of doors for you.

➤ Contact information: You do want people to contact you, right? Well then, please do what 98% of all other LinkedIn users do not—put your contact information in the text of your profile. Include an e-mail address and phone number that people can use to contact you. Need another phone number? Read about my1voice.com in Chapter 4; it's free and so is a Gmail account.

**Get the free mobile app at**
http://gettag.mobi

# Chapter 9

# Digital Breadcrumbs

## Plugged In—Turned On—Tuned In

The medium is the message.

—MARSHALL McLUHAN

So, your resume is done. Your cover letter is complete, and you're feeling pretty good about yourself. Any employer who reads it will immediately know that you've got the right stuff. Great! Now what?

Guerrilla, resumes, cover letters, and job boards are active tools that require your continuous involvement. Now you need to learn how to put Social Media on autopilot to help employers find you ... and beg to hire you! It ain't hard.

## ■ THE MILLION-DOLLAR QUESTION

How can you make employers knock on your door and ask you to interview for a job?

British battlefield strategist Liddell Hart summed it up years ago when he coined the term the "indirect approach." It means you don't keep banging headfirst into the problem—that just makes it worse. Attacking the trenches head on in World War I is a tragic example. Instead, you do something surprising that maneuvers around the blockage.

In World War II, the Nazi army used an indirect approach when it attacked through the supposedly impassable Ardennes Forest and swept around the Maginot Line behind the French army.

Today, going around human resources and straight to the hiring managers also requires an indirect approach using the Web. You leverage the tools they already use every day to actually make it easier for employers to find you.

# ■ THE MAGIC OF SEARCH ENGINE TECHNOLOGY

How do you apply the indirect approach to job hunting? You start by leveraging the changes in recruiting to your benefit and make it easier for people to find you. Reading the following brief history on the evolution of Internet recruiting will be worth your while.

In the late 1990s, job boards like Monster were heralded as the future of recruiting and foretold the future demise of headhunters. Ironically, headhunters made use of job boards long before employers, helping them to flourish. The job board industry quickly grew from several dozen million to several billion. Here's where the train went off the tracks. Somewhere along the way employers decided that they would not pay headhunters a fee for candidates the headhunter found on a job board.

It soon became common practice for employers to check job boards before extending an offer to a candidate. If the employer found the candidate's resume on a job board or in its own application tracking system, the employer would refuse to pay the headhunter.

Well guess what? For obvious reasons many headhunters stopped posting to job boards or presenting candidates found on job boards. Headhunters started to look for passive candidates using search technology, targeting people who were *not* registered on job boards. Ironically, job boards became a way to find disgruntled employees whom a recruiter might target to replace with one of his candidates.

In the old days, a headhunter would spend a lot of time networking, but many young headhunters who were new to the industry found cold-calling unpleasant. One solution was to embrace technology. And they did. Headhunters have been at the forefront of search technology from its inception. Headhunters Googled you long before you even thought to Google yourself.

Despite a recession and high unemployment from 2001 to 2003, many employers were finding it hard to find the right candidates. Many reasoned that the best candidates were employed and not looking, and the billion-dollar staffing industry jumped in and helped promote the idea. Right or wrong, around about 2004, passive job candidates became the most prized by employers. And that idea remains top of mind today with most employers.

Today as profits continue to be squeezed and budget cuts hit the HR department, recruiters and hiring managers have followed the head-hunting industry's lead and are increasingly using search engines and social media sites to find those passive candidates who appear to be an exact fit for their needs. Keyword searches in communities of interest have replaced the tedious telephone spadework that recruiters have long used. This is evolution.

Sites like LinkedIn, Spoke, and Jigsaw are staples in every re-cruiter's bag of magic tricks. They can use tools like Google to per-form a keyword search and "x-ray" those sites and find anyone they want. Right now, you are far more likely to be Googled by an employer than found on a job board or inside an applicant tracking system (the "black hole"). That, or we'll track you down through LinkedIn.com (the number one way), Facebook, Twitter, or other social media sites.

This is fantastic news for you. It means that your career success only requires you to continue doing your best work and letting people know what you are involved in—via LinkedIn and other types of social media. If you have a great reputation, the right people will discover you. They will want to work with you. They will want to hire you. Guerrilla, having your phone ring with job offers is much easier than trying to get a call back. Do you see where we're going with this?

## ■ BE EASY TO FIND

In this section, we describe how to use Internet tools that recruiters rely on and further explain how to use those very same tools to bypass gatekeepers and contact hiring managers.

But first, let me emphasize that you need to manage your Web pres-ence, or online identity, the same way you monitor and manage your financial credit statement. The Internet is often your first interview—it is where you make your first impression, so please be certain that your Internet presence will get you to the second step—the face-to-face interview or a telephone call. Make sure that what's out there reflects you at your best.

## ■ WHAT DOES GOOGLE SAY?

Admit it, you've Googled yourself.

Good. Keep on doing it, and do it often so that you can see what employers, recruiters, and headhunters see if they search for your name. But what if they don't know your name? Did you know that you can buy your own name as a keyword, directing searchers to your blog or web site? Well, you can. How cool is that? How strategic can you get? You can also buy keyword phrases that you can have lead directly to you. "Exhaust system engineer Detroit" would have been a good combination for some of the people who were at the SAE World Forum I referenced in the introduction.

---

### GUERRILLA WISDOM

#### *Employment 2.0*
#### James Durbin

As the wave of information unleashed by the Internet continues to overwhelm recruiters, your ability to stand out in the online crowd adds a new dimension to your job search. It's no longer good enough to be a good or great employee. Broadcasting your abilities in search engines and social media sites, even when you're not ready to switch jobs, is something you'll need to learn how to do.

The good news is that small actions you take now can help insulate you from the turmoil of the job market. Building a comprehensive online presence now gives you the advantage in both current and future searches.

Here is your must-do list for employment 2.0:

1. *Sign Up for LinkedIn*. LinkedIn is a social networking service that allows recruiters to search for you by title, school, company, and geographic location. Take the time to fully complete a winning profile, reach out to a few friends, and accept invitations when they are offered. Also make sure your LinkedIn URL is attached to your e-mail signature. Having a LinkedIn profile is like wearing a Rolex in a hotel bar: It says you're looking without having to be obvious about it.

2. *Update your online directory information at ZoomInfo, Naymz, and Jigsaw.*

3. *If you have a blog, post on it frequently with your name and title.* Add descriptors like your current projects, technical expertise, and examples of anything you have done that shows up in the public record. Add conferences, meetings, user groups, and leadership positions in the community.

Be specific with your expertise—try to imagine what a recruiter might type into a search engine. Include niche software you have used, complex projects you have run, and descriptions of your certifications. The goal is to be obvious but not too obvious.

4. *If you don't have a blog, offer to guest post at blogs that discuss your industry and your metro area.* Take advantage of their search engine ranking to put your name within easy reach of a Google search for your industry.

5. *Write articles for trade publications, newspapers, and the local company newsletter.* Recruiters seek out expertise, and someone who is published is going to have a better chance of getting noticed than someone who keeps his expertise confined to company e-mail.

6. *Sponsor or start a networking event for your specialty in your local area.* The truth about networking groups is that the most benefit goes to the people who start the group. Why not make that you?

7. *Go to Ning.com and search for industry sites in your area.* Even if the group isn't active, a complete profile with contact information will be a big fat target for a researcher.

8. *Get involved in online discussions about your industry.* This is the single best way to showcase what you know without actively asking recruiters to call you. If you aren't currently looking, take an hour a month to look for discussions where you can answer questions and demonstrate your expertise. If you are looking, make it an hour a day. LinkedIn Answers, Yahoo Answers, industry forums, and Google Groups are all good places to start.

These suggestions are all good, but the most important piece of advice I can give you is to set aside your fear and your pride and start immediately. You spend most of your time doing your job, and the danger is that you'll find yourself siloed within your organization at the worst possible time. The truth about networking is you need to do it before you want to see results. Trying to jump-start a job search is a lot harder when no one knows your name. Following these steps will make you easy to

*(continued)*

(*Continued*)

find online, and they'll also sharpen your abilities and reputation in your current position. If your corporate recruiter keeps finding you when looking for that next executive position, the call you get might be from the inside.

James Durbin, The Social Media Headhunter, www.socialmediaheadhunter.com
LinkedIn: www.linkedin.com/in/jimdurbin.

## ■ BEYOND JOB BOARDS AND NETWORKING—WHEN BEING PASSIVE CAN BE A GOOD THING

You know about job boards and you know about networking, but how much do you know about recruiting for passive candidates? Some recruiters think that the best candidates are the ones who aren't out there looking, so they use clever tools to find people who fit their search criteria but who are likely still in a job. How do you make sure that they can find you when they're looking for someone to fill a job for which you would be a perfect fit? Make yourself known in the places they search.

Recruiters hunting for the perfect passive candidate use search tools like Google and ZoomInfo to locate candidates at competitors' companies who have the skills and experience they seek. Again, you need to make sure you can be found and that might include actually building a web site and marketing it. Web summaries on sites like ZoomInfo, as well as blogs, provide personalized URLs that can be used as crawlable home pages on the Web and are good opportunities to showcase your work and interests (more about this later in this chapter).

GUERRILLA MISSION

*Are You Zoomable?*

Google is just the beginning. Now I would like you to go to ZoomInfo at www.zoominfo.com (see Figure 9.1), where any information that is publicly available about you is summarized. Many of the top recruiting firms—including yours truly—and the Fortune 500 use ZoomInfo.com to cut their search time for candidates in half. If recruiters can pull down a hundred well-qualified prospects from ZoomInfo, why would they run an ad or call around asking "Who do you know?" They wouldn't—*full stop.*

Figure 9.1    Zoominfo home page.

This is probably the easiest thing I will ask you to do for your career. These are easy digital breadcrumbs to leave and will bring job offers knocking for years to come. Follow these instructions to optimize your summary.

➤  Make sure your title or a description of your job function is specific enough that you will be found.

➤  Add missing information and correct inaccuracies.

➤  Upload a phone—that's secret headhunter code for "call me."

That is all you need to do, and, as you will soon realize, it is very beneficial to your career. As I always say, if you are not Zoomable you simply don't exist. You are invisible to the very people who are looking for people with your skills.

## ■ DIGGING INTO THE WEB TO GET TO HIRING MANAGERS

When you've struck gold and actually see a perfect job advertised, or you've found the perfect company but no jobs are listed, the HR department isn't the only avenue in. ZoomInfo allows you to click on its advanced search link and search by company. To refine the search, it offers an on-demand product where you pay per search to refine the target list by company, job title, location, and other areas of specialization. Make sure you open your search process to include all the tools available to you and take advantage of those that are being used by leading employers, which, of course, means going to LinkedIn, Facebook, and now Twitter, to see:

1. If the company has a corporate page and who is connected that you may know.
2. What jobs the company has listed or is tweeting about.
3. Whether the company has an alumni page or list of followers, as may be the case with Twitter.

Don't forget virtual sites like SecondLife.com and virtual job fairs. You don't have to get dressed up for a virtual job fair, and you can visit the site on your own schedule.

### WARNING

Only read the following section if you want recruiters to find you and offer you the best jobs before anyone else. I am serious. By taking the advice that follows, you will always be one of the first people that they call when they have an opportunity. If you're naturally shy and can't handle being popular, don't read any further. For the rest of you, here are six unconventional—and *free*—weapons to heighten your visibility. Building them is easy and there are lots of shortcuts for smart Guerrillas:

1. LinkedIn, see Chapter 8.
2. Your eResume.
3. Your blog.
4. Your web portfolio.
5. Your personal web site or Visual CV profile (www. visualcv.com).
6. Facebook, Twitter, and MySpace.

I put them in this order because of their usefulness, ease of construction, your control over the content, and the search engines' propensity for indexing the content. You can control the first five. MySpace, Twitter, and Facebook accounts, while free, are subject to each site's particular terms and conditions which, if you violate them, can result in having your site taken down. I also find that there are a lot of people who cannot stay off their Twitter, MySpace, and Facebook accounts once they're on them, which wastes valuable time you should be using to actively hunt. As well, search engine rules change almost daily, so relying on SEO (Search Engine Optimization) techniques to force your page to the top of the page in search results is nearly impossible.

---

### ➤ LinkedIn

Refer to Chapter 8 for a detailed discussion of LinkedIn and how to create your profile.

### ➤ Your eResume

An eResume or home page is a critical part of your job search. It does not replace the need for a personal web site; it complements it. An eResume, short for electronic resume, is also a lot faster to create than a web site. You can incorporate your eResume into your personal web site.

Guerrillas don't wait for jobs to come to them; they go after them, and an eResume is a valuable weapon. Properly done, it will make you easier to find for recruiters on the Internet and that's exactly what you want. Most people wrongly believe that posting their resume to a few job boards will make it easy for the whole world to find them. Do not tell them differently, let them continue to think that way ... it will lessen your competition.

In reality, job boards account for about 3% of the available jobs. Monster and CareerBuilder, for example, each have approximately 75,000 customers. While that's huge, it represents just a fraction of the 10,000,000 employers in the United States. For many small- and medium-size businesses, posting jobs on a job board is expensive, not just because of the posting fees but also because of the administration time spent responding to unqualified candidates. Instead, many firms are learning how to direct source candidates themselves.

Internet recruiting courses—the one that recruiters attend—teach students how to use Boolean search strings in search engines like Google, Bing, Yahoo!, and others. A well-constructed search string can turn up the resume or home page of an individual who wasn't even looking for a job—an individual referred to as a passive candidate. For many reasons, passive candidates are often perceived as being more valuable than active job hunters. You want to use this knowledge to your advantage now to find a job and continue to do so to keep new opportunities knocking at your door.

---

### GUERRILLA TIP

➤ Save time—use your word processor to save a copy of your chronological resume in HTML format. (Keep your Guerrilla Resume for direct contact/marketing activities. With an eRe-sume, more is usually better.)

➤ To do this, click on "File" in Word's menu bar, followed by "Save as" in the File submenu. When the "Save as" box appears, type a name for the file in the "File Name" box. Lastly, select the "Save as type" box and select "Web page" (*html)" and save your document. That's it. You're done.

➤ Linking strategies—if you are using Word you can easily go through your resume and highlight key words and then click the right mouse button to bring up the command box, which will permit you to make a hyperlink connection.

Make hyperlink connections to each of your past employers. Recruiters like to do Boolean searches for employees who are currently or were formerly working for specific employers—say Cisco or NYNEX. Also link yourself to professional organizations like IEEE, American Quality Association, or Boy Scouts—whatever is relevant to the type of job you want to be found for.

➤ Free hosting—if you don't yet have a personal web site to host your eResume, you can get a free one by typing this exact phrase into Google: "Directory of free website page and image hosting providers." Then select the best one for you.

➤ Meta Tags—use your meta tags wisely as they can greatly increase your chances of being in the first 10 to 20 resumes returned from a search. Don't know what a meta tag is or how to use it without going back to school to get a PhD in geek? Again, just type "How to use meta tags" into Google and you'll find an article that will explain it in layman's language. If you are more visually inclined, type the phrase into YouTube and watch how it is done. Here are some good tips to get you started:

➤ In the title section put in the word "resume" and your full name. You have just 60 characters and that's your best use of them.

➤ In your description section use the words that best describe you.

➤ The keywords section needs to reflect those keywords an employer is likely to use to find someone like you. Remember to use nouns not verbs—expressions that are descriptive and job related like "project manager," "policeman" "electrical engineer," or "retail manager" work well.

➤ Keywords for job titles. Although your current or most recent job title may be construction manager, include other relevant ones. To find a list, peruse job listings and include job titles for any job for which you would honestly be qualified.

➤ Keywords for locations. If you live in New York but would consider relocating to another city, then let employers know by including those places in your keyword list for locations. Also consider using telephone area codes because many recruiters keyword search area codes when they want to cover suburbs attached to a main city.

➤ Keywords for certifications/affiliations. Group together. Include board memberships if they're relevant.

*For Example:*

<title>Bob Smith—Resume</title>
    <meta name="**description**" content="Bob Smith construction manager for ABC Co. in Chicago specializes in high-rise commercial construction—20 years experience.">
    <meta name="**keywords**" content="construction manager, construction supervisor, commercial, Chicago, New York, 212, building, ABC Co, ">

Google the competition—run a Boolean search yourself at Yahoo or a key word search at Google. Find the highest ranked resume. Right click on it and then use the "view" command to see the contents of their HTML tags. Then copy it or improve upon it and update or change yours. Keep experimenting with the selection of keywords until your resume comes up first.

## ■ HOW TO CREATE AND POST A WEB PORTFOLIO ONLINE

The key to lifelong employment is being found—easily. Ultimately, this means you need to always be marketing yourself somehow, even when you have a job. Not an easy task unless of course you leverage technology and establish a full online portfolio.

If your work speaks for itself, why not introduce it to the widest audience possible. The following sites (and yes, there are more that allow you to showcase your expertise whether you are a designer, lawyer, or short-order cook) have no restrictions beyond tasteful and legal guidelines and your imagination in terms of what you can promote. Look at these sites and establish your online portfolio:

➤ Carbonmade: www.carbonmade.com/. Carbonmade helps you build and manage an online portfolio web site. Especially good for designers, illustrators, and digital media professionals.

➤   Shown'd: www.shownd.com. Whether you're a photographer, graphic or web designer, illustrator, writer, videographer, or "that guy," you're going to need a portfolio.

➤   VisualCV: www.visualcv.com. A free, multimedia online resume that sets you apart from the competition and allows you to upload audio and video clips. Think you can take your camera and shoot some of your projects and upload them? Yes! Also link to articles you've written or appeared in.

Now, with these sites not only do you get to showcase your portfolio, you may even land a freelance gig.

➤   Guru.com: www.guru.com. With more than 1 million registered members, Guru.com is the world's largest online marketplace for freelance talent from lawyers to web designers. I have hired more than a few people from this site for work on my web sites, graphic design, and editing.

➤   Elance: www.elance.com. Expert programmers, designers, writers, translators, marketers, researchers, and administrative contractors with tested skills.

Need more options? Type this search string, along with the name of your industry, into Google: "free portfolio website." Play around with your wording until you find one you can use. Chances are good that recruiters already look for people like you on that site. Remember, it's all about being easy to find.

Although home pages are a primary sourcing method for online recruiters, they aren't the only ones. Two other weapons are gaining ground—quickly.

## ■ YOUR WEB SITE

Building your web site is simple. You already have most of the content. Nontechies (us normal people) shrink at the thought of creating a web site because it's complicated. That doesn't have to be the case. For years, I have been referring people to three great sites where you can buy a ready-made template that you can customize to fit your own needs.

The first is Templatemonster.com at www.templatemonster.com. Historically, the advantage of using a template has been that you save time by not needing to master the technology first, but you do it at the cost of good looks. Frankly, looks matter. If a web site doesn't look good, people will not bother with it. CEO David Braun has assembled a top-notch team of graphic artists who build and release up to a dozen new templates every day. These sites are pure eye candy and cost as little as $25. Guerrilla, you can't beat that. If you like one of the templates but cannot program it yourself, go to Guru.com or Elance.com and start a bidding war for your project. Yes, you too can hire a freelancer.

Two other web site creation options include, 1and1.com and Godaddy.com. In both cases you can choose a template and publish it to the Internet in minutes through their online, menu-driven, self-serve web sites. The content is all you need to provide.

However you choose to get your site up and running, here are the major sections you need to include:

➤ Home page

➤ Contact page

➤ Resume or experience page with all your resumes on it: Guerrilla, Extreme, ASCII, and so on

➤ Interests or links page

➤ And any optional pages you deem appropriate

*The content of those pages must do the following:*

➤ It should engage the reader.

➤ It must present a clean, professional image.

➤ Be consistent. It should present the same brand you are trying to achieve with your resumes and cover letter.

➤ It should have a call to action—you need to tell readers what to do next or, at the very least, make it easy for them to get hold of you.

➤ If you write a blog, there should be a link to it.

*If you want to be seen in the best possible light as a potential employee, then your web site should not:*

➤ Appear folksy or cute

➤ Link to any questionable web sites of a religious, political, or sexual nature

➤ Contain pictures of you and your family—especially young children—because you don't know who is looking at the site and for what reason

➤ Include your home address

➤  Make mention or hint of your marital status

➤  Your home phone number (get a second line or use e-mail)

➤  Show personal information of any kind that could lead to identity theft, such as your Social Security number or driver's license number

Recruiters (whether they work for the employer or themselves) search the Internet for keywords. If you have a "Projects" section, you need to have hyperlinks that connect as described in the e-resume section, with links to:

➤  Your current and past employers

➤  Associations you belong to (use both the full spelling and the acronym, as you never know how someone will search)

➤  Articles in which you or your project are mentioned

➤  University and colleges you have attended

➤  Special certifications you have received (again, use both the full spelling and the acronym. For example: Chartered Accountant, CA, C.A.)

➤  Anything else that would prompt a call or inquiry from a curious recruiter

Most of the content for your web site will come straight from your resume. Keep your writing short and tight. The site's purpose is to prompt the reader to call you, not to answer all questions.

Darryl Praill's site is a great example (see Figure 9.2). It's engaging, informative, and bold like the man himself. See what he's done that you might incorporate into your site. www.darrylpraill.com

# ■ YOUR BLOG

A blog is a powerful addition to your web site.

A blog is an electronic journal that has been made available on the Web for others to read. The activity of updating a blog is *blogging*, and someone who keeps a blog is a *blogger*. Blogs are typically updated using software designed for people with little or no technical background. Thank goodness.

Your strategic use of a blog can make you a prime target for employers and headhunters. Why? Because you're making it easier for people to find you on the Web, and just think of it, no more waiting

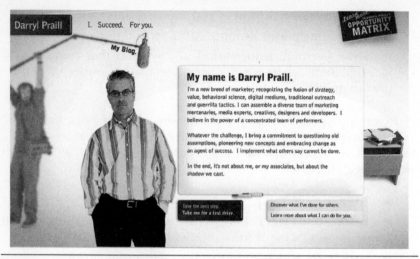

Figure 9.2    Darryl Praill's web site.

for your blue-haired web designer to update your site. You can post to your blog yourself. Having your own blog gives you credibility and a forum to demonstrate your expertise. If you're not an expert, you can become your industry's oracle by linking to other bloggers, articles, news sources, and web sites. You build your credibility by highlighting what others are doing. For example, if your goal is to be hired as a teacher, you can talk about the latest developments in K–12 or ADHD.

Best of all, blogging can be done for free. Check out these sites to start your Guerrilla job-hunting blog:

- ➤ www.typepad.com
- ➤ www.wordpress.com
- ➤ www.blogger.com

If you are not certain what to write about, then go to www.blogsearch.google.com and look at what other bloggers are doing. BlogSearchGoogle.com will allow you to keyword search any subject. (There's that term again—you should get used to hearing it because finding things on the web—and being found on the web—relies on understanding how to exploit keywords.) Fire up your web browser, surf over to www.blogsearch.google.com, and enter the keywords that are relevant to your area of expertise. In fact, while you're there, create a blog alert (on the left-hand side of the screen). Now, read what other people are writing about. It is that easy.

From a personal branding perspective, your blog is a billboard on the Internet. Use it to get people to stop at your web site, read your resume, and call you for an interview. Blogging can help you find a job in the following ways:

➤ Increase your visibility because search engines love blogs.

➤ Demonstrate your critical thinking and communication skills, which employers look for.

➤ Establish and legitimize you as an expert in the field/function you want to be recruited into.

➤ Brand you as informed and savvy.

➤ Invite discussions and inquiries (so you would be wise to invite comments to start the conversation).

Being easy to find is the first step in securing your career future. If you do it correctly, you may never need to go looking for a job again because you're making yourself easy to find. Being found is what you want; it enables you to market yourself 24 hours a day at little or no cost. Make certain to link your blog post to your web site, LinkedIn account, Facebook and/or MySpace account (look on each site in the Q&A section for instructions—it's pretty easy). Typepad will do this automatically for you with the widgets (mini applications) available on its site.

Does this work? That's all you should really care about right now. Can investing a little time doing this actually pay off?

Adam Swift started a blog on mixed martial arts in his spare time while completing his law degree. Mark Cuban found him, bought the blog www.mmapayout.com, and offered Adam a key role in his organization in the process.

---
**A WAR STORY**
---

*Adam Swift*

During my second year of law school, I realized I didn't want to be a lawyer. I had always had a passion for sports business, particularly for the promotional aspects of professional wrestling as a child, and later mixed martial arts (MMA). Since I had entered law school, MMA had exploded into one of the fastest growing sports in the world. I decided to give it a shot and began mailing resumes and making phone calls to the leading companies in the industry. After months of frustrating cold calling, I realized that if I was going to land my dream job, it was going to take a more nonconventional approach.

I read *Guerrilla Marketing for Job Hunters* over the summer before my final year of law school. One of the strategies discussed was the use of blogging in order to demonstrate expertise and become more accessible to headhunters. I decided to implement this strategy by starting a blog dedicated to the business of MMA. I've always enjoyed writing and figured that at worst I would find a fun hobby.

MMAPayout.com was born in September of 2007. It didn't take long for the blog to develop a following and start to produce networking opportunities. My timing couldn't have been better as almost simultaneously a contract dispute broke out in the UFC (the Ultimate Fighting Championship), allowing me the chance to put my legal education to work. The exposure I gained covering that story generated some professional writing opportunities with magazines. I was able to parlay that into more networking opportunities and even a little extra cash.

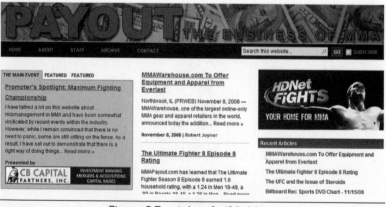

Figure 9.3    Adam Swift's blog.

By the spring of 2008 I was being sought out by the *New York Times* and the *Washington Post* for my expert opinion. I had also begun receiving feelers from various employers about potential job opportunities. The site even produced a fairly lucrative part-time consulting practice, and I counted among my clients a billion-dollar public corporation.

Shortly before graduation, about nine months after I started blogging, I accepted a position with Mark Cuban's HDNet Fights as manager of Marketing Alliances. Mark and Andrew Simon, the CEO of the company, had become familiar with me by reading my blog (see Figure 9.3).

---

Adam Swift is the manager of Marketing Alliances of HDNet Fights (www.hdnetfights.com), one of the leading MMA organizations in the country, founded by Mark Cuban.

---

### GUERRILLA TIP

Don't bad-mouth your current or former employers; it could cost you your current job, and it certainly could turn off prospective employers. The point of blogging is to get a job, not lose a future opportunity.

---

## ■ FACEBOOK AND MYSPACE

Facebook has more than 500 million users—that's right, more than half a billion users. If Facebook were a country it would be the third largest in the world—right behind China and India. Do you think recruiters are using it to find passive job hunters? You bet they are. Every day and with equal regularity.

I can here you saying, "Geez, Dave, this is a lot of work". And you would be right, but there are a few tricks you can use to decrease the time it takes to be found, and being found is still a lot easier than looking for a job. Remember, thousands of headhunters, recruiters, and employers may be looking for you right now, and if they can't find you, well, then your next job may go to a lesser qualified more Internet-savvy individual. It doesn't have to be so. You already have most of the information you need to start. Just recycle it from your resume, blog, and web site—that way, you'll know for certain that there is consistent messaging. Remember, if you want to be found by recruiters but not give them access to your entire life, play with your privacy settings. Take me, for example. Anyone can see my bio and favorite quotations, but I have to friend you if you want to see more.

Make sure that each Web presence you create links to the others. This increases your ranking in Google and moves you to the top of the list. Invite your friends and colleagues current and past. Join GROUPS that are in line with your professional interests. Lastly, check out the employers you target by searching for their corporate profiles.

## ■ BRANCH OUT THROUGH FACEBOOK

Branchout.com is a new social networking add-on for Facebook that looks like it will have similar functionality for job hunters as LinkedIn.

> *BranchOut helps you expand your career network to include absolutely everyone you know on Facebook. It's an incredibly powerful tool—but also a lot of fun to explore.*
>
> *Every time a Facebook friend joins BranchOut, you see where they used to work, where they work now, and where their friends work. You'd be surprised how many connections you have at companies you've always wanted to work at—all through friends of friends. If you're looking for your dream job, these connections can open the door.*\*
>
> *\*http://tinyurl.com/23mcn2d*

### GUERRILLA INTELLIGENCE

*Crush Your Job Search Competition with This Unique Facebook Technique*

**By Barbara Ling**

So you're looking for a job and it seems that no matter what hidden rock you uncover and turn over, you spy the following words blazing out at you:

Use Social Networking to connect with prospective employers. . . . *Use Facebook!*

*Facebook? Excuse me?*

Well, actually, Facebook truly *can* be a very important tool in your job searching career—but it has to be used wisely. *Very* wisely.

You've probably heard Facebook horror stories, in which recruiters/potential employers terminated the careers of individuals because of unsavory photos or language discovered on a candidate's Facebook wall, right?

The above ... not good at all!

Yes, you're a quality job seeker, and yes, you should always present a strong professional appearance to the world. But as Facebook encourages interactions, your friends might post inappropriate content to your wall, thus sullying the way you come across. What to do?

Enter Facebook Fan Pages—but Facebook Fan Pages with a dramatically useful career-buffing edge.

You're familiar with Fan Pages, right? Generally, they focus upon a business or product or group or cause or, well, just about anything in which one can have an interest.

The neat thing about Facebook Fan Pages is that you can create and share any content you'd like and categorize said content on specific tabs. That means you can add a Welcome tab, a Resources tab, a Current News tab ... anything that strikes the imagination!

Now, apply this to yourself. Hands down, you're *the* best candidate for the dream position for which you're searching. How can you showcase that to your best advantage *and* attract industry leaders, industry recruiters, and other thought leaders at the same time?

After all, unless you've already branded your name in your industry, chances are people will not get excited about a Facebook Fan Page that's solely about you. Sad to say, but it's true.

However, these individuals certainly would be far more willing to join and network on a Facebook Fan Page that furthers their own careers. Think about it—let's say that you're looking for a job in the teaching industry. What are your future employers/recruiters searching for? Besides sterling candidates, of course, they want to stay abreast of:

➤ Applications of technology in education
➤ Role of mobile phones in education

*(continued)*

(*Continued*)

➤ Professional educational associations

➤ Key educational organizations

Not to mention dealing with:

➤ Union politics

➤ Bullying

➤ Zero-tolerance

and the like. Right?

Well then.

Just think how you'll come across to prospective employers and recruiters if you yourself create such a Fan Page for your industry; one that actively demonstrates to visitors of all levels that not only are you aware of what's important to them, you freely offer those resources to build a community that enhances *their* careers.

The benefits to this strategy are endless. Career leaders who wouldn't normally give you a thought (as they don't know you exist) would definitely give such a valuable industry-specific resource their time and consideration. And, if you add a custom Facebook Fan Page Welcome tab, you can introduce yourself as the author of that comprehensive resource—and direct visitors to your LinkedIn profile or personal resume portfolio site.

And the best part of this is that it can be done for free.

Do you realize what that does? It effectively bypasses the need for recruiters/HR folk to join your Facebook network; instead, they see you presented in the very best possible light of all, that of the author of a key industry resource that's built via the wonders of Facebook. Go the extra mile in your creation of this Facebook Fan Page and you can eventually gain the reputation of an industry subject matter expert as well.

That's not something to be taken lightly whatsoever. Remember, Guerrilla job seekers proactively choose to position themselves head and shoulders above the rest. Using the common social networking platform (Facebook) to demonstrate your industry knowledge (Facebook Fan Pages) and funnel interested hiring parties back to your professional credentials (LinkedIn, your resume portfolio site) is one very effective Guerrilla technique.

*Take advantage of it today.*

---

Barbara Ling is a 13-plus year veteran Internet entrepreneur who specializes in demystifying the Internet and teaching others how to powerfully make it work for them. Learn more at www.barbaraling.com or www.linkedin.com/in/barbaraling.

## ■ TWITTER

The best use of Twitter—aside from stalking headhunters (see Chapter 4)—is for being found. Even if you don't tweet more than once a day, you can become the oracle of your industry by following the major players and retweeting their posts. Pretty simple, right?

To be found, make sure you use all of the 160 characters allowed for your bio to best advantage. Think keywords. Link to your web site or blog for further information. Look at Figure 9.4 to see my Twitter profile. I use the keywords for which I want to be found in my bio and link to my business web site Perry Martel International. I am a part-time writer and a full-time headhunter, so that is what I emphasize.

**David Perry**

**@RogueRecruiter** Ottawa, CANADA

*Headhunter| Executive Recruiter| C-level | High Tech |*
*Author| Guerrilla Marketing for Job Hunters | Blogger |*
*Job Hunting | Ottawa CANADA*
http://www.perrymartel.com

Figure 9.4   David Perry's Twitter bio.

### GUERRILLA INTELLIGENCE

*How to Be Popular on Twitter*

**The Recruiting Animal**

Here are nine steps to help you increase your appeal and attract a following on Twitter.

*(continued)*

(*Continued*)

1. First you need a name. It can be your name or it can reflect your interests. Human Resources expert Margo Rose became HRMargo. Make it easy to understand at a glance. Separate joined words visually with capital letters: TheresaGarabedian not theresagarabedian. Use words that mean something, not a bunch of incomprehensible letters. Use an underscore when you have to. If MikeJones is taken, Mike_Jones will have to do.

2. Next, you need a bio. Start with your job title. Then list special areas of expertise. For instance: Industrial Engineer. Lean Manufacturing. Six Sigma. 5S. Cellular Manufacturing. Leave out your religion, marital status, and children. (Include them on Facebook.) Include relevant, commonly searchable keywords. Many recruiters don't include the word "recruiter" in their bios. That's dumb. How are you going to find them? If you're looking for a job, say, "Searching for a new position." Don't brag.

   Twitter allows 160 characters. You don't have to use all of them. Use the web link for your LinkedIn profile. From there, you can link to other sites.

3. Your picture in the Twitter stream is a tiny square. Only bright, bold designs and closeups can be seen. Use .@picnik.com, a free online photo editor, to crop, sharpen, and brighten your picture. Let me stress this: Dark pictures are too dark. If you like, use a cartoon (called an avatar).

4. To market yourself you need an audience. On Twitter, you want people to follow you. How do you get followers? On Twitter, search a keyword that reflects your interests. If you're into lean manufacturing search every variation of the term including leanmanufacturing, #leanmanufacturing and #lean. (On Twitter, searchable keywords have a number sign in front of them and are called hashtags.)

   Do the same thing on @Listorious (http://listorious.com). Twitter lets you put related people into lists under a common heading and Listorious searches those headings. Use @Tweepsearch to search Twitter bios.

> Follow almost everyone you find. Half will follow you back. Mass-delete those who don't with @Twerpscan.
>
> 5. Now post links to interesting articles with your brief comments. (Shorten links with http://tinyurl.com/ @TinyURL, http://bit.ly @bitly, or http://is.gd.)
>
>    People are hungry for mentions, so if someone else posts a good article, retweet it manually so that it's clear it comes from you. People notice RT retweets. If someone RTs your posting, you can post a thank-you or retweet something of theirs. To be noticed, you have to post a lot (but not a lot of garbage). Don't post hackneyed quotations. That sucks.
>
> 6. Direct selling is not common in social media. Twitter is for learning, networking, and putting yourself on display. People notice you and see you're smart. They check out your bio. When you get to know them you can ask if they can suggest any leads. There's also a chance a recruiter might find you.
>
> 7. Republish your tweets on a regular blog. This increases your chance of being found in a Google search of your keywords.
>
> 8. Check out Twitter job boards like @JobShouts, @Tweet-MyJobs, and @TwitJobSearch.
>
> 9. For a full book about job search on Twitter, see *The Twitter Job Search Guide* by @Susan Whitcomb, @Chandlee @ CEO Coach. (I'm in there, too!)
>
> Is Twitter worth the time? If you like it, yes, but it cannot be your priority.
>
> ———————
>
> The Recruiting Animal hosts a rowdy online radio show for recruiters and career pros at RecruitingAnimal.com.

# ■ VIDEO RESUMES

If you make a video resume, direct it at one specific employer. Have a very specific message that you want to deliver and talk to the camera. Show your audience the rock star leader they could hire and not a deer in the headlights. Don't read a script from cue cards—no one wants to hire a phony-baloney. Though video resumes may seem interesting on the surface, their application has not been widely successful. Given the cost, and most people's propensity for being average in the looks department (I aspire to average!), there is a better, more powerful alternative.

The use of audio in conjunction with a well-constructed resume is the happy medium. Most people in most professions aren't hired based on how they look. You probably were hired based on your experience, ability to communicate effectively, and other skills. Being able to highlight those skills, in conjunction with your resume, will catapult you into a league of your own when competing with all the other hopeful candidates for a hiring manager's attention.

Several head-hunting firms, in a bold move to differentiate their services, have begun using a tool that adds an audio play button to your resume. When they forward a candidate's resume to their client, the hiring manager is able to get a glimpse into your speaking ability, your composure, your attitude, and professionalism, combined with a clearer understanding of your specific skill set—all by clicking the button.

Bright idea? No! It's brilliant.

Imagine for a moment how much better you could present your candidacy to an employer if they were able to listen in while a professional recruiter interviewed you—pulling out all the information that employer needs to understand to make a hiring decision. I only wish I had thought of it. I spoke to the inventor Jerry Albright recently and he confirmed that there was nothing preventing job hunters from using Verbal Summary. So, if you're thinking about recording a video resume, check out this web site first: www.verbalsummary.com. It may present you in a better light. Oh yes, and you'll save about $5,000—not to mention the public humiliation—by not doing that video.

---

### Guerrilla Intelligence

*Targeted Advertising with Facebook*

**Willy Franzen**

Traditional career experts will tell you that "job wanted ads" never work. It's been done a million times, and it never delivers results. If you asked about Facebook as a job search tool, they would probably tell you that your embarrassing pictures from college days can only cause trouble. "It's a good way to lose your job or never get hired in the first place. Stay away from it." This well-meaning advice is dead wrong.

As a business owner, I've used Facebook's targeted advertising platform myself to bring college grads and internship seekers to my web sites. Since Facebook allows advertisers to target their ads to individuals at a given workplace, I've also dabbled in using the advertising to reach employers who might be interested in advertising jobs on my web site. I quickly realized that job seekers can also use Facebook to target employers. To test my idea, I organized an experiment with five recent college graduates. I encouraged each to design a Facebook ad and target specific companies they would like to work for. Their ads included a picture, a quick note about why they wanted to work for the company, and a link to an online version of their resume. The results were almost immediate—all enjoyed some level of response. One received dozens of e-mails from people willing to help her land a job at their company.

Facebook ads won't instantly land you a job but they will open the door to new opportunities and get your resume to the top of the pile. By using creativity to stand out, you can make a positive initial impression.

To get started with your ad campaign, all you need is a Facebook account, a credit card, and some sort of publicly accessible online resume (a solid advertising campaign can be done for under $20). Once you have those, head over to www.facebook.com/ads and use the simple interface. You could have a campaign running in less than 10 minutes.

The most important thing that you must do is write your ad copy specifically for each employer you target; it's amazing how changing a few words can drastically change the number of people who click on your ad. Once your ads are running, monitor them. Try different variations.

If you do it right, you should have employers knocking on your door to talk about their jobs. From there, it's up to you to impress them and seal the deal.

*(continued)*

(*Continued*)

For a step-by-step guide on how to manage your own Facebook job wanted advertising campaign, type the following into Google's search box, "Use Facebook Ads to make employers hunt you down."

Willy Franzen is the founder of One Day, One Job (www.onedayonejob.com) and One Day, One Internship (www.onedayoneinternship.com), two sites that help college students find entry-level jobs and internships. He can be reached at Willy@onedayonejob.com.

## ■ KEEPING IT TOGETHER

Are the opportunities to promote yourself online starting to overwhelm you? Do not become discouraged. Start with LinkedIn and branch out as you have time. *Note*: Branchout.com is a Facebook application that is looking to replace LinkedIn's functionality. Now, why even bother with other sites at all? Simply put, LinkedIn is a business and it can change the rules on how people use its site at will. More important, more than a few employers have started to comb through LinkedIn profiles of their staff looking to see who might be looking for a new job—not something you ever want to happen.

So, unless you are between opportunities, do not be overly aggressive when you use LinkedIn if you suspect your employer is watching. Instead, be active. Be social, and we'll find you.

Of course, there's nothing stopping you from combining LinkedIn, Facebook, and other social media to launch a smart bomb.

## ■ HOT OFF THE PRESSES: ABOUT.ME

As we were going to press, a brand new service launched called About.me. About.me allows you to consolidate your web presence in one place so people can get a clearer picture of your interests, talents, and experience which you scattered across the Internet. Best of all, you can decide exactly what your personalized About.me home page looks like. Co-founder Ryan Freitas, pictured in Figure 9.5, is a perfect example. From Ryan's About.me page, you can connect to him on

Figure 9.5   Co-founder Ryan Freitas' About.me home page.

Twitter, LinkedIn, Flicker, Tumblr, and so on. More important, with About.me anyone can:

➤ Create a personal, dynamic profile page (think splash page) that points users to your content around the Web (versus depending on Google search).

➤ Understand how many people see your profile and what they are first interested in, which is good to know when you're a job hunter.

Very cool and insightful.

This is brand new, so if you missed the opportunity to buy your name as a dot-com, you might want to go register yourself right now.

## ■ TAG YOU'RE IT!

Imagine for a minute being able to direct an employer to a page you created with a message dedicated just to them or a portfolio of your work or a video of you speaking to them. How would that strengthen your brand, Guerrilla? Enter Microsoft with Microsoft Tag. With the free Microsoft Tag software you can create a tag like the one shown on the next page that will connect a person using a smart phone to your message.

Microsoft says it best:

*Microsoft Tag is a new kind of bar code that connects almost anything in the real world to information, entertainment, and interactive experiences on your mobile phone. Tags are free to create and use. You can add them to your ads, posters, product packages, display it on your web site, billboards, clothing ... the list is endless. When you scan a Tag using the free Tag Reader application on your mobile phone, it will automatically open a webpage, add a contact to your address book, display a message, or dial a number—there are no long URLs to type or SMS messages to send. Anyone can create Tags for free. And unlike other kinds of bar codes, Tags are fully customizable. You can create your Tags in black and white or colorful Tags that visually represent your business or personal brand in a spectacular manner.*
*http://tag.microsoft.com/overview.aspx*

Get the free mobile app for your phone
http://gettag.mobi

Mobile is a natural progression of the Internet. It's still at the intrigue stage. That said, using it would be a good example of your Guerrilla tactics. Imagine a resume being sent with a Tag. Or the coffee caper where the letter has a Tag. The possibilities are near limitless. Microsoft's technology is free. And free is prime Guerrilla pricing. Go to http://tag.microsoft.com/consumer/index.aspx, read the white paper and case studies, then figure out how you're going to incorporate this with your business card, Guerrilla Resume, cover letter, and so on. Then show me your best stuff by sending an e-mail to G3@perrymartel.com.

# Chapter 10

# Commando Tactics

## *15 Breakthrough Strategies That Work*

*Those who say it cannot be done shouldn't interrupt the people doing it.*

—CHINESE PROVERB

So far we've shown you a few new techniques for finding opportunities and for helping others to find you. Want to turn up the heat on the competition and take things to the next level? If you've ever heard me speak or been subjected to one our Job Search Boot Camp seminars, you know I firmly believe that anything worth doing is worth doing well.

Always bring your A-game to every opportunity by diving into this chapter and choosing the tactics that will work best for you.

## ■ #5: THE COFFEE CUP CAPER

This works with any hiring manager, in any sector, anywhere they speak English and drink coffee. And it has produced a hit rate of 50% to 63% in interviews secured.

Here's the deal.

You will send a box to decision makers at target employers.

Inside the box will be three items:

1. Your Guerrilla Resume (printed in full color).

2. Your Guerrilla Cover Letter, with a closing paragraph that says, "Can we meet for coffee?"

3. A paper cup from Starbucks or another well-known coffee shop.

*Action Steps*

1. Go to Starbucks and ask for empty cups. They give them to you for free. (Don't ask how we know this. We just do.)

2. Send the boxes via FedEx 2Day or UPS Ground, so you can track the shipment online and know exactly when it is delivered.

3. Call 30 to 60 minutes after you get the delivery notification and ask, "Did you get the coffee cup?" Of course they'll answer yes. Then ask, "So, are we on for coffee? How's Thursday morning look for you?" Be gently persistent and try to set a date. And be prepared to sell yourself shamelessly if they ask why they should meet with you. Show off the research you've done on the company. Have your Guerrilla Cover Letter and resume in front of you and use them as a script.

Caution: Can you use the U.S. mail to deliver your package? If you want to save a few bucks, you can. You can also save a few bucks by cutting your own hair instead of letting a professional do it. But is that a good idea? Use FedEx 2Day or UPS Ground.

**Get the free mobile app at**
**http://gettag.mobi**

## ■  #58: BECOME THE EXPERT

You can become recognized and branded as an industry expert by writing and producing a newsletter. All you really need to do is summarize best practices—add your experience or comments—print and mail it. When you send a newsletter with topical information that's actually useful, employers may recognize your name when you telephone, making them more likely to take your call. When they, in turn, are looking to hire someone with your expertise, you're likely to be one of their first calls. Here are some useful guidelines:

➤ Newsletters should be one to four pages but no longer.

➤ Summarize lengthy pieces and refer the reader to your web site for the full-text version.

➤ You can dress up the newsletter without breaking the bank by using preprinted paper from companies like Paper Direct (www.paperdirect.com/).

## ■ #9: WRITE A WHITE PAPER—FOCUS ON A HOT TOPIC

This is just like producing a newsletter but you only need to do it once, and you can reuse it until the topic falls out of vogue. Summarize the industry pundits and then offer your own take on it. Read up on a hot topic like VoIP (voice over internet protocol) and write a 10- to 15-page summary linking it to your industry. A hot topic like VoIP will have effects on every industry in the United States, but you need to concentrate on what's important to your sector. Call some of the more quotable people you discovered during your research and interview them for your own piece. Ask them for feedback before you publish. Print it and distribute it.

➤ Mail it to employers you want to work for.

➤ Make it available electronically for e-zines.

➤ Send it to business publications as a possible article.

➤ Send it to trade publications relevant to the industries you have targeted for your job search.

➤ Allow other publishers and editors to use your white paper as long as they include your byline, e-mail address, and web site URL.

## ■ #57: THE TROJAN THANK-YOU NOTE

Everyone's face lights up when they see one of those little envelopes that are peculiar to thank-you note cards—those tiny little 4 × 4 white envelopes with barely enough room to write a name and address on the front and a return address on the back. Fold your resume and

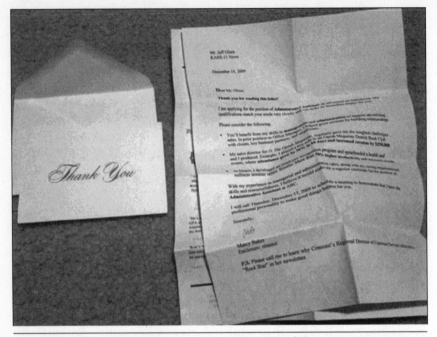

Figure 10.1    Use thank-you note envelopes to deliver your resume.

cover letter together carefully until they fit inside and then mail it (see Figure 10.1).

➤ Don't use labels; address each one by hand.

➤ Use this technique around any holiday—Christmas, New Year's, Fourth of July, and so on.

➤ Use a small, tasteful stamp.

## ■ #29: SEND HALF OF YOUR RESUME

First, find a company you want to work for. Write a compelling cover letter describing why you are a good fit, pointing the receiver to the enclosed curriculum vitae (CV) for further information. Don't seal the envelope and don't enclose a CV. They'll think the CV fell out in the mail. Wait for the phone to ring; speak to the hiring manager personally, engage in a conversation, and sell yourself shamelessly. (This tip comes compliments of Matt Foster, managing director, CVO Group at www.professionalpeople.com.) In addition:

➤ Use high-quality stationery.

➤ Make sure the letter fits snugly in the envelope so it doesn't fall out.

➤ Ensure your phone number is on the cover letter.

## ■ #157: SEND A LETTER STATING YOU ARE OVERQUALIFIED

Send your resume and a cover letter that states: "It will appear obvious from my resume that I'm overqualified for the job you advertised, so let me tell you why you should interview me and consider 'supersizing' your opportunity." Compose a bulleted list of three to five benefits you think the employer might be interested in. Close the letter saying something to the effect that "I am old enough to have already learned from my mistakes, so my experience is more cost effective than a more junior person. In a few months, or years, you'll need to send them for training to upgrade their knowledge, whereas I come fully equipped to do the next job, too." Then:

➤ Point out any certificates or advanced training that you already have that someone in that job might be expected to acquire.

➤ Show you are already qualified to do the next position, too.

➤ Point out any retraining allowances or incentives employers might be eligible for if they hire a more seasoned person.

### GUERRILLA INTELLIGENCE

*Be Your Own Recruiter with E-Mail Marketing*

**Joseph Nour**

Most people think of e-mail marketing as a way for businesses to promote products or services by sending thousands of e-mails. Guerrillas understand they can use it to stay in touch with prospective employers on a one-to-one basis, too. Let me give you an example.

Let's say you're a marketing professional seeking a communications director position with a growing company. In addition

*(continued)*

(*Continued*)

to your resume, you have an electronic portfolio showcasing some of the best work such as brochures, advertisements, sell sheets, and published articles. In most cases, the only chance you'll get to share your portfolio is when you get to the interview stage, but you know that if potential employers could actually see some of your work up front, your chances of quickly finding the right job would dramatically improve. E-mail marketing can provide the vehicle for you to do just that.

With e-mail marketing you can provide your contacts with regular samples of your work through a monthly e-newsletter with web links to published articles or to your blog. It's a great nonintrusive way to enhance your mindshare. The first step is to build your opt-in e-mail list. Include your professional contacts as well as recruiters and those recruitment services that your company may be using.

A best practices e-mail marketing service should offer a host of features including:

➤  On-demand online access

➤  Tools for helping you grow your opt-in e-mail list

➤  Easy-to-use tools for quick e-mail campaign creation

➤  HTML templates for newsletters, e-cards, promotions, and so on

➤  Campaign tracking and reporting features

➤  Automatic CAN-SPAM compliance

➤  Image hosting for uploading captivating images to enhance your campaigns

Take advantage of the metrics and tracking reports to see who opened your e-mail and the specific content they clicked on. Use this information to follow up personally with those who showed a clear interest in what you have to offer.

Here are a few more useful tips to specifically aid your job search:

➤  Keep your e-mail as short as possible.

➤  Tease them with the e-mail message and get them to click to your resume, online portfolio, or blog—you want to hook them, not pitch them.

➤ Keep it personal—use the mail merge functionality so all of your contacts receive a personally addressed e-mail. If your e-mail looks like a bulk or mass mailing, your recipient is less likely to read it or respond.

➤ Use HTML so you can get the advantage of tracking, but keep it simple.

➤ Spend most of the time on the top three inches of the e-mail; it's what they see if they are using "preview" in Outlook.

➤ Ask them to forward the e-mail to other colleagues who may be looking for someone with your skills.

➤ Spend time on your subject line—legally, it can't be misleading and it must reflect the contents of the e-mail, but you want to make it punchy.

➤ Does it look like spam? Send a copy of the e-mail to yourself and see if you'd open or delete it unread.

➤ Always use both first and last names in the "from" line—most people assume mail from Lily or Irene or any other first-name-only person is spam.

Attachments equal viruses in my mind. I have never opened a resume from someone I didn't know that came as an attachment—ever. If the resume wasn't in the body of the e-mail, it was an immediate delete.

Joseph Nour is CEO of Protus IT Solutions and owner of Campaigner, an e-mail marketing service for small- to medium-sized businesses. Access a free trial as well as tips, webinars, and other resources at www.campaigner.com.

## ■ #11: E-MAIL CHAIN LETTER

Take a list of 20 companies you want to work for and send an e-mail to everyone you know, asking them to read the list to see if they know anyone who works at any of the companies. Ask them to contact you if they do, so that you can ask for a referral. Finally, ask them to forward your e-mail message to 10 more people. (We've learned that this tactic does not work for Washington, D.C. lobbyists.) A few tips:

➤ If you e-mail your list to 10 people and they e-mail it to 10 people and . . . within four cycles, you have covered 10,000 people.

➤ Only include your phone number if you don't mind having people call you.

➤ Don't put anything in the letter you wouldn't want a stranger to read.

➤ Put your name and e-mail address at the top of the message in a "From": salutation, so the reader can find your coordinates quickly.

➤ Do not do this if you are currently employed.

Caution: Only ask people to forward your message to 10 people. More than 10 and people won't do it. Why, we just do not know. Perhaps people struggle to find more than 10 friends. The point is, in test after test, people who asked their contacts to forward the message to more than 10 friends failed. Don't be a failure—follow the instructions. My daughter Christa (the young lady at the start of the book who combined this with a Facebook ad) started getting results the same night. For most people it takes 24 hours. Oh, and by the way—do not do this on a weekend; that, too, has proven not to work.

## ■ #131: SEND ARTICLES AS A FOLLOW-UP AFTER AN INTERVIEW

Sending an article to a hiring manager with a simple note like: "I thought you might be interested in this ..." is a great door opener. The trick is to find something that is truly helpful to the person in his job. You can uncover potential needs by doing a search through Google for position papers the person may have presented or to see what the company's competitors are announcing by way of new products—and let the hiring manager know. I know people who have landed great jobs by doing this. Keep these tips in mind:

➤ Articles are easy to find by using search engines.

➤ Use the alert system at Google (www.google.com/alerts) to keep you up-to-date on subject areas of interest to your targeted employers.

➤ Magazines usually have electronic editions.

➤ I find photocopies work best because very few people bother to do this anymore. Also the photocopy will stay longer on the person's desk. It may even be passed on to other staff members who could be hiring.

➤ Keep your contacts through this medium to a maximum of once every three weeks.

➤ Make sure you send a personal note, even if you send an e-mail clipping.

## ■ # 183: DISTRIBUTE A BOOKLET

Write a booklet with information relevant to your industry and give it away. Everyone loves a freebie, so give away something that demonstrates your expertise. I designed, wrote, and distributed a free booklet on how to do a reference check correctly, entitled "Don't Hire a Liar" (see www.perrymartel.com). It subtly points out the benefits of using a professional like myself when hiring (see Figure 10.2). Here are some ideas:

➤ Link to your web site, e-resume, or blog.

➤ Give the booklet away electronically.

➤ If you send a printed version, indicate where the recipient can get extra copies for colleagues.

➤ Advertise it on your web site and those newsgroups frequented by hiring managers in your target market.

## ■ # 69: CALL HUMAN RESOURCES

Heresy? No, there's a method in my madness. Call the human resources department and ask what outside agency or third-party recruiting firm they use. Why? Two strategic reasons. First, any human resources person will immediately ask why you want to know. To which you answer, "I've been to your web site and I understand that you're not looking for someone with my skill set right now, but the agency you use may be dealing with other firms—so I guess I'm looking for a recommendation from you." If they don't press you for an interview, insist on knowing whom they use and why. Keep these tips in mind:

➤ People in human resources love saving money on fees, so they may try to hire you directly.

➤ Getting a referral from one of their customers will ensure an agency gives you special attention.

Figure 10.2   This free booklet is available at www.perrymartel.com.

➤ Always ask for the name of a specific person and their direct dial number.

➤ Get permission to use the human resources manager's name as a reference.

➤ Ask if they personally know of any other companies that could make appropriate use of your skills.

➤ Send them a thank-you note with a copy of your resume to keep on file.

## ■ #10: WRITE A CASE STUDY

Write a case study that showcases your skills. This could be as simple as a coveted client you sold or as complex as a new product you helped introduce to the market. Send the study to firms that have needs similar to those emphasized in the study. Not only do you get to showcase your writing as well as your research and analysis skills, it demonstrates your business acumen. For example: Did you establish an innovative compensation program for resellers that increased sales and decreased spoilage or returns? This is a big deal in retail, where 90% of profits are lost due to returns. Try this:

➤ Choose an example that builds your credibility with your targeted employers.

➤ Results that would be of interest to a potential employer include increased efficiencies, new marketing techniques, and new or different distribution channels.

➤ Areas that would be promising include:
  ➤ Sales/marketing: distribution channels
  ➤ Manufacturing: Just-in-time (JIT) inventories
  ➤ Operations: Enterprise resource planning (ERP) systems

## ■ #77: PREPARE A COMPETITIVE ANALYSIS

Do a competitive analysis on one of your targeted employer's products and send it to the president or vice president. People assume that all companies keep up to date on their competitors, but this is rarely the case. Most companies don't have the budget or the ability internally to remain aware of best practices. Your piece will likely be most welcome. Follow these suggestions:

➤ Focus on companies that are direct competitors of those you want to work for, not your own company.

➤ Readers need to get real knowledge out of reading the piece.

➤ Use graphs and charts wherever possible because people like visuals.

➤ Make it only as long as it needs to be.

➤ Offer to share your primary research if the company is interested.

---**A WAR STORY**---

*Martin Buckland*

I'm certain you've heard of Wall Street, and not just the movie, but have you ever heard of Bay Street, the financial heart of Canada? Recognizing the significance of North America's leading financial districts, can you imagine becoming a personalized, walking billboard advertising your value to the masses? Well, my Guerrilla connection Joseph Cunningham did, and he prospered by doing so.

Joseph, a senior Bay Street executive, had limited his job search by simply utilizing online job boards, thinking this method would generate attention for his intriguing background and secure interest in his qualifications. After 15 months, he realized this passive approach was not working.

Under pressure, financially and personally, he decided to take a more aggressive approach, which was intimidating to his reserved personality. Taking the bull by the horns, Joseph prepared a compelling Guerrilla statement to address and captivate an audience within his own environment: *"Shrewd finance leader with a depth of knowledge in capital markets seeking a new opportunity. Any leads?"* To maximize the message, he prepared business cards and a two-sided, wearable placard worn over his disheveled suit and advertised his message on Bay Street for three days walking between two intersections during peak, pedestrian traffic periods. Securing both positive and negative attention, Joseph continued his aggressive pursuit.

On day three of his quest, one of my clients encountered Joseph while proceeding to an ExecuNet networking event held close to Bay Street that evening. My client was intrigued by this innovative approach as he was also in career transition and invited Joseph as his guest to attend my Toronto ExecuNet meeting. This was Joseph's first, and only, networking event during his arduous and frustrating job search.

At ExecuNet that evening, he wore his two-sided advertising message and gave a compelling and emotional elevator speech to a silent, attentive, and captive senior-level audience. This memorable infomercial captured the attention of a high-level executive at one of Canada's largest financial institutions. A constructive dialogue resulted in a referral to a decision maker, culminating in a fast-tracked interview process. Within six weeks of attending ExecuNet with his Guerrilla message, Joseph successfully returned to work in his field of expertise as a Director of Capital Markets.

---

Compliments of Martin Buckland, president and principal of Elite Resumes, www.aneliteresume.com.

---

## ■ #71: WRITE A BROCHURE

Create a brochure instead of a resume. This is a great way to find temporary or contract work leading to a full-time position. Send the brochure to your target group. Speak to their needs on the front cover. Profile your projects and accomplishments on the inside three flaps (use one of the inside flaps for quotes from your references). Reserve the back panel for your mini bio. Include a photo if you're good looking. In addition, do the following:

➤ Hand-address the envelope you mail it in.

➤ Buy glossy brochure paper for your laser printer.

➤ Keep the copy short—it's a teaser.

➤ Make sure your address and contact information are easy to find.

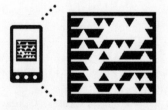

**Get the free mobile app at**
**http://gettag.mobi**

*Do You Exist to Recruiters? Simple Search Engine*
*Optimization for Job Seekers*

### Donato Diorio

In mid-October 2010, my friend David Perry called me and shared some of his insight.

"Donato, in the Detroit area, there are hundreds of exhaust system engineers, yet when I do a Google search, I can only find a handful of them."

David was explaining this while speaking to a group of recruiters. "This is a problem; most engineers are not on the radar of recruiters." I agreed with David.

The backstory: A recruiter's first step in finding a candidate is his own database. Next, recruiters leverage the Internet for candidates. Job boards, social media sites, and open web searches are the tools of the trade. Only after the immediate sources are exhausted do recruiters start the process of "direct recruiting"—looking for new candidates via referrals and many, many conversations.

Most job seekers don't understand this.

If you are not in the recruiter's database and you are not present on the Internet, to the recruiter, you don't exist.

David has impeccable timing. Over the last year, I had been absorbing all I could in the realm of search engine optimization (SEO). In my own initiatives, I had earned the top spot in Google many times. "How can SEO help job seekers?" I wondered.

While on the phone, I did a quick Google search for "exhaust system engineer." David was right; few of these engineers were available via a search engine query. Next, I proposed a hypothesis to David. He liked it.

October 19, 2010, I registered ExhaustSystemEngineer.com. It cost about $8 from GoDaddy.com.

Using Wordpress.org, I set up a blog and hosted the domain for an additional $20 for the year. No technical knowledge is needed. If you don't know how to do it, the people at Go Daddy are very helpful. Total cost: $28.

Next, I added a few excerpts from articles about exhaust systems. The single paragraph had links to the original article.

After adding some content to the site, I found some articles about exhaust systems to comment on, leaving my blog address. (It is important here to leave real comments and show an interest in someone else's work, otherwise it is seen as comment spam.)

The last step was to sign up for a Twitter account and create the username ExhaustEngineer. My first tweet was an announcement of my blog, ExhaustSystemEngineer.com. The total time spent to do this exercise was about one hour. If you were doing it for the first time, it might take you two to three hours to get familiar with WordPress.

On October 21, 2010, two days after registering the domain, creating a blog, and adding some content, the first Google search result for Exhaust System Engineer was ExhaustSystem Engineer.com, as seen in Figure 10.3.

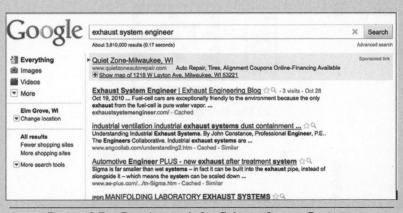

Figure 10.3   Google search for Exhaust System Engineer.

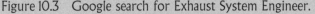

If I were a real exhaust system engineer, the next step would be to add my resume and contact information to the blog and keep it updated with fresh content. In the time after the writing of this article, David and I are going to find a real exhaust system engineer looking for work and give the person a chance to showcase his background and talents. We will detail our

*(continued)*

(*Continued*)

adventures on David's (www.GM4JH.com) and my blog (www.idonato.com).

Remember, if you are not present on the Internet, you don't exist to most recruiters. The difference between being found or not is taking action.

---

Donato Diorio is the founder and CEO of Broadlook Technologies (www. broadlook.com), a software company servicing thousands of recruiters worldwide. Donato's in-depth knowledge combined with his high level of energy and enthusiasm, make him a highly sought-after speaker, thought leader, and educator on best practices in recruitment, sales, and search engine optimization. Donato's blog can be found at www.donato.com.

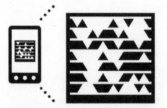

**Get the free mobile app at**
**http://gettag.mobi**

■ 21:TEMP TO PERM

The temporary help industry employs nearly two million Americans on any given day. Temping is a multibillion-dollar industry. This is a great way to break into a company through the backdoor. Remember, employers hire from within first, so it's to your advantage to already be there. Although there may not necessarily be a lot of firms hiring people on a full-time basis, there are probably a lot of firms that can afford one day a week or more. Here are some ideas to open the door to temp work:

➤ Market yourself as a "Top gun for hire." A good rule of thumb on what to charge is 1.6 times your previous daily wage.

➤ Try to get hired for full days not half days.

➤ Ask the employer to provide parking.

➤ Invoice weekly.

## ■ #94: AUDITION

It worked well for the people on *Survivor* and *The Apprentice*, so why not you? Produce a video, burn it on CD or DVD, and distribute it to potential employers. Keep it tasteful and highlight the results you achieved on one or two projects. Suggest you have coffee to discuss how these employers might use your skills. If you have video editing software, you can burn your own copies for less than $2, complete with the box. In addition, do the following:

➤ Use a DVD box because you can tuck a resume inside the front cover.

➤ At the beginning of each video, tell the employer why you're interested in working for the company.

➤ Talk about the research you did to conclude the company is a good fit for your skills.

➤ Highlight accomplishments that would be of interest to this employer.

### DON'T TRY THIS AT HOME

Have you seen the movie *Jackass*? There's an obvious benefit to out-of-the-box activities that bring you to the attention of employers. There is also a real danger of crossing the line and doing something in poor taste or that puts you or the employer at risk. Here is an example pulled from the pages of the *Montreal Gazette*:

The job hunter hoped his resume would land him an interview. What he got was the attention of the bomb squad. The man was arrested after he included his CV in a ticking package left in a Montreal marketing firm's washroom last month. It was his way of drawing attention to the application, as he was among 400 contenders vying for six paid internships. The 24-year-old didn't get the job but he did get charged with public mischief. He had handed the receptionist an Arabic newspaper

*(continued)*

(*Continued*)

with a note alerting her to the ticking parcel in the men's washroom, police said. At a time of heightened concerns over terrorism, the package raised the specter of a bombing. Montreal police evacuated the company's building. Later, police discovered the package was harmless. It contained a metronome—a device used by musicians to help maintain rhythm and tempo—along with the candidate's CV.

### GUERRILLA TACTICS

➤ Be bold!

➤ Be passionate!

➤ Be creative!

➤ Be tasteful!

➤ Be safety conscious.

➤ Be image conscious.

➤ Enlist a personal army of helpers.

➤ Offer a reward to anyone who helps you secure an interview or job.

➤ Don't do exactly what others have done recently.

**Get the free mobile app at**
## http://gettag.mobi

Part

IV

# Your Guerrilla
# Job-Hunting Campaign

# Chapter 11

# The Force Multiplier Effect in Action

## 14 Sample Campaigns

Take time to deliberate, but when the time for action has arrived, stop thinking and go.

—NAPOLEON BONAPARTE

Is your head spinning? Would you like to get a sense for how other people have combined ideas and tactics to craft their Force Multiplier Effect? Read on.

We faced an interesting dilemma when creating this latest version of *Guerrilla Marketing for Job Hunters*; our case studies were plentiful and powerful. The stories needed to be told, and shared, so that you can learn from others' success. Unfortunately, we have more success stories than room. So what did we decide to do? We decided to follow our own advice and integrate old media tactics with new media platforms.

Before, you might have simply sent in a resume to a hiring manager, but if you follow our advice now you might send in a cover sheet and a link to your web site whereupon the hiring manager would see your pictures, your videos, your blogs, your accomplishments, and anything else that made sense to help you get the job. You'll see that we open up each successful case study with the situation, and we wrap it up with what was accomplished.

Now you can learn how they achieved their results, conveyed in their own words—often with video or audio, by going to the specified web page dedicated to their story. Personally, we think you'll love the approach. I would like you to read their stories and be inspired. These Guerrillas have had the courage to try something new. They are my personal heroes and I hope you will take the time to drop a note to them on LinkedIn.

I chose the following examples because each employs different combinations of tactics, and I even learned some new ones from them. The weapons and tactics you choose will be unique to your situation.

These successful Guerrilla Job Hunters represent every gender, race, age, and career point; student, professional, personal contributor, manager, and executive—because the tactics will work for anyone.

## ■ CASE STUDY: GAIL NEAL

*I took a commission-only sales job at a cemetery in August of 2008. I thought it was the ultimate recession-proof job. I was wrong— almost a year later I was actually more broke than when I started. It was time to find something else to do. Easier said than done. The unemployment rate in Detroit, Michigan, was 25 to 30%.*

Read Gail's story at: www.gm4jh.com/g3downloadpage/gail-neal. End result: Gail landed a job seven weeks after going Guerrilla.

## ■ CASE STUDY: TOM MCALISTER

*I was in a challenging spot, professionally. But a combination of Guerrilla tactics, personal branding, and fortuitous timing got me back in the game. Several events conspired to create Brand Man, my fictional alter ego. The first was the economic crisis and the subsequent implosion of the job market. I knew there would be lots of qualified candidates applying for the same positions I was targeting. Plus, I was at a disadvantage because I had been doing contract and freelance work for the previous year and a half.*

Artist: Sina Grace.

Read Tom's story at: www.gm4jh.com/g3downloadpage/
tom-mcalister.
End result: Tom abandoned conventional job search protocols to become a stand-out comic.

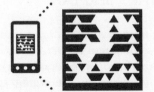

**Get the free mobile app at**
**http://gettag.mobi**

Artist: Sina Grace.

## ■ CASE STUDY: BILL MCCAUSLAND

*During the financial crisis, my well-paying sales and marketing position within the automotive industry in southeast Michigan was eliminated. Living in one of the worst job markets, how do I beat the odds by not only finding employment but advancing my career?*

Read Bill's story at: www.gm4jh.com/g3downloadpage/
bill-mccausland.
End result: Bill landed a job in eight days by doing one thing.

## ■ CASE STUDY: STEVE COBAIN

*I had been working in the financial services industry since 1981. Having achieved senior executive-level status, the corporation I worked for (a very well-known global financial services organization) let me go after more than 20 years of service. To be fair to all parties concerned, when I left my last employer, it was actually more of a mutual parting of the ways. Nonetheless there I was, unemployed for the first time in my life and in my 50s and not sure what I was going to do. Because we have been living in the worst employment market period since the great depression of the 1930s, I knew competition for any job at my level would be stiff and I wondered, "Who will hire someone at my age? Will I have to sell my home and move away from family and friends?"*

Read Steve's story at: www.gm4jh.com/g3downloadpage/steve-cobain.
End result: Steve went from zero offers over 14 months to six offers in five weeks—each of which was created just for him.

## ■ CASE STUDY: MARY BERMAN

*I had gotten laid off from my job of 11 years in advertising. When the Big Three took a dive here in Detroit, so did the automotive print business. I knew the job market was going to be tough, but I thought with my advertising/marketing background, I would be able to brand myself in some way and land a job without any problems. I made cards to pass out, attended networking groups, and even developed my own web site. I worked hard networking and put numerous hours in on the computer sending out resumes. I did more than most and thought I would have some success, but this job market turned out to be a tough one; they were getting 800 to 1,000 resumes for every job I applied for. Here I was, seven months later I had not had one interview!*

Read Mary's story at: www.gm4jh.com/g3downloadpage/mary-berman.
End result: "Coffee Cup Mary" was hired in seven weeks.

## ■ CASE STUDY: KENRICK CHATMAN

*I was one of 700,000-plus professionals who lost their jobs. I was fairly confident that I would land a comparable or better position quickly, like I had done previously in my career. Three months later, I quickly realized that this job market was the worst that many Americans and I have faced in our lifetimes. Likewise, I knew I needed to really distinguish myself from the competition.*

Read Kennrick's story at: www.gm4jh.com/g3downloadpage/kenrick-chatman.
End result: Kenrick built a community, which led to an offer in a town where no one is hiring.

### GUERRILLA INTELLIGENCE

*Beyond the Job Boards, Corporate Career Sites, and Traditional Job "Reqs"*

**Peter Clayton**

The popularity of social networks, video sharing sites (YouTube, Vimeo, Veoh, Mediafly, Viddler, Y!Video, DailyMotion, Metacafe), as well as audio and video podcast interviews freely available on iTunes, Zune, and podcast aggregation sites such as spokenword.com and podcast.com, can provide you with invaluable insights regarding a company, a specific job, and *actionable information* you can use when researching or contacting individuals at your target companies.

*(continued)*

(*Continued*)

Many organizations, large and small, are utilizing YouTube to post career-related videos. Before making those phone calls, and certainly before interviewing, search YouTube for company videos. Twitter has become a popular platform to post jobs and promote corporate initiatives. A number of companies, like TweetaJob, have come online in the last couple of years to help companies Tweet their open positions. Use sites like Twellow to find individuals in your profession to connect with and recruiters within companies you've targeted.

I produce a career and leadership podcast called TotalPicture Radio. Since 2005, I've recorded over 500 interviews. These are in-depth podcasts that include many senior executives at Fortune 500 companies. Are you trying to network your way into Research In Motion (BlackBerry), Nike, Deloitte, Ernst & Young, Wyndham Worldwide, IBM, Taleo, Unisys, Booz? Do a keyword search on totalpicture.com for companies you've targeted. Listening to the interviews with these executives will give you great insights and a lead-in to a phone call that few will have the good sense to use: " Hi ___, I just listened to your interview with...." Immediately, you've shown you're far more resourceful—and more genuinely interested in the organization—than 90% of the people trying to get in the same door.

There are a number of podcasts targeted to careers, recruiting, human resources (and probably your profession), easily found. If you have a smart phone or an MP3 player, this is great information you can access from anywhere—commuting to work, on a treadmill, cooking dinner, wherever—information that could provide the key to unlock the opportunities you've been looking for.

Chris Russell, serial entrepreneur, founder of AllCountyJobs.com, GreenJobSpider.com, and JobsinPods.com, produces a career podcast called Secrets of the Job Hunt. The Bill Kutik Show is a biweekly podcast hosted by Bill Kutik, a leading independent industry analyst with 20 years of experience in the HR technology field. If you want real insights on how recruiting is done today, and the applications and systems companies use to manage their career sites and human capital, have a listen. BlogTalkRadio hosts a number of podcasts with recruiters and HR professionals. The HBR IdeaCast and Knowledge@Wharton are great for keeping up on important trends and the latest issues business leaders are discussing.

I'm a partner with Chris Russell on Jobs in Pods, "the only podcast where real employers, leading recruiters, and staffing agencies talk about their jobs and how to get them." I encourage you to have a visit. Why? Because most of these interviews are with the *hiring managers*.

Back to the title of this segment: beyond the job boards and company career portals. On Jobs in Pods, you can *hear* the hiring manager (or recruiter) tell you specifics about the job, and what impresses them in a job interview. You will not get that reading a job listing. Is this company a good cultural fit for you? Does this sound like the job you really want, and do you meet the qualifications? By listening to the "jobcasts" on Jobs in Pods, in less than 10 minutes you'll have a very good feel for the company and the position.

All of these resources and tools will help you make informed decisions, focus your Guerrilla Mind, add context to your tactics, and deploy the greatest, most potent weapon in your arsenal: the telephone.

Peter Clayton, the "podcast protagonist," is a practitioner of all things "tradigital," having created breakthrough media for many Fortune 100 clients. In 2005, Peter developed the first career and leadership podcast: TotalPicture Radio. The show has grown to become a well-known and influential voice in the recruiting and HR community. Find Peter on LinkedIn at www.linkedin.com/in/peterclayton.

## ■ CASE STUDY: KEVIN WATSON

*My reality was that the high-tech meltdown resulted in an unprecedented increase in the probability of experiencing a permanent layoff, the likes of which had never been seen in the sector or the rest of the economy. Those laid off saw a steep decline in their earnings. Among those laid off, four in five (80%) did not find jobs in tech and about two in five left the city.*

Read Kevin's story at: www.gm4jh.com/g3downloadpage/kevin-watson.

**NAT'S JOBS**
America's 1st Job Alert System

Search here for jobs... | Go

Nat's Jobs | Todays Jobs | Join | New Jobs | Contact | Press | FAQ | Nat's Friends | RSS FEED

Home >

### Find Your Next Job Before Someone Else Does

*NatsJobs.com – the 1st nationwide Job Alert system!*

**FREE 24/7 UPDATES** – every job filtered for relevance

**JOB TRACKER** – track every job you respond to regardless of its origin.

**NORTH AMERICAN COVERAGE** – we monitor all the major & minor job boards including Monster, LinkedIn and Craigslist as well as niche sites and newsgroups – so you don't have to.

**Use Nat's Jobs** *It's Free*
..and stop spending hours surfing those large job boards - Life can be this simple!

**Latest News**

- **Jobs in Memphis, TN (11/04/10)**
  4 November, 2010, 11:48 am
- **Jobs in Miami, FL (11/04/10)**
  4 November, 2010, 11:18 am
- **Jobs in Austin, TX (11/04/10)**
  4 November, 2010, 10:28 am
- **Jobs in Seattle, WA (11/04/10)**
  4 November, 2010, 10:09 am
- **Jobs in Bristol, VA (11/04/10)**
  4 November, 2010, 9:54 am

*More than 5,988,267 Opportunities Found Since May 1st 2009!*

*A Smarter way to job hunt!*

I use to track new opportunities by going from job board to job board but each visit would take 10 or more minutes. It doesn't take that many sites before you have spent your entire morning.

My computer runs 24/7 looking for new jobs and e-mails them to you so you don't have to. This simple approach allowed me to know what position(s) are vacant in a fraction of the time (*and not miss any*). I have a good job now so you are more than

Ads by Google

**Looking For Employment?**
Find a New Direction For Your Life: Train Online & Start a New Career.
www.cd-ed.com/Goodb

**Hiring in Gatineau**
Bilingual

Figure 11.1   Nat's Jobs job alert system.

End Result: Kevin Watson and his wife Nathalie found jobs using a system Kevin built to feed them new job leads every day (see Figure 11.1).

## ■ CASE STUDY: CHAD LEMKE

*I was a first-career executive and had spent all or most of the previous 12 years expanding my responsibility and furthering the careers of those around me. Sometime after the third ownership change, I found myself negotiating the terms of my release from the VP role that had been my pinnacle accomplishment. It was the end of an amazing run. The concept of finding a new career was completely foreign. You don't exactly look in the classified section of the local newspaper for your next executive-level position. The prospect of finding my next opportunity was as much*

*exciting as it was scary. Okay, more scary than exciting. I just
wanted to get back to work.*

Read Chad's story at: www.gm4jh.com/g3downloadpage/chad-lemke.
End Result: Chad built a brand new network from scratch in weeks to
receive three offers.

## ■ CASE STUDY: DARRYL PRAILL

*It's interesting how life works out sometimes. While I began my
professional life as a computer programmer, I'd slowly evolved
my career from creating bits and bytes to instead marketing bits
and bytes. And I was good at it. Life had been good to me and I
felt that I had accomplished a level of success that very few ever
achieve. But life has a way of setting you straight, of ensuring
your head doesn't get too big and that your humility remains in
check. Eventually, life caught up to me, too.*

Read Darryl's story at: www.gm4jh.com/g3downloadpage/darryl-
praill.
End result: Darryl and fellow job hunter Allan Zander had seven offers for the pair of them as a team in a city that had 65 percent
unemployment in their sector.

**Get the free mobile app at**
http://gettag.mobi

## ■ CASE STUDY: ERICA C.

*Having been a self-employed business owner for the past eight
years, it hasn't been necessary for me to undertake a job search
for quite some time, and I quickly realized the task of landing a
job [that I wanted] was going to be the biggest challenge I've faced
to date.*

Read Erica's story at: www.gm4jh.com/g3downloadpage/erica-c.
End result: Erica landed her dream job in an entirely new industry where she had absolutely no experience.

## ■ CASE STUDY: JADE N.

*I was a soon-to-be college graduate in the United States on an international student visa. I was looking to relocate to a different state with minimum industry experience. Oh, and this story takes place in the middle of the financial meltdown of 2008. Additionally, I had to find a job within three months, which is when my student visa expired. Was I crazy? Just a tad, but I knew what I wanted and one way or another I was going to get it.*

Read Jade's story at: www.gm4jh.com/g3downloadpage/jade.
End result: Jade moved from New York City to Washington, D.C., and then landed her dream job in the nick of time.

## ■ CASE STUDY: GRANT TURCK

*I needed a job in 2009, but like getting a movie made in Hollywood I knew it wasn't going to be easy, especially in California where the unemployment rate was already over 11%! I would need to stand out, but how? Armed with the knowledge from* Guerrilla Marketing for Job Hunters 2.0, *I crossed my fingers and chose my secret weapon: Facebook Advertising.*

Read Grant's story at: www.gm4jh.com/g3downloadpage/grant-turck.

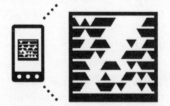

**Get the free mobile app at**
**http://gettag.mobi**

End result: Grant went from being in the dark to the center of the spotlight when his Facebook ad caught the attention of bloggers and employers alike, resulting in four offers in just three weeks.

## A WAR STORY

*Jim Moens*

I had recruited a young guy (very early 20s) for a visual basic developer position at one of my clients. He had a two-year computer science degree and had been working for a year-and-a-half to two years as a sort of one-man IT department for a very small, rural manufacturer. He did it all—programming, networking, support—you name it. The day before the interview, he and I met for lunch. He brought along his laptop and proceeded to show me how he had developed an application for my client, based on information he had gleaned from me, the client's web site, and other sources. He had been working on it every evening for the past week, and it was most impressive. Good functionality, slick interface, intelligent use of technology . . . simply awesome. The day of the interview came and went. He did well, just as I had expected, but we were a bit nervous. Another, more experienced programmer had applied on his own and interviewed as well. I spoke with the client just after he had made the decision to hire my candidate. He stated the deciding factor was (no surprise) the "home brew" application my candidate had developed. It proved, in one fell swoop, that he could, without a doubt, do the job, and perhaps most important—that he wanted it more.

Compliments of Jim Moens, owner, SearchWorks at www.searchworkscareers. com.

■ CASE STUDY: JEFF KRUZICH

*I became part of the great American layoff trend in September of 2009. Having been in sales for over 20 years, I was confident I would be able to find another sales manager job. Five years earlier I had been laid off and had another position within three months, so I wasn't worried. I had interviews with three companies within the first two months and made it to the final two for two of those companies. One, the job got put on indefinite hold, the other they hired someone who had industry experience. Now it was December 2009 and everything came to a screeching halt. There were no new postings on the Internet and every lead I had vaporized.*

Read Jeff's story at: www.gm4jh.com/g3downloadpage/jeff-kruzich. End result: Hired in seven weeks, just two days before getting married.

Figure 11.2   Greg Quirk's web site.

## ■ CASE STUDY: GREG QUIRK

*Companies are looking for people who are innovative. You are not going to put yourself in a worse position than you are now by trying something new, and you will be surprised by the results!*

Read Greg's story at: www.gm4jh.com/g3downloadpage/greg-quirkgreg-quirk/.

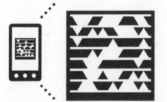

**Get the free mobile app at**
**http://gettag.mobi**

---

### GUERRILLA INTELLIGENCE

*In Case of Emergency, Break Glass*

**Harry Joiner**

What you are about to read assumes that you will continue to run a conventional job search, complete with cold calls to recruiters, job board resume submissions, and chicken-finger networking events. And the reality is that if you make $100,000 or more per year, the following method might not work. You'll need to take a more traditional approach. But if you can settle for a lower paying job, then here's what I like to call the "Any port in a storm" blitzkrieg job search method.

**Step 1:** Collect yourself. Not too long ago, my 12-year-old son, an aspiring Eagle Scout, brought home a copy of the *U.S. Army Survival Manual*. I swear, this book reads like a job search guide—at least as far as the mental conditioning aspects are

*(continued)*

(*Continued*)

concerned. The Guide mentions 10 personal qualities required to survive in a life-threatening environment. They include:

1. Being able to make up your mind.
2. Being able to improvise.
3. Being able to live with yourself.
4. Being able to adapt to the situation—to make a good thing out of a bad thing.
5. Remaining cool, calm, and collected.
6. Hoping for the best but preparing for the worst.
7. Having patience.
8. Being able to "figure out" other people—to understand and predict what other people will do.
9. Understanding where your special fears and worries come from.
10. Knowing what to do to control them.

Don't those tips apply to a desperate job seeker?

I have seen my own career crash and burn this century, and I know from experience that not only will you survive it, but, if you are cool headed, you can also emerge from it with a higher paying, more fulfilling job than you had before. Just relax. Your anxiety is like your skin color: There is nothing you can do to change it.

You can manage your anxiety with prescription medications, but basically you are going to have to deal with it yourself. Freaking out won't help you survive. In fact, it will only make things worse—and then you'll *still* have a problem. Anxiety adds no value. I know what I'm talking about. Simply inhale. Hold it. And exhale. Now lock and load.

**Step 2:** Make sure your former employer will give you great references. Preferably, they should do this in writing on an undated letter on their letterhead. This letter will be added to the envelope you prepare for Step 6, so don't let your former employer slide on this. Good references are a *must*.

**Step 3:** Call a bunch of nonprofits and ask them if you could work there in a white-collar capacity for free one or two days a week while you look for a new full-time job. After you see Step 6, you'll know what you are going to be doing with the other three days a week.

Call 50 nonprofits if you have to. You'd be amazed at how tough it is to get a job working for free, but you must persevere. Job One is being able to look an HR manager square in the eye when she asks you, "So, what have you been doing in your free time?" because nobody wants to hire a victim!

Tell the HR manager that you are working at such-and-such a charity, "because you have always believed in the cause, and now—thank heaven—you have a couple of days a week to give back to society." Now you have gone from being a victim to being a positive-outcome-oriented survivor who can make lemonade out of lemons. *Plus*—and this is a big plus—you can put the nonprofit on your resume and use it as a reference. It's a beautiful thing.

To find nonprofit organizations, check out www.guidestar. com, a database of more than 1.7 million nonprofits.

**Step 4:** Order some nice stationery from an excellent stationer. Make sure it's nice, because you want it to reflect well on you. There is no point in being unprofessional. Time is of the essence, so first impressions will count for a lot. I use a thermographed "house linen"-weight paper from Reaves Engraving, Inc. (www.reavesengraving.com), but you can use any stationer that has a similar quality product. Get the matching envelopes and business cards. Five hundred should do it. It's a small investment to make in your career.

**Step 5:** Rewrite your resume and prepare a nice sales letter. There's a cottage industry around resume writing, so I won't get into it here except to say that you need to have a hard-hitting metrics-rich bullet-pointed resume. The law of specificity applies. Odd numbers work best. Your resume must highlight verifiable, concrete accomplishments such as:

➤ "Increased sales in XYZ category by $47,215 in Q2 2006."

➤ "Decreased distribution costs by $17.61/pound by renegotiating truck leases."

*(continued)*

(*Continued*)

➤ "Reorganized shipping and receiving workflows for a savings of $12.41/case."

You get the idea. This goes back to the comment about being able to "plug and play" in any company.

About the cover letter: The best cover letters are actually written in the "problem/agitate/solve" format. Google that to see what I'm talking about. The master of sales letter writing is Gary Halbert. Google him, too. Without being long-winded here, you want to write a letter to the head of the company function in which you'd like to work, for instance, *Dear Sales Manager, Dear CFO*, or whomever.

Then start off with an honest opening sentence like, "I stopped by briefly today to apply for a job. I have no idea if you are hiring, but even if you aren't—I think I could be of value to you."

Then simply provide a bullet-pointed laundry list of ways that you could help them on a full-time, part-time, project, or interim basis. Give them some affordable no-strings-attached staffing options. Again, position your needs honestly in a way that they can identify with—and profit from.

Why such over-the-top honesty? Because hiring managers are busy and they are not expecting such an honest approach. It will catch them off guard because it's true. It's completely without pretense. Hiring managers love that.

**Step 6:** Cold walk buildings. You are looking for full-time, part-time, temp, interim, project, and seasonal work to get you through your job search. You can work from their office or from home. You have a computer with Internet access.

*The only goal in doing this is to meet enough people to get called in for a real interview.*

Nobody is going to get hired on the spot with this plan. However, if you *do* meet the sales manager on the first visit, simply say:

*"Look, I know you are busy, but I'm looking for a new job in this geographic area. The envelope contains a cover letter and my resume. I have no idea if you are hiring or not. My only objective in stopping by was to position myself as a possible resource for your company. Obviously, I have enough guts and tenacity to knock on*

*doors—but I'm decent enough not to be pushy. Kindly review my resume and let me know if you'd like to meet for a regular interview. That will give both of us some time to do our homework on each other. Otherwise, perhaps you can pass my resume along to a local friend who is hiring. Okay?"*

Now clearly, it takes nerves of steel to pull this off—but people did this type of thing during the depression. And B2B (business-to-business) sales people do this every day.

Remember that desperate times call for desperate measures, and if you just lost your job and you are not tied to a particular industry and you are almost out of cash and have kids to feed, then what I have written is a fairly good game plan for getting out and collecting no's—the most time—honored way to get to yes there is.

---

Harry Joiner is an executive recruiter specializing in integrated marketing and new media. In addition to being a regular contributor to MarketingProfs' Daily Fix, Harry has been featured in MarketingSherpa's Great Minds in Marketing series and received coverage in USAToday.com, AdWeek, and the *Wall Street Journal*'s *Career Journal Online*. Reach Harry at www.linkedin.com/in/harryjoiner.

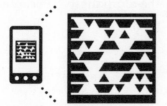

**Get the free mobile app at**
## http://gettag.mobi

# Chapter 12

# Hand-to-Hand Combat

## Winning the Face-to-Face Interview

The first one gets the oyster, the second gets the shell.

— Andrew Carnegie

As competition for customers, market share, and profitability intensifies, understanding what makes an organization effective and which levers to pull to improve financial performance are critical. So much has changed and you have to adapt. If you're doing things the way they used to be done, you need to stop and update your approach because you will blow the interview and waste your time.

As a Guerrilla job hunter, your strategy has been to appeal to an employer's core need to make money, save money, and increase efficiencies. Combining those needs with elements from the New Value Table (Table 2.1) produced a winning resume that secured interviews. Now, you want to get multiple offers so that you can make a good choice for you, your career, and your family.

## ■ FOCUS ON THE EMPLOYER'S GOALS

High-performance companies consistently hire doers—go-getters—at all levels. Innovation, creativity, perseverance, and leadership are the key levers for success. That's why they want to talk to you. Now you just have to deliver on your brand's promise at every interview. Here's how.

What you're ultimately selling during an interview are those elements of your background, skills, and personality that can make a significant contribution to the company. Your potential contribution will be weighed against the cost of a bad hire. You have to battle their FEAR, DOUBT, and UNCERTAINTY.

If they make the wrong choice, at minimum, they are wasting time and money. At worst, a bad choice could jeopardize the recruiter's or manager's job, perhaps even the success of the company. A lot is at stake.

Your mission is to neutralize the employer's concerns by eliminating fear, doubt, and uncertainty.

## ■ BUILD YOUR STRATEGY AROUND THE EMPLOYER'S EXPECTATIONS

You will meet four general groups of decision makers during interviews. Each group requires a tailored strategy. Each group has an agenda that you must focus on.

The groups are:

1. Senior executives
2. Hiring managers
3. Human resource managers
4. Corporate recruiters

### ➤ Senior Executives

Even if you are not seeking a senior executive role, executives look for similar things from all candidates, so understanding their perspective will help you position your accomplishments accordingly. By the way, that is the first thing they look for—accomplishments.

Executives want to see a lot of recent accomplishments and understand the specifics. They need to know how your accomplishments can translate into success for them if they hire you—even before they interview you.

Executives also look for:

➤ Honesty and integrity: A well-principled person whom people trust and who can build shared values throughout the organization.

➤ Intellectual capacity: The ability to make quick, solid decisions in tough, competitive environments.

➤ Intensity: The capacity to create a deep level of trust among their staff and create an energy-charged, enthusiastic environment.

➤ Passion: An unrelenting drive to leave a positive mark on the organization that is not driven by money or power.

➤ Work ethic: A resiliency that allows you to persevere, no matter how difficult the task.

## ➤ Hiring Managers

Hiring managers are the people you will work for directly. They are most interested in accomplishments specific to their area of the business. Moreover, they want to know how your accomplishments can translate into success for them personally.

Here's what else hiring managers may look for:

*Technical Competencies*

➤ Proactive: Do you embody a forward-thinking, proactive mind-set beyond your immediate function?

➤ Focus on results: Can you recruit a quality subordinate team and get them working together, to generate high levels of performance?

➤ Smart: Do you have a strong intellect, coupled with pragmatism and pure common sense?

*Business Intelligence*

➤ Budget conscious: Do you understand the critical importance of cash? Do you watch expenditures as an entrepreneur would, or simply spend knowing your paycheck and benefits will come, no matter what?

➤ Judgment: Do you have the ability to deal with novel and complex situations where there is no history or road map?

➤ Customer focused: Do you understand how the industry and marketplace work?

*Emotional Intelligence*

➤ Persistence: Can you drive programs to successful fruition? Are you self-motivated?

➤ Empathy: Do you have the ability to connect with employees and customers?

➤ Stamina: Do you demonstrate a built-in unrelenting drive to succeed?

### ➤ Human Resources Department

Human Resources has concerns that go beyond those of hiring managers and executives. HR is also interested in your overall fit with the company's core values and culture—your relationship intelligence. The people in HR look for the following attributes:

➤ A fit with the current and next job: How easily can you move up as the company grows? HR will consider your qualifications for the next job because an upwardly mobile person eases their burden for succession planning and improves their department's return on investment (ROI).

➤ Ability to fill a gap in the management mix: Good coaches know their relative offensive and defensive strengths and make trades accordingly. Likewise, smart HR managers understand their organization's strengths and weaknesses and will seek to complement, not replicate them.

### ➤ Corporate Recruiters

These are a company's internal recruiters. More often than not, if you respond to a newspaper ad or job posting, a junior staffer will be the first person to assess your qualifications. The irony of tasking a company's least qualified employee with the responsibility of acquiring its human capital assets probably hasn't escaped you—but that's reality.

Recruiters are often left to figure things out on their own. At a minimum, they have to compare candidates against a list of stipulated skills or abilities. If you have the exact skills you make the cut—if not, you're out. They have a lot to lose professionally by recommending someone who is not qualified. Some people have said that these people might not know good credentials if they slapped them in the face. They can't read between the lines. Here's how to give corporate recruiters what they are looking for:

➤ Tailor your response to exactly what was advertised.

➤ Work experience: Tell them how your experience fits their opportunity. You have to connect the dots for them.

➤ Goals: Your short- and long-term goals must be in line with the opportunities for advancement.

➤ Personality: Chemistry and cultural fit between you and your coworkers is critical. Find out what "type" they hire ahead of time. Call someone who works there.

➤ Communication skills: Written and verbal communication skills are becoming increasingly critical as the global marketplace evolves. Demonstrate your ability to listen effectively, verbalize thoughts clearly, and express yourself confidently.

➤ Image: Junior people are easily impressed by an appropriate ensemble, so dress for the part you want, not the one you currently have. They'll mentally compare you to their image of the group you'll be working with. When in doubt, overdress two levels above business casual.

➤ Knowledge of the company: Recruiters expect you to be as enthusiastic about the company as they probably still are. Make sure you read everything on the company's web site. Don't waste their time by asking questions you should already know the answers to.

---

## GUERRILLA INTELLIGENCE

### 10 Tactics HR and Hiring Managers Won't Expect

#### Cindy Beresh-Bryant

Companies have job openings because they have a problem and need a solution—that's where you come in. Generally speaking, when interviewing, companies are interested in three things:

1. *Can you do the job?* Do you have the requisite knowledge, skills, and abilities (KSAs) to perform at or above their standards?

2. *Do you want to do the job?* Do you articulate the right work ethic, desire, and energy?

3. *Will you fit into their culture?* Organizations tend to hire for skills, but they fire for fit. While hiring managers are often concerned with skills, HR is likely tuned into cultural fit. To be successful, you have to demonstrate both.

*(continued)*

(*Continued*)

*Tactics HR Won't Expect*

1. At the beginning of the interview ask what the successful candidate will look like or what the performance expectations are for the successful candidate. While most interviewers have been trained to avoid asking leading questions, they won't expect this type of question from a candidate, especially at the beginning of the interview; human nature is such that they'll likely be caught off guard answering the question and provide you with critical information that can be used to successfully frame your answers.

2. Know what message (strengths/accomplishments) you want to get across during the interview. Answer questions in two parts—what they want to know and what you want them to know.

3. Leverage success stories framed as PARs (problem, action taken, and result) to highlight the value you'll bring to the organization. Be succinct; limit responses to two minutes.

4. Ask your own probing questions to measure reactions: "Did I answer your question fully?" or "Am I being clear?" It will demonstrate your sensitivity to the interviewer's needs and help establish rapport.

5. Be prepared to take a leadership role, especially with an unskilled interviewer—get your message across articulating your accomplishments using those PARs.

6. Avoid discussing salary—he who gives a number first loses negotiating power. If backed into a corner, give a salary range rather than a finite number. Base your range on competitive data.

7. Never leave an interview without establishing the next steps. Ask for a specific date and time that's best to follow up—and then actually follow up.

8. Send handwritten thank-you notes to each interviewer; include something of value—a timeline of how you'll spend your first 60 days on the job, a solution to a specific problem discussed, resource materials (book, DVD, and

so on), anything that demonstrates the leadership they can expect from you.

9. Be tenacious. Continue following up every five to seven days. To avoid the gatekeeper, call early in the morning, during the lunch hour, or late in the afternoon when they are likely away from their desks.

10. If you don't get the position—don't quit. Continue building the relationship and demonstrating value; periodically stay in touch, send relevant and useful information such as newspaper or magazine articles, refer high-caliber candidates for other openings, and so on. This will ensure you stay top of mind in the event that another position becomes available in the future.

Cindy Beresh-Bryant is the owner and president of HR Solutions by Design, LLC, offering small and mid-sized business a competitive advantage through HR outsourcing and consulting. She is also author of *The HR Café* and a monthly newsletter: *The People Pages—Strategic HR News and Solutions*. Visit her at www.TheHRCafe.com, LinkedIn: www.linkedin.com/in/cynthiabereshbryant or www.hrsolutionsbydesign.com.

## ■ THE INTERVIEW MINEFIELD

The most common way people gain entry to a company is through an ad or referral, starting the process at the bottom of the chain of command. As mentioned, the corporate recruiter is the person who is least likely to understand your potential and has the most to lose by recommending you, so his natural tendency will be to do nothing.

Traditional job-hunting methods will expose you to a minefield fraught with booby traps. As you advance each successive level up the chain of command toward the final decision maker, you risk being eliminated. After the company finally does make you an offer, it will be subject to an excruciatingly detailed reference check and yet another opportunity for you to be eliminated.

For most job hunters, interviewing looks like the diagram in Figure 12.1.

The lower down the chain you begin, the more people there are who will need to approve of your hiring, and therefore, the more hurdles you'll have to clear. Luckily, the opposite is also true.

Figure 12.1 The interviewing chain.

## ■ NAVIGATING THE MINEFIELD

As a Guerrilla, you've been trained to attack weak points. The higher up in the organization you begin, the fewer people you need to satisfy, and the closer you'll be to an offer.

Executives have a macro view of the industry, of their business, and of skill sets. They're more interested in what you're capable of doing for them in the future than in dissecting your life story. Executives have more experience hiring and tend to make quick, gut-level decisions with little validation. So, you should always aim to begin your job hunting in the executive suite.

In the best case, Guerrilla interviewing resembles that shown in Figure 12.2.

Or in the worst-case scenario, it resembles that shown in Figure 12.3.

When you start at the top, you can get an offer without meeting anyone else. Executives have authority to make an instant hiring decision and have a mandate to continuously talent hunt for the whole company. They're the only people who have that macro view of the company's needs. When an executive passes your resume down to a hiring manager with a note saying, "get a hold of this candidate," or "looks good," it's much easier to get an offer. If you think that's simplistic—boy, are you ever wrong! Headhunters work with senior executives for a reason—they can make decisions quickly and efficiently.

Figure 12.2 Best-case Guerrilla interview.

Figure 12.3    Worst-case Guerrilla interview scenario.

## ■ PREPARATION—UNDERSTAND THE MEETING'S PURPOSE

The employer believes you'll bring something to the organization. What exactly is that? Are you being interviewed because they have announced a specific opening, or did something in your approach pique their interest? To prepare for the meeting, you need to understand the reason for their interest.

If you're being interviewed for a specific job, they'll tell you and you'll know what to focus on. If it's a general, nonspecific get-to-know-you interview as a result of your unsolicited approach, you need to focus on the requirements you uncovered while researching the company. If they're in line with your accomplishments, then that's likely the reason for the meeting.

Personally I've always found being direct gets the best results. The easiest thing to do is simply ask, "How much time do you think we'll need?" and "What's your agenda?" They'll tell you. If they don't tell you, it means they definitely have a pressing problem that your background indicates you can solve—but they don't want to show their hand. In that case, you'll need to focus on what you've accomplished over the past five years. This is more work, but it's not impossible.

If you ever find yourself in an interview where you're unsure of the agenda, quickly ask, "Where would you like to begin our conversation?" If they say, "Tell us about yourself," then you should ask, "Where would you like me to begin?" Where they want you to begin is what they're most interested in. Focus on their interests.

Projecting the image of a stellar can't-do-without candidate comes with practice and preparation. There are three things you need to do:

1. Complete a T-account exercise.
2. Build your storybook.
3. Rehearse your message.

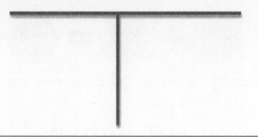

Figure I2.4   The T-Account exercise.

## ➤ T-Account Exercise

There's no substitute for this exercise. A sage headhunter taught it to me years ago. The exercise requires you overlay your accomplishments on the employer's needs. This preps you to talk about your accomplishments, long-term goals, as well as strengths and weaknesses in the context of the specific job you're interviewing for.

I know this sounds too easy—too common sense—too logical, but it's not. In my experience, few job hunters spend time thinking about how their experience and skills relate to a job until they're actually asked. I've seen people blow it when they were asked the simplest question: "What do you know about our company?" That is the perfect opportunity to explain what you've learned and how your experience makes you their perfect candidate. Too often, even the most senior people wing it.

Draw a line down the middle of a page. List the employer's needs on the left side and your skills and accomplishments that prove you can do the job on the other (see Figure 12.4). In the interview, you'll be able to point out these compatible assets for the employer. You'll stand out as organized and prepared. Grab a blank sheet of paper and do it now. You can recycle this exercise in your thank-you note.

## ➤ Analyzing Your Strengths and Weaknesses

All employers ask you about strengths and weaknesses. It's one of the few questions you can absolutely guarantee. Yet, it's numbing how little forethought most people give to this question. This might sound asinine, but I've actually had people who, when asked about weaknesses during an interview, either couldn't come up with any or replied, "I don't believe I have any." Candidates who say they have none—I guess they are, in their own mind, perfect—will find that Mr. Employer will view them in a highly negative light. So much so, that once they state they have no weaknesses, the game is over. And I mean over. This is a disastrous interview blunder. Assess your weaknesses in advance of an interview.

### Guerrilla Mission

*Strengths*

Now that you've completed a needs analysis with the T-account exercise, you need to list your top 10 strengths. Grab a piece of paper and list them in bullet form. Stop. Do it now. This is important.

Now look at your strengths. Which of those applies to the job for which you are being interviewed? If you were the interviewer, would that be enough? Would you spend your last dollar to acquire you? If your immediate answer is "yes," proceed to the next exercise on weaknesses. If you said "no," congratulations for being so honest; you have just saved your interview from certain disaster. You're running these exercises because, like a pro sports coach, you understand that practice makes perfect and game day is no time to practice. Run through this exercise until you've listed five strengths to support the job's requirements.

*Weaknesses*

Run the same exercise, only this time list your weaknesses as they apply to the job. Now pick a weakness you've been working on and detail what you've done to correct it. Are you short-tempered? Don't mention that one. This is not true confessions time. Interviewers expect you to pick something "light." That's what candidates do. Please don't disappoint them. What you're going to do that most candidates don't think to do is demonstrate your follow through. Right after you reveal your weakness, you're going to explain what you've done to correct the matter.

You might prepare an answer like this:

*I was told a few years ago that my budgeting wasn't good enough. I had never received any formal training, so I immediately registered in a night class. On my last review, my supervisor noted how much improvement I'd made. My budgeting skills are now well above average. He did me a big favor.*

Congratulations. In this example, you told the interviewer:

➤ What the problem was (budgeting)
➤ Why it was a problem (no training)
➤ What you did to correct it (night class)
➤ What the results were (improved skill level)

Moreover, you've also shown that you are open to constructive criticism and most important, that you are prepared to act on feedback. Most employees are not. If the interviewer is keeping score, you just received double bonus points, because employers will hire someone with average skills and great attitude over a self-confessed superstar any day.

---

### ➤ Build Your Storybook

Following the T-account exercise, you need to turn your strengths and accomplishments into memorable stories because everyone likes a good story. More important, people retain ideas more easily if they're presented in the form of a story. After hours and hours of interviewing, it's often difficult for interviewers to distinguish one candidate from another unless one of them—that'll be you—really grabs their interest with a great story.

Storytelling has other advantages:

➤ When you link ideas for the interviewer, you're far more likely to engage the listener's interest and leave a favorable impression.
➤ The conversational tone relaxes your interviewer and will turn an interrogation into a conversation.
➤ Storytelling appeals to an interviewer's gut feel and innate ability to hire people with promise.

➤ Given two people who are equally qualified on paper, an employer will tend to hire the best storyteller, because the person is perceived to have superior communication skills.

Unlike the fairy tales you heard as a child, your stories are based on facts. They portray you as a modern-day hero—confident but not arrogant, decisive but not overbearing, driven but not maniacal. You must provide accurate illustrations of the significant goals you've achieved and the skills and training you mustered to achieve them. You get to play the part of the hero who vanquished the dragon.

Which accomplishments prompted the employer to want to meet you in the first place? Those are the stories to use. The key elements of each story relate to the requirements—be they in administration, sales, marketing, engineering, operations, or something else—you outlined in the T-account exercise.

For example, you have discovered from your research that the employer needs to be able to bring new products to market in a timely manner and you have 10 years' experience in new product development. Your story might sound something like this.

*Mr. Employer, in the summer of 2009 our major competitor, in an attempt to run us out of business, began giving away a product that they claimed had the same features as our mainstay product. Not surprisingly, revenue plummeted 90% in our next quarter. The bottom fell out of our stock. Several of our key development and salespeople quit. In response, I led two small teams of six engineers on a mission to develop our next-generation product and to expose the weaknesses in the competitor's offering. Within five weeks, we discovered serious design flaws in the security layer of their software that made the user's data vulnerable to hackers. We staged a demonstration of our findings for our sales and marketing team. They designed a counterattack that stopped our competitor in its tracks. Meanwhile, my second team added major functionality to our core product. When the flaws in our competitor's product became front-page news, my team was ready with a bulletproof upgrade. We did all this in less than nine weeks. Company revenues surged 15% higher than our previous best quarter.*

What is the interviewer likely to infer from this story?

➤ You rise to the occasion when confronted with difficult situations.

➤ You can lead under pressure.

➤ You can execute a strategy.

➤ You're a team player and a team captain (because you kept saying "we," not "I").

You're a . . . you're a . . . It'll be a long list of positive attributes leading the interviewer to conclude, "We've gotta have you on our team!" And that's what you want.

The interviewer will infer all positives and will start to ask "how" questions:

➤ How do you manage?

➤ How did you keep them focused?

➤ How—how—how.

Guerrilla, he's hooked. This is exactly how you want him to react. Now you get to lead them into a natural discussion on the similarities between what you've done and what they need. Make sure you prepare a few more anecdotes to reinforce your positive attributes.

➤ **Rehearsing Your Message**

From your T-account, pick out instances where you used those skills successfully. Prepare three relevant stories for every interview. Use these to create analogies during the interview. Starting with your most relevant accomplishment, write a two- or three-paragraph story. Bulleting the sequence of events may make it easier to write the paragraphs. The act of writing forces you to organize your thinking and etch the details in your mind for easy retrieval. Now read the paragraphs out loud. Does your story sound like you're talking or does it sound like you're reciting something you've memorized? Your story must be delivered in a conversational tone.

Practice telling the story until your words and facial expressions appear natural. In an interview, your ability to retrieve information quickly is important. It'll boost your confidence and surprise the interviewer, who will expect the usual period of silence while inadequately prepared candidates contrive their answer.

Your ability to rapidly recall the details of a story affects whether you'll be invited back and if you'll get an offer. I recently watched a sales VP candidate crash and burn during an interview. While his answers were perfect and naturally delivered, he paused for three or four seconds before he answered each question. In an interview, that's a long time. For every moment an employer watches you think, you lose credibility. You need to be prepared to speak within one short breath after the other person stops talking. The employer must see you as being confident and prepared.

Interviews aren't real life. Everyone knows that, but it won't stop the interviewer from forming a real-life opinion on your candidacy. You can know your job better than anyone in the world, but if you freeze during the interview process, the interviewer isn't likely to care. If you can't just naturally "flick a switch" and perform like a Hollywood actor, you'll need to rehearse with the zeal of a drill sergeant. If you practice long enough, you, too, can deliver an Oscar-winning performance.

## GUERRILLA WISDOM

### Emotional Intelligence and Your Career Portfolio
**Anita Martel** *RGR*

Having an up-to-date emotional intelligence assessment has become one of your greatest assets in your job search strategy. Why? Because by doing so, you've reduced the risk the hiring manager has in hiring *you*.

An emotional intelligence assessment gives you concrete and valid evidence that complements your resume and provides tangible proof to a potential employer. Hiring managers are risk adverse and by making their job virtually risk free, you have just given yourself a leg up on the competition. The added plus to having your emotional intelligence assessed is that you can speak with complete confidence during an interview. You gain valuable insight that you can use to your benefit. By knowing your strong points, you can further build on them and use them to position yourself advantageously. By the same token, by knowing your weaker points you can specifically concentrate on improving them. It is strongly recommended that you retake the test at two- to three-year intervals to reevaluate your progress over time.

In the workplace an ever-increasing number of employers are choosing to use emotional intelligence assessments to ensure a greater fit of potential and current employees within their

*(continued)*

(*Continued*)

company culture. It is becoming more and more obvious to to-day's companies that their workforce can no longer be managed in the traditional style. That is, today's employee is no longer just a part of the puzzle that completes the big picture but has become the process by which to do it. Organizations are now filled with highly educated knowledge workers that, as a team, have become this process. This is, in essence, what will give one company a distinct competitive advantage over another, and today's companies are specifically looking for that edge.

On the personal side of things, since none of us live in a vacuum we can clearly see how our personal lives always end up trickling into our professional lives at one time or another. We develop relationships with everyone around us. How well we manage those relationships can have a significant impact on both our professional as well as personal lives. Having vibrant, healthy relationships has become the core competitive advantage in today's workplace.

So what exactly is emotional intelligence? "Emotional intelligence is the unique repertoire of emotional skills that a person uses to navigate the everyday challenges of life" (Multi-Health Systems, 2008). It is the awareness of one's emotions and the ability to use those emotions to strengthen one's performance. Simply put, emotional intelligence is often referred to as common sense or street smarts.

Research has demonstrated that an individual's emotional intelligence is often a more accurate predictor of success than that person's IQ. No matter how intellectually intelligent someone is, his or her success is still governed by how well the individual can communicate ideas and interact with peers. As opposed to IQ, which is said to be set early on in life, your emotional intelligence can be substantially strengthened and developed with appropriate training and thus can be improved considerably. Since emotional intelligence is elastic, those who lack it can gain it and those who have it can augment and develop it further.

Now many emotional intelligence tests exist on the market and all claim to be the best. I have researched a great number of them and keep coming back to one in particular. The BarOn EQ-i assessment is by far the most comprehensive on the market.

It assesses interpersonal and intrapersonal skills, stress management, adaptability, and general mood with many other areas within these categories. Several different reports can be generated, including one on leadership, and its versatility allows individuals to track and work on their emotional intelligence. As well, a company wanting to have an accurate predictor of best performers or a comparison/fit for potential employees can also use it. It is used worldwide, is available in several different languages, and has been scientifically validated. It can be taken online and completed in about 40 minutes. You receive a clear and easy to read written interpretation of your results, recommendations on what to do to increase your emotional intelligence, and a debriefing session with a certified administrator.

Remember, you are creating your career portfolio and whatever you can add to it that will put you a step ahead of the competition is essential. All good career portfolios will include a summary resume, a detailed resume, a number of references, and an up-to-date emotional assessment.

Anita Martel is a partner of Perry-Martel International and a Certified BarOn EQ-i administrator. She is devoted to helping leaders, individuals, and teams increase their effectiveness and attain their full potential. For more information or to take the test you can e-mail anitam@perrymartel.com.

## ■ HOW TO ANSWER QUESTIONS

Answer questions with a one-two punch—a short answer followed by a long answer. For open-ended questions, I always suggest you say, "Let me give you the short version. If you need to explore some aspect more fully, I'd be happy to go into greater depth."

Answers of less than 30 seconds are generally insufficient, but answers over three minutes are too long. This is an important detail. In the first instance, you'll come across as light, lacking knowledge, depth, and insight—not the impression you want to be making. Long answers right off the bat, though, could brand you as being too technical or boring. You need to strike a fine balance, and this one-two punch does it. In the end, a question like, "What was your most difficult assignment or biggest accomplishment?" might take anywhere from 30 seconds to 30 minutes depending on the detail—but let the interviewer draw the details out of you.

Always remember that the interviewer is the one who asked the question. Tailor your answer to what the person needs to know without a lot of extraneous rambling or superfluous explanation. Why give a sermon when a short prayer will do?

# ■ HOW TO PREPARE FOR THE BEHAVIORAL INTERVIEW

 Download available

The interview isn't just about your stories. Beyond the purely technical questions specific to each job, I have listed the typical questions interviewers ask. These are behavior-based interview (BBI) questions. If BBI is new to you, don't panic. It was designed to reduce hiring errors by focusing on a job hunter's past experience and behaviors instead of relying on an interviewer's gut-level decision-making ability. BBI questions actually focus on the core components of your accomplishments. That's good for you.

If you have experience with traditional interviewing techniques, you'll find the BBI different in several ways:

1. The interview will be structured to concentrate on areas that are important to the interviewer, instead of allowing you to concentrate on areas that you think are important. (The T-account exercise and a thorough understanding of the job description will give you all the clues you need.)

2. Rather than asking how you would behave in a particular situation, the interviewer will ask you to describe how you did behave in a similar situation.

3. The interviewer will drill you for details. You'll have no time to speculate. (Now you know why we've spent so much time detailing your accomplishments.)

If you prepare reasonable answers to the following questions, you'll be well on your way to acing your interview, no matter who is conducting it.

*Strengths*

➤ What key factors have accounted for your career success to date?

➤ What do you consider to be some of your most outstanding qualities?

➤ What is your greatest strength or asset?

*Weaknesses*

➤ What aspects of your current position could be better performed, and what kind of improvement could you make?

➤ If we asked two or three of your peers who know you well to be somewhat critical of your performance, what two or three improvement areas would they likely identify? Why?

➤ If you could, what two things would you most like to change about yourself to improve your overall effectiveness—and why?

*Job Performance*

➤ What have been your last three performance evaluation ratings? Why?

➤ In what areas does your performance excel?

➤ Why, in your judgment, are certain businesses successful?

*Personal Style*

➤ What kind of operating style do you feel is not conducive to good performance? Why?

➤ What basic values and beliefs do you feel are important to good performance?

➤ How would you categorize the traits and attributes of a good manager? Why are these important?

*Management Skills*

➤ What are some of the techniques you use to motivate poor performers?

➤ Give me some examples of how you have used these techniques.

➤ What results did you get?

*Communication Skills*

➤ Give me an example of a complex communications problem that you faced.

➤ What made it complex?

➤ Why was it difficult to communicate?

*Integrity*

➤ If you caught one of your most valued employees doing something dishonest, what would you do?

*Assertiveness*

➤ If your boss told you that you had a "stupid idea," but you knew it was a very good one, what would you do?

*Risk*

➤ What factors most influence your willingness to take a risk?

*Analytical Skills*

➤ What is, perhaps, the most complex business analysis you have had to make?

➤ What factors made it complex?

➤ How did you tackle this task?

*Perseverance*

➤ Describe a work situation where you knew you were right, but the odds of winning were such that you felt you had to abandon your position?

➤ What odds did you face?

➤ What approaches did you use?

How did you do? I can't overemphasize the need to practice your answers to these questions. If you can, you should rehearse with a nonjudgmental friend. If you don't have any friends, rehearse in front of a mirror with a tape recorder. (Make a mental note to acquire some friends in the future.)

Ask and answer the questions one-by-one, and when you're finished, watch or listen to the tape. Do you sound confident? Are your answers complete? Would you hire you? Lastly, did you notice your facial expressions? Did you look happy, relaxed, and natural; or did you look like someone who needed to pass gas? Practice, practice, practice—until you feel confident and look terrific!

## GUERRILLA WISDOM

*Winning in the "Red Zone"— A Special Section of the*
*Guerrilla Playbook*

### Charles Timmins

Stewart received word that he'd been selected as one of four finalists invited to the round of interviews. Four members of the leadership team—the CEO, President/COO, CFO, and Chief Talent Officer—would interview all finalists over a four-day period. An offer would follow. Stewart wisely asked for and was granted permission to be the final candidate interviewed.

After three rounds and seven interviews over a three-week period, Guerrilla Stewart had made it to the "Red Zone," those final 20 yards to the promised land—the end zone. And as a Guerrilla, he knew he had to prepare differently for his upcoming interviews with the senior executives in order to push the ball over the goal line—exceeding their expectations.

Each interview round had enabled Stewart to clarify and confirm the essential requirements of the position, and how he measured up. Stewart began to realize that the original job description represented a narrow view of what he really would have to do to realize minimal success in the job. His Guerrilla questions elicited insights into other areas of need that existed around the position and its stakeholders. He also sensed that potential upside existed to realize dramatic gains within his function.

Stewart's previous operations assignments required that he go before the Executive Committee of his Fortune 500 employer quarterly. He earned a reputation for consistently distilling complex ideas (with detailed supporting data) into a clear, concrete, and concise summary, with insightful analysis and actionable recommendations to achieve leadership's vision for the business units.

He chose to leverage this brand attribute by formulating a presentation that would serve to guide the interviews and provide all the executives with a consistent perception of his candidacy.

(*continued*)

(*Continued*)

Stewart created a four-part, written presentation to position himself as the "Ideal Candidate."

*Section One* consisted of an extended T-account exercise, detailing a point-for-point match. He incorporated throughout the document company-specific language that he had heard in the prior seven interviews.

*Section Two* addressed those unarticulated needs and potential opportunities using the same T-account exercise. Putting these out on the table would trigger a deeper level of conversation with each executive. Strategically, Stewart sought to reshape the job specification from what the company wanted to what he felt they needed, showcasing tangible examples of his prior successes. Introducing these new selection criteria, Stewart hoped to shift the executive team's perceptions of the other candidates as being less qualified to address the broader requirements.

*Section Three* offered a forward-focused summary of the advantages and benefits of Stewart's credentials, talents, and potential to deliver results. These he would reinforce with verbal success stories.

*Section Four* contained his "Killer Questions." After each of the prior interview rounds, Guerrilla Stewart had assumed an ownership mind-set, putting himself in the senior leaders' shoes. He also behaved as if he were already in the job—researching everything he could to formulate intriguing questions for the senior leaders. Stewart knew that one or two well-crafted questions would reveal more about his competence than any clever answer he could offer. And, he was proven correct.

Stewart presented his counteroffer, he asked his new boss, "What really differentiated me?" Smiling, his boss said, "Your presentation got the senior team to reevaluate what we really needed to do better in order to become more competitive. We need that kind of thinking around here. It just feels right."

And, this is the music that Guerrilla Marketers long to hear.

---

Charles Timmins is the founding principal and chief innovation officer of *PMA, LLC*, a Philadelphia-based career strategy firm. Known for his contrarian advice and Guerrilla tactics, Charley works with 6-figure executives and professionals to help them *"stand out authentically"* to land career opportunities that make a real difference. Visit him at LinkedIn: www.linkedin.com/in/charlestimmins.

## ■ HOW TO ANSWER THE "F" QUESTION

If you were fired from your last job, you should expect to be asked why. What are you going to tell them? The truth! How you tell them is the important point. Use truthful, positive information to put yourself in a favorable light—and modestly explain what you've learned from the experience. Outline the steps you've taken to upgrade your skills or change your behavior to ensure it won't happen again. If it was a personality issue, then briefly state the following, "I'm open to working overtime but can't work 70 hours a week." They'll conclude your former boss was a slave driver without your having to say so. If you don't make a big deal over it, neither will they.

## ■ HOW TO ANSWER THE "L" QUESTION

Many people have been answering this question lately. Layoffs happen all the time. It's a fact of modern-day life. It's not personal, so don't take it that way. Explain in 30 seconds or less how it came to be and why you where chosen: seniority, geography, nepotism, whatever the case. If the company went through seven layoffs and you were in the last round, that's positive news you should impart. Practice describing your situation from the employer's viewpoint. Work through any feelings of anger or bitterness beforehand. You'll score points for professionalism.

## ■ DRESS FOR EXCELLENCE

I don't care how many times you've read, "dress like the interviewers," it's bad advice. You dress in the best clothes you have, no exceptions. Guys, there are only two colors when it comes to suits: navy blue and charcoal gray. Shoes are black with matching black socks (if you wear white socks, I'll find out and personally hunt you down). If you have body art, you should cover it. Invest in yourself—buy a Brooks Brothers shirt. It'll provide the best return on $75 you ever get.

Women should wear conservative business attire, appropriately buttoned. Perfume and jewelry should be kept to a minimum (only one pair of earrings).

## ■ HOW TO RECRUIT AN INSIDE ADVOCATE

During your research, I hope you found the phone number of the interviewer's executive assistant. If not, call and get it now because the day before the interview you're going to recruit that person onto your team. Here's how to recruit your interviewer's most trusted confidant: the day before the interview, call the assistant and say:

> Hello my name is [your name goes here] and tomorrow at [the time for the interview goes here] I am scheduled to meet with [the interviewer's full name goes here]. I just wanted to call and ensure that [interviewer's first name goes here] schedule is still intact.

Wait while the assistant verifies it is. Thank the person and hang up the telephone. Making this call telegraphs the assistant two key subliminal messages that work in your favor:

1. You value your time.
2. You value their time.

Guerrilla, how many people do you seriously think would risk making that call? Not many. In my experience, candidates never confirm an interview once it's set up. By calling, you indicate the interview is not the most important thing you'll do that day. What do you think that does to your leverage?

In sales school, rookies are taught to never confirm an appointment once it's set because it gives the other person an opportunity to back out. What they neglect to point out is that by risking rejection, you can actually strengthen your position. The other person assumes, "This guy must really be important." This enables you to walk into the meeting with confidence. This has never backfired on me.

Moreover, tomorrow the only person the interviewer's assistant will remember is you. You are likely the only person who has ever called to confirm. That speaks volumes about your self-esteem. To the assistant, your simple gesture is indicative of how professionally you'll interact with them if hired. Personal assistants, secretaries, and receptionists can have enormous influence on your success. Be rude even once and you'll torpedo your chances.

## ■ THE ABSOLUTE LAST THING YOU DO BEFORE BED

It is often the simple questions that trip people up, so before you turn in for the night, review your answers to the following two questions:

1. Why do you want this job?
2. Why do you want to leave your present company, or why did they leave you?

Most candidates stumble on those basic questions. Don't be caught speechless!

## ■ GAME DAY

What most candidates don't realize is that the job is already theirs. Guerrilla, the interviewer is seeing you because they want to hire you. They have a problem you can solve and they acknowledged as much the second they agreed to an interview. The issue now is to convince them they're not making a mistake. Essentially, it's up to you not to drop the ball.

The first few seconds will set the tone for the interview, so look the interviewer straight in the eye, smile, and say, "I've been looking forward to meeting you." If the person asks why, go for it. The game's on and you have the ball. Most employers want "can do," "will do" employees. Start your meeting off like any other business meeting by laying out why you're there. Don't waste time with idle chitchat about the weather or the big game last night. The employer will be grateful.

In order of importance, an employer will consider the following factors at a first interview:

➤ Character
➤ Relevant accomplishments
➤ Drive
➤ Initiative
➤ Communication skills

Throughout the meeting, the interviewer will be determining whether you have what they need, not only through your stories but also through your body language. Yes, body language.

## ■ THE SCIENCE OF BODY LANGUAGE

Sixty-five percent of all communication is nonverbal. There has been a lot of hullabaloo on the science of body language and its value in job interviews. What your gestures say about you could make a difference in your interview success. For example, are you lying when you tug at your ear or is your ear just itchy at the wrong time? A trained professional will know the difference. Your interviewer is probably not a trained professional, but many interviewers think they can read body language. I've read many of these books and few agree on what means what, so let me give you a quick primer on the subject. I promise this won't require a personality makeover.

Interviewing can make people nervous—on both sides of the desk. The interviewer has an hour or less to decide if she ever wants to see you again. Generally speaking, a blind date isn't this stressful. You want to put your best foot forward and appear to be the kind of person you really are, even when you're nervous. Here are some tips to help you do that:

➤ Relax and be yourself. Just be more polite!

➤ Offer a firm handshake. In the United States, three pumps up and down is sufficient.

➤ Maintain eye contact when you're talking, but don't stare. Focus on the interviewer's nose if direct eye contact bothers you. Avoid looking down into your lap.

➤ Sit facing the interviewer, not off to the side.

➤ Lean slightly forward and look attentive. It indicates you're interested in what the person is saying.

➤ Keep your hands out of your pockets and away from your face—especially your nose! Excessive gesticulation is distracting.

➤ Keep your two feet planted squarely on the ground. Crossing your legs may be misinterpreted as a defensive move and that you have something to hide.

If you can remember these points, you're covered in the body language department. If you forget some of this advice, don't panic. Focus on the interview: The minutia is not as critical as many of these books would have you believe. Oh yes, I almost forgot, tell the truth and your body language won't give you away.

## ■ YOUR GUERRILLA INTERVIEW STRATEGY

Your mission: to impress interviewers so much they handcuff you to the desk for fear you'll escape. Don't laugh! It could happen.

> Not that long ago, I was interviewing with a client who was particularly impressed with the candidate I'd recruited. It had been a long and difficult project because of the rare skill set we were looking for, but the interview was going as planned. At one point, the president became so excited he dragged his four vice presidents in to meet the candidate as well. The interview ran for six hours—well past the allotted time. We had to bring in lunch for the seven of us. In the end, we only let the candidate go home after he promised to review our offer with his wife that night and call us first thing in the morning. (Yes, he signed on.)

This candidate understood the number one Guerrilla job-hunting tactic and how to use it. Unusual? Yes! Rare? No. Similar events have transpired many times during my 22 years of recruiting. Okay, never with handcuffs—but you get the idea.

## ■ YOUR NUMBER ONE TACTIC

Sell first. Buy later. Here's what I mean. No matter how much research you've done, no matter how eminently qualified you are, no matter how great the width of your smile, your first objective is to get them to like and want to hire you. In the beginning, it's not about you—it's about them. Your mission is to sell-sell-sell! Let me explain.

Even if you've never sold a thing in your life, you can do this. Once they're sold on you—you get to buy while they sell-sell-sell! Let me explain.

Interviews have three distinct stages. During the first two stages, you sell. During the third you turn the tables and make them sell to you. Here's how the interview should unfold.

### ➤ Stage 1: The Warm-Up

The warm-up general discussion is designed to get to know you. Let the interviewer lead. If he asks you the time-honored opening question, "Tell me about yourself," there's only one way to respond: "Where would you like me to begin? Where should I start?" By using this method, you subtly telegraph that your thoughts are well organized, and you want to understand the intent of the question. Be prepared to jump into your primary reason for being there. They have a need you can satisfy. Ply them with stories and analogies but don't be overbearing.

They'll question you about the specifics of those jobs that interest them. The more time they spend on a subject, the more relevant it is to the position, so don't be too quick to move the discussion to your interests. You're not running the show, they are—for now.

Listen carefully to the interviewers and be direct. Bring your success stories forward. By focusing on results, you demonstrate how you can make them money, save them money, and so on. Ensure that you're answering their questions completely. Ask, "Is there anything else you'd like to know about this?" or "Does that answer your question?" to make sure that you have delivered the details they need. Ask questions that are on topic and in line with theirs. Ask for clarification if you don't understand a question or need more details.

### ➤ Stage 2: Detailed Discussion of Qualifications

This stage involves an in-depth technical discussion of your key skills as they apply to the position. Demonstrate your current industry knowledge by talking about their business, market position, and any new products their competitors have rolled out.

Many interviewers don't know how to interview to get the information they need to make a hiring decision. Guerrilla, it's your responsibility to ensure they get it. To take the lead tactfully, ask some "how" questions that will steer the conversation toward the strengths you want to emphasize:

➤ How has XYZ affected [insert pertinent area of company]?

➤ How are you dealing with [insert pertinent topic]?

➤ How do you think X will affect the industry over the long term?

Pull these questions together from the data you discovered when you called people who used to work at the company (Chapter 7, Guerrilla Networking). Be prepared to answer this question yourself and engage the interviewer in conversation. Prepare three "how" questions before you go. You don't have to agree with the interviewer's opinion but you do have to listen. Some interviewers will challenge you just to test the depth of your character. Have your facts ready and be prepared to drill down to the tactical level to explain the who, what, where, when, why, and how of your major accomplishments. By discussing how they relate directly to the position, you demonstrate your ability to hit the ground running.

If the interviewer says something outrageous, bring the discussion back on track by saying, "That's interesting." Or "I hadn't thought of that," and then ask another question. Don't get into an argument.

*I recently watched a candidate lose a job offer because he got into an argument with the president over a minor technical issue that wasn't even germane to the technology. In the ensuing moments, the candidate aptly demonstrated that he was not open to new ideas or anyone else's opinion. He answered our biggest concern without being asked directly. We continued the search and hired someone else a month later.*

Don't let that happen to you—even if you're right—you're wrong. By the way, the candidate was right, in terms of the technology discussed, but he approached the tête-à-tête as an absolute authority. In this case, my client wanted a leader, not a dictator. Not 15 minutes earlier, the candidate had been emphasizing his inclusive leadership style. The moral of the story: Be ready to be tested.

### ➤ Stage 3: Closing Discussion

Finally, after the interviewers have interrogated you and are satisfied that you're the real deal, they'll politely ask if you have any questions. They'll assume they've already answered them during the interview and won't expect any. This moment of truth separates the winners from the losers, so to speak. Asking the right questions will lead the employer to the inevitable conclusion that you're the right candidate.

## ■ TAKING CHARGE OF THE INTERVIEW

Your personal question period is an important event. It gives you a final opportunity to separate yourself from the pack. Here's where your copious research comes into play. When someone asks us deep thoughtful questions, we think the person is smart and important, don't we? Think about this for a minute. You can turn this behavior into a strategy to create demand for you. If your interview didn't go very well or was only so-so, this is where you can make up ground and overtake your competition. If it went as well as I expect it will, here's where you ensure you get the offer.

### ➤ Becoming Their Top Choice

By asking the right questions, you can learn the company's real weaknesses and map them to your accomplishments right in front of the interviewers. It's a curious thing, to watch employers start nodding their heads. When you see telltale side-to-side head movements, don't panic! It doesn't mean no. It means, "Yes." It signifies, "I can't believe this guy understands my problems." The interviewer is thinking, "I should have been selling this guy. Here he's been assessing me the whole time! I can't let this one get away!" Now watch the interviewer start to sell you and sell you hard. They've now handed control over to you. Once you are at this point, ask all your questions and carefully drill down on their answers.

## ■ QUESTIONS DESIGNED TO SEPARATE YOU FROM THE PACK

Download
available

1. Can you explain to me how your business philosophy has changed/evolved over the past five years? How does this compare to your competitor X? The answer tells you what the company values most. It will tell you whether the company is product- or market-driven and where its weaknesses lie. If the company hasn't changed in five years, it is either a runaway success or blind; either way, your opportunity to make a real impact could be minimal.

2. How does the company deal with the inherent conflicts between quality and the timely delivery of new products? This tells you how realistic the company is and whether its alpha- and beta-testing processes are well run. It also gives you insight into how the different departments operate. Anything less than total cooperation between kingdoms is a recipe for disaster—everyone works on "Internet time" now.

3. What industries or outside influences affect the company's growth? This tells you how the company minimizes the downside and maximizes the upside. Many external influences can impact a company's success. A smart company will be able to recognize these external influences and leverage them.

Like a good lawyer, you need to know the answers to these questions yourself. Your questions should lead the interviewer to focus on those areas that demonstrate your strengths.

---

*The Killer Question*

Here's how to leverage every interview you're on and get five more interviews. Ask this question during your interview:

*Ms. Smith, in my research I found the following competitors [name up to five]. Can you please tell me what they're doing that keeps your executive team up at night?*

Why do you ask this? You're giving them the opportunity to brag first and then confess their concerns so that you can:

➤ Assess how you can best help them achieve their goals.

➤ Use the data points you've been given on their competitors to turn around and approach them for a job as soon as you've finished that interview.

Very Guerrilla. Look at it this way. Maybe they'll hire you. Maybe they won't. This is just a preliminary business meeting with no guarantees on either side, but where the interviewer is definitely going to use everything you say to his or her advantage. You should do the same. If the interviewer confesses concerns about a competitor, why shouldn't you use that to your advantage? Get on the phone to the hiring managers at the competing firms and tell them, "I just came back from an interview at ABC Company and given what they told me about you and why you keep them up at night, I think I'd rather work for you! Can we have a coffee?"

---

## ■ HOW TO ASK FOR THE JOB

The goal of every interview is to get an offer: an offer for the job or an offer to interview more. Your goal in the first interview is to be asked back. It is highly unlikely you'll be hired in one interview although

I've had it happen. There are two closing questions—as we call them in sales—that are appropriate for your first interview:

1. "Who will I meet in the second interview?"
2. "When would you like to schedule our next meeting?"

*Warning*: If the interviewer wavers in any way, here is the question you must ask. Don't interrupt and don't argue.

"Is there any reason you would not consider inviting me back for a second interview?"

"But, but, but . . ." I can hear you saying now, "Dave, I think things went well, why in the world would I want to bring up any negative feelings?" Why? Because they didn't offer you the job, so there are negatives and you want to address them now while you're across the table from them.

Let me put this another way: Do you know the number one reason employers pass on certain people? They think you can do the job. You've proven you're qualified; they're just not completely convinced you're going to be really happy in this job. Duh! Maybe they think you're overqualified. Or that it's not quite what you are looking for. Maybe you're an A candidate and they know their company is only a B+.

Well, you can't get them to change their mind after you've left, but while you're sitting there you've got a near 100% chance of turning it around. By asking them to tell you what their concern is while you're still sitting there, you get to explain away that concern with new/more information. Just look the interviewer in the eye and say: "Here's why I'm very interested in this job. I want this job. And, I'm going to stay in this job for a long time if you give me the opportunity."

That should overcome their "buyer's remorse."

If the interviewer has misunderstood something you said, say, "I see; what gave you that impression?" Again, let the other person talk until you feel confident you can address his concerns. What you are doing is erasing any fear, doubt, or uncertainty that you will stay. Book the next interview there and then by asking the following two questions.

1. Are there any presentation materials I should bring?
2. Who, besides yourself, will make the final hiring decision? Will I be meeting with them as well?

At the end of the final interview, you want to ask:

> ➤ "What challenges would you have me tackle first?"
> ➤ "Is there anything preventing you from extending an offer to me?"
> ➤ "When would you like me to start?"

If you get less than a yes, circle back and ask, "Is there any reason you would not make me an offer?"

Throughout the interview process, you must maintain your enthusiasm for the job. Your objective is to get the offer and then think about whether you really want it. Many people mistakenly try to decide if they want the job during the interview. Big mistake! This will distract you during the interview, and your lack of focus will be apparent to the interviewer. Focus on getting the offer.

## ■ CONCLUDING THE MEETING

When you're just about ready to go, ask the interviewer one last question: "Is there anything else you think I should know about the company or this position?" This signals that you've finished. If the person likes what he's seen, he will say something to regain control. Tell him you're interested in meeting the key people you'll be working with if he thinks there's a good fit. Now shut up.

Go home and write a memorable thank-you note.

## ■ HOW TO HANDLE MONEY

There's only one way to handle money; defer the conversation until you know you want the job. Memorize the following line for when you're asked about salary expectations:

> *I like this company and I like the opportunity, but it's premature to discuss potential compensation until we've mutually agreed there's a good fit both ways. Wouldn't you agree? What is the next step in your process?*

That's the only answer you need. It brands you as bright, confident, and self-assured—exactly what they want. If they come back with the old "We just want to make sure we're in the range" line, you must say, "I'm certain you'll be fair." That statement will stop them in their tracks. It accomplishes two goals. In their mind, it signifies money isn't the most important issue—which every employer likes to know, and it forces them to the bargaining table. You want them to get you to the table. You'll learn how to close the deal in Chapter 13.

**Get the free mobile app at**
**http://gettag.mobi**

## ■ HOW TO FOLLOW UP BETWEEN MEETINGS

Download
available

You need to get the download off the GM4JH web site because I want you to actually listen to a good voice mail.

### ➤ Second and Third Interviews

It is rare that anyone is hired on the first interview these days. It happens, but normally only at the most junior levels. Even presidents will want you to meet their senior executive team before making an offer, no matter how impressed they may be. No one wants to upset the delicate team dynamics they have in place. Directors, of course, will have you meet their vice president. The lower you are on the corporate hierarchy, the more likely you'll meet several people in the process.

You know that being invited back for second and third interviews means that the company is interested in you and you're interviewing well. Make sure you continue to sell yourself just as you did in the first interview. Don't assume the first person who interviewed you has passed on the details of that meeting.

Generally speaking, you need to ask everyone in the process the questions you asked the first interviewer. Plan your agenda so you know what you want to cover in the interview. Work on improving areas that may have been perceived as weak in the first interview. An employer's decision-making process is less rational than you might think. You want everyone you meet to like you. Once you've made it into the "acceptable" category, getting the offer is a matter of fit. Make sure you get a business card from everyone you meet. Thank-you notes need to go to each interviewer separately.

### ➤ Tips for Other Types of Interviews

➤ Telephone interviews: Phone interviews are used to screen candidates out—not in! The screener's job is to decide whether you warrant an in-person interview. Your job is to convince them you do by sounding enthusiastic and by convincing them this is *the* job you want. Screeners don't necessarily know what the job entails and may not care by the time they get to you on the list. It is your responsibility to tell them how your skills and accomplishments fit the requirements.

When someone calls you to do a telephone interview, make sure you can actually take the call. If you can't speak at the moment, tell the caller and arrange for a time to return the call, or ask for a minute to walk into a conference room and change phones. Very few people will refuse you a moment to get organized, and it could make the difference between receiving a so-so or a superstar rating. Take a few minutes to get ready by reading your resume and reviewing the company's ad.

➤ Board or group interviews: If you're faced with a panel of interviewers, the first thing you want to do is to walk to the end of the table and shake each of their hands and ask each participant for a business card. When you sit down, lay the cards out on the table so that each card faces its owner. When you begin to answer questions, you can address them by name. This will impress the interviewers and build your confidence.

When asked a question, look directly at the questioner when answering. Don't worry about the rest of the panel. If multiple people ask you questions at the same time, answer the first one completely before moving to the next. It is quite all right to ask the speaker to please repeat a question. Be genuine and relaxed, especially if you sense they are trying to irritate you. They may try to see how you react under pressure.

# 13

# Negotiating the Deal

## *How to Bargain with Confidence*

The worst thing you can possibly do in a deal is seem desperate to make it. That makes the other guy smell blood, and then you're dead. The best thing you can do is deal from strength, and leverage is the biggest strength you can have. Leverage is having something the other guy wants. Or better yet, needs. Or best of all, simply can't do without.

—Donald J. Trump, *Trump: The Art of the Deal*

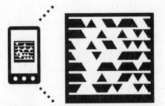

**Get the free mobile app at**
**http://gettag.mobi**

Congratulations. You've been through all the interviews. You like the organization and the job—it's a good fit. The organization likes you, too, and offers you the position. So now what? How do you make sure you get the best possible deal?

Guerrilla, you've been setting up the close from the first moment you walked into the employer's office. You looked sharp, acted smart, and came off as self-assured by not talking about compensation—a real "A++ Player." Carry that same behavior into the negotiations.

Candidates who net the best results approach the negotiation process with a blend of positive attitude and preparation.

The following information is important to your financial well-being whether you are an individual contributor or a senior executive. Some of the entitlements and strategies may not apply to your current situation, but the strategies and tactics are valid for every new hire. As we go through the material, think about how you can apply these techniques.

## ■ PROJECT A WINNING ATTITUDE

Unlike many business deals that are short-lived and transactional in nature, employment negotiations are relationship driven and can last a lifetime. It may be acceptable to thump your fist on the desk to gain a concession buying a car because you're not likely to see the salesperson again; however, you'll likely see the employer's negotiator every morning at the water cooler. You may get a small special consideration but at what cost—being labeled a horse's ass? The uncompromising aloofness of a candidate who doesn't give a damn bespeaks such a wealth of self-confidence that the client may figure there's something to it, but if you don't deliver, you'll be dispatched with equal indifference.

In negotiations, flashy, bold, or arrogant behavior is a detriment. Approach the negotiations, instead, with detached enthusiasm coupled with the ability to walk away. If any old offer is acceptable, you have nothing to negotiate—but you must negotiate because you risk alienating the employer if you don't. After all, it's no fun for the fisherman when the fish jump into the boat.

You don't want to appear so excited that they offer you less than top dollar. Conversely, don't run them off by appearing indifferent. As a headhunter, I never worry about the brash ego-driven candidates—they're easy to close—it's the quiet ones I have to keep an eye on. Your leverage rests with your confidence in your ability to do the job. You don't need to sell. The employer must sell you. But first, you need to understand what you're buying.

## ■ PREPARING FOR NEGOTIATIONS

Research equates to power. That's absolutely the case now. Before you receive an offer, you need to create a checklist of your needs and expectations. Guerrilla, if you don't plan like this, you may find that in the rush and excitement of accepting the position, you forgot or missed important elements. Winning at this stage requires you to look beyond salary and deal with the complete package.

You established your value to the company in terms of how you're going to impact its bottom line when you wrote your resume. That is truly how you negotiate. You don't just negotiate at the end when the deal comes up. That is a specific skill you develop and that you use throughout the interview process. You've laid the seeds for negotiation all along the way. That's how you really have success, by linking your skill to accomplishments, bottom-line value, and revenue to the company.

## ■ NEGOTIATE WITH THE FINAL DECISION MAKER

Before you start, make sure you understand who you're negotiating with. Some employers use the timeshare-vacation-approach. They send in the HR manager or some other junior functionary to have the preliminary discussion and isolate your hot buttons. After several hours of discussion, this individual suddenly needs management approval. You don't want to discover at the last minute that your hard-fought concessions were all for naught and you're facing a new negotiator.

If the offer has come through a headhunter, you need to understand the recruiter's role in the negotiation. Typically, it's in their best interest to get you as much money as possible because their compensation is tied to yours. You'd be wise to gauge your recruiter's skill at negotiating before turning your life over. Many recruiters lack the depth of knowledge and breadth of skills necessary to negotiate a complete package. In some cases, they're more interested in closing the deal as quickly as possible. If this happens, the smart Guerrilla remains firmly in the driver's seat.

Use your recruiter as a sounding board and a platform to launch trial balloons. If the employer gets agitated, it'll be with the recruiter, not you. If something goes wrong, just deny—deny—deny. The employer may step in to finish the negotiations and the recruiter will still get paid—it's all part of the game.

## ■ NEGOTIATE YOUR POWER BEFORE YOUR PAY

This may seem at first a little backward. Doesn't your title determine your salary? Well actually, no. It's the depth of your responsibilities that determines how much an employer is willing to pay you. The greater your level of responsibility, the richer your pay packet. Therefore, it's in your best interest to negotiate your duties and responsibilities before tackling compensation. You and the employer must have the same understanding of your responsibilities and the specific performance standards that gauge your success.

Performance standards must be observable and measurable; they can't be subjective or your performance becomes open to interpretation, making your bonus subjective as well.

For example: a subjective clause in a contract might read, "Increase sales." An objective statement would read, "Increase sales by 15% in 12 months." Only the second clause can be measured.

If during the interview process, you agree to shoulder more responsibility than the employer originally envisioned, document it at the time, so that when you negotiate compensation, you can both make an apples-to-apples comparison. By supersizing the responsibilities of the job (do you want fries with that?), you push compensation upward. The easiest way to negotiate the salary you want is to increase the responsibilities of the job. You must document the following:

➤ Title
➤ Reporting structure
➤ Authority
➤ Accountability
➤ Number of direct staff
➤ Specific performance standards
➤ Committee responsibilities, if any

Any increase in authority or responsibility that you can document will amplify your compensation package. If the increase in responsibility is not documented and the job description stays the same, there's no justification to raise your salary. You and the employer need to have the same view of the position's scope before the offer is made. Your initial strategy is to increase the compensation package in light of the increased responsibility. That way, the employer's first offer is already inflated and probably closer to an acceptable level requiring only minimum negotiation.

Once you have the details of the job finalized, it's up to the employer to come back to you with a reasonable offer. You have two choices here. You can either tell the employer exactly what it will take to close the deal or you can let them make an offer. After investing this much time in interviewing and negotiating, most employers will come back with a reasonable offer because they don't want to repeat the process with someone else. By the time they get to this point, the employer already has a pretty good idea of what the market is paying for this position and what the company can afford. As a headhunter, my strategy is to aim for the absolute top dollar and settle a few bucks below. It's in your best interest to let employers think they've won. This shows that you are flexible.

## GUERRILLA WISDOM

### *Social Media and Job Hunting—A Lawyer's Perspective*
### Heather Bussing

Potential employers use social media, too. They will Google you and see if you have a Facebook page. If your information is available, they will look at it.

They are doing due diligence to find out more about who you are and to see if it's worth both your time to set up an interview or take the process further. This is perfectly legal. If you put the information online and they can find it, they can look at it.

The only thing that is illegal is if they eliminate you as a candidate because you are a member of a protected class based on your race, color, religion, sex, national origin, pregnancy, age (over 40), or disability. Some states and countries have broader protections that include marital status, ancestry, medical condition, and sexual orientation.

It is perfectly legal to eliminate you as a candidate because you get drunk, do drugs, have bad taste, lack discretion, or drive a Honda. Employers can discriminate based on your clothes, Halloween costumes, purple hair, nose rings, enlarged ear lobes, or tattoos. They can also discriminate based on your posts on Twitter, MySpace, and personal blog—as long as it is not related to a protected factor.

Some job seekers tell me they want the employer to know who they really are because they don't want to work for someone who won't accept them. That's fine. It's just that the chances of having a good working relationship are so much better if you

*(continued)*

*(Continued)*

both focus on what your qualifications are and the work to be done. So the judgments go both ways.

I have also heard that some job seekers are being advised to alter their name or identifying information on job applications and their resume so that they can say that damaging information online is not really about them. This is a bad idea for a number of reasons.

The federal government gets extremely touchy about your tax identification and social security information matching the payroll information for tax purposes. Immigration and Homeland Security also get excited if someone is misrepresenting who they are. So you will have to give the correct information to the employer at some point.

Misstating information on an application, particularly about your identity, is at best grounds for questioning your truthfulness and at worst, fraud. Either way, it would probably be grounds for termination and is definitely not a good start to a new job.

---

So be you. But don't put things online that you don't want strangers to know about you. Direct market instead. Heather Bussing is a California employment and business lawyer who likes to prevent problems before they become lawsuits. Contact her through LinkedIn at www.linkedin.com/in/heatherbussing.

## ■ ESTABLISHING YOUR BOTTOM LINE

Download available

Do you know what your bottom-line salary must be? "More," isn't a number. Most people have an idea of what they would "kinda like to make," but rarely do people know exactly what they need. Fewer still know what they want prior to the offer. Failure to establish your bottom line may place your current lifestyle at risk or, at the very least, leave money on the table. It's important to know those details, but it's even more important not to tell the employer. Ideally, you want to start negotiating well above your minimum amount and if all goes well, never approach it. Guerrillas won't wait until the last possible moment; they'll tally up the cost of their lifestyle well in advance of the employer's first offer.

All employers think about salaries in ranges of high and low. Many subscribe to salary surveys. You can find out the inside skinny on thousands of companies—for free—by going to Glassdoor.com. Your future employer's industry association will likely have a salary survey, too; pick up the phone and ask. If you can't get access to it, then do your own. Call their competitors. You'd be surprised how much information you can get from a human resources department if you tell them you are a researcher—which you are. The download provides a detailed list for researching compensation requirements.

## ➤ Negotiating Benefits

Compensation is more than just your base salary, but employers will be focused primarily on the base salary because it's a fixed cost and in some cases, such as insurance, it determines the cost of other benefits. From your viewpoint, though, almost everything you don't have to pay for directly is money in your pocket.

Maybe you noticed that I did not list a cell phone as a benefit. Companies will try to tell you it's a benefit; in reality it's an electronic dog collar. Many of the newer phones have GIS (geographic information systems) positioning technology, making it too easy to track you down—via satellite—on your day off. Ask for a monthly allowance instead.

## ➤ Tuition Forgiveness

This is not the same as an education allowance. Tuition forgiveness deals with the money you already invested in your education. For example, you may have financed an advanced degree in nursing, and now each month you have a student loan just as you might have a loan for a car or house. If you're in a hot area like IT security or nuclear medicine, you may be able to get the employer to assume your education mortgage.

Now's the time to stop reading and download that sheet I referred to two sections ago, if you haven't already. Take a hard look for any items you currently pay for that you could ask the employer to cover. Insurance programs can be very costly and you pay for them with after-tax dollars—double ouch. The employer will gladly provide extra benefits if he thinks that you will accept a lower salary. Let him reason that way for now.

Remember, benefits are great, but they're not spendable dollars. You maximize your cash flow by having the employer pay for your benefits. Always maximize the employer's portion of the coverage because you're not taxed on benefits. Well, okay—in Canada benefits may be taxed, but in the United States you're taxed on your gross salary, not your total package including benefits. Frequent-flyer miles are the only exception; if the company gives them to you and you use them, the IRS will tax you.

## GUERRILLA MISSION

Download
available

Download this compensation checklist right now. It will help you determine what you have now, and how much each item costs. What benefits can you reasonably expect the employer to pay for? What would you like them to pay for? Make a list now so you know what you're going to be negotiating for and the monetary value of each item.

Using a checklist ensures you won't have regrets later. It also demonstrates your business savvy. Be alert, employers may try to trick you by focusing on your total compensation instead of your salary. Instead of focusing on the $40,000 salary, the employer will try to sell you on the $52,000 package (base plus benefits). In most employee/employer negotiation schemes, it's to the employer's advantage to load up the benefits component to lower base salary. Of course, Guerrilla, you'll be prepared to counteract this. You want the highest possible salary and great benefits, too.

## ■ YOUR STRATEGY

Take the lead. Do not make the mistake of letting the employer define the issues for you. You must negotiate salary last. Why? Simple: The employer will be focused on the big number—your salary—to the exclusion of all else. You want to nibble—just a little—and then a little more. Talking about the little items first will earn you a string of rapid concessions on items like insurance, professional fees, and vacation. If the employer wants to be the hero on the salary front, who are you to deny them? A true winner gives wins away, so let them feel like they're winning. For the time being, focus on increasing the value of your benefits by 50% to 100%. It's still money for you and there's no ego involved in their giving away benefits.

### GUERRILLA TIP

If you are relocating and you already own a home, make sure you don't get stuck with two. Have a clause put in the employment agreement that states in effect that you'll endeavor to sell your house but if, after two months, the house is not sold at fair market value, the company is responsible for buying your former home outright or paying your mortgage until such time as the house is sold. This is one of those benefits you want to think about from the outset, but only table as an "afterthought" just as you're reaching to sign the employment agreement. Essentially, you need to have all the other points of the agreement in writing before you try this. Don't worry, you're not going to shock the employer; they were just holding their breath hoping you wouldn't bring it up. Shame on you if they succeed.

On several occasions, I've needed to go above and beyond even this. I have gone so far as to negotiate the moving of a director's wine collection from France. In another case, we bought a manager a home and moved his daughter's horse.

Nothing, it seems, is beyond reason as long as the employer is convinced the company needs you. Remember though, parity is important in an organization, and some of the things you request may be denied because they would shake up the organization's existing compensation ranges and structures. If this is the case, don't push further—the organization isn't likely to budge and you will lose.

---

## ■ THE PSYCHOLOGY OF THE DEAL

After several go-rounds on benefits, you'll likely be close to settling in to negotiate salary. When you think that time has come, then you may want to raise the following issues as much for the opportunity to secure them as to give them away:

➤ Signing bonus

➤ Severance

➤ Earlier-than-scheduled compensation review

➤ Guaranteed minimum first-year bonus

How you deal in the final negotiations will be a telltale sign for the employer on how well you will negotiate for the company. This is especially important if you are seeking a purchasing, marketing, or sales position. You don't want to cave, but you do want to be seen as being logical in your rationale and considerate of their position.

Throughout the negotiations, you may hear comments or questions like the following, and you need to be prepared to deal with them in a logical and matter-of-fact style:

➤ If we make you this offer, will you accept it right now?

➤ What will it take for you to accept the offer?

➤ What other way can we structure this deal so that it would be acceptable?

➤ What do you think is fair-market compensation for someone like you in this city?

➤ How low can you go on each dimension of the compensation package?

My advice is to remain cool and stick to your agenda. An employer who is asking you these questions is trying to close you. The psychology of the deal dictates that you never, ever accept an offer on the spot. If you say yes immediately, it weakens your position now and in the future. Always ask for a day to review the offer with your significant other—even if that's your mother. You may want to say something like: "I'm very interested in joining your team, and I'd like the night to discuss it with my significant other. Is that okay with you?" (This is especially relevant if the job requires relocation.)

Your uncommon courtesy will buy you the night—or longer—to mull over the details and ensure you haven't missed anything.

## ■ BREAKING AN IMPASSE

When negotiations come to an impasse, and they always do, it's your responsibility to continue driving the deal. Be prepared to ask questions and keep the negotiations alive and moving forward. Asking the following questions demonstrates your sincere interest in coming to an agreeable offer.

➤ What flexibility do you have on: salary, signing bonus, annual bonus, or anything else?

➤ How about considering other dimensions of the package, beyond annual salary and job title? For example, signing bonus, annual bonus, vacation, retirement plan, and equity.

➤ What other differently structured compensation packages can you offer?

## ■ NAVIGATING THE GAUNTLET

Most people are reluctant to negotiate because they either feel greedy or have a hard time asserting themselves. Yet these same people are quite effective when acting on behalf of their company. Guerrilla, if this describes you, it is okay. Your remedy is at hand—do it for your family. Think what a difference an extra $5, $10, or $20,000 could make in little Timmy's life. By negotiating for those you care about most, you'll negotiate a better deal. It's never just about you.

## ■ BODY LANGUAGE

You need to be conscious of your body language. Be aware of the messages you are sending. There are times when the negotiation can be a real grind. Don't get rattled. Don't let them see you sweat. Telegraph what you want the employer to see. If you are smiling and your palms are face up on the table, those are signs that you are open and receptive to what they are saying. If, instead, your eyebrows are furled and your fists are clenched, I have a pretty good idea what you're thinking. Drink lots of water. No coffee or alcohol. Take frequent bathroom breaks on purpose if you need to compose yourself.

## ■ ASK FOR A LITTLE—GET A LOT

If you are negotiating an hourly wage, remember that every dollar per hour represents $2,080 per year. Most employers like to talk salary. For salaries less than $50,000, focus the employer on the dollar per hour amount. Simplify and minimize the concession you need. For example, it's easier to get an employer to agree to an increase from $20 to $24 per hour than to get them to agree to a $48,000 salary when they budgeted $40,000. Which do you think is more palatable for the employer? Asking for $4 more per hour is nothing—$8,000 causes unnecessary headaches but you're still talking about $8,000.

You may also run into one of the following scenarios, and you need to decide in advance your course of action (I have a few suggestions):

➤ The employer acts like its doing you a favor.

➤ The employer appears cordial until you dig your heels in.

➤ Someone besides your future boss is doing the negotiations.

The employer wants to strike the best deal possible. All kinds of games may get played. Disarming the employer can be as easy as turning your hands palm up on the table and saying, "You look a little tense, is everything all right?" That phrase will force even the most hardened negotiator to lighten up. Try it.

## ■ CLOSING THE OFFER

Get it in writing. Keep notes during the negotiations explaining what was agreed on. Date stamp your notes. When the final draft is completed, read it closely to make certain that the final offer reflects what you've agreed on. If years down the road you notice a discrepancy, you won't be able to correct it. You get one shot at doing this right.

When the final deal is done, pay a lawyer to review the terminology of the contract or letter of employment for unforeseen pitfalls (e.g., noncompetition clauses that would force you to move to Alaska if you wanted to pursue your profession with another employer in the future). Employ the lawyer to read the terms and conditions for ambiguity only, not to renegotiate or add to the contract. Most lawyers are deal breakers not deal makers, and you don't want them to kill your deal.

Finally, don't talk yourself out of a deal—know when to shut up. Once it's done, it's done. Move on quickly to another subject. I need to emphasize the importance of talking about anything but the deal once it's done. Talk about the weather or the big game. Avoid anything that sensitive people can dispute.

## A WAR STORY

### The Good, The Bad, and the Great!

*Cindy Kraft*

Jack and I started working together during the wind down of his CFO duties postmerger. Like many senior-level finance executives, he had held a number of positions over the past seven years and his positioning, through no fault of his own, was one of a job hopper. Added to his angst was the fact that his salary had taken numerous dives through the various moves.

Jack had set some high goals in anticipation of accepting a new position, including compensation, corporate culture, and relocating to a specific geographic area. He was resolute in his determination to make a *right* move rather than *any* move.

Jack built two foundational documents that served as the driving mechanisms in deciding whether to take the positions he was offered. The first document was value driven. He identified his top eight values and analyzed each position offered (including compensation and culture) against those values. The second document was a list prioritized around "must haves," "wants," and "frankly, don't care about" in his next role. This was his road map for entering into serious negotiations to get what he wanted.

The "must have" list contained items he was unwilling to negotiate—they were the items that would make or break the deal; the wants list contained items he would be willing to negotiate in order to get a must have; and his "don't care about" were his ace in the hole. He put these items on the bargaining table and then magnanimously threw them out as he continued to negotiate for the things on his must have list.

Through the course of our nine-month journey, Jack received numerous offers, which he turned down because they did not meet his requirements and/or his values. The decision to say no took great courage on his part as he remained firm in his desire to make the right move, not any move ... despite the search taking longer than he anticipated.

With a clear and compelling value proposition, great patience, and hard work, Jack did indeed get his "right" job. He was able to relocate to his desired geographic location with the company paying his relocation costs as well as buying his house in this stalled housing market; ask for and receive the salary he desired, which was well above the salary from his previous position; and also obtain every one of his "must have" perks.

A compelling value proposition and the confidence to clearly articulate his value to prospects enabled Jack to powerfully negotiate his desired compensation ... and get everything he wanted. Sweet!

---

Cindy Kraft, The CFO-Coach, www.cfo-coach.com www.LinkedIn.com/in/cindykraft.

---

## ■ HOW TO KILL YOUR DEAL

It goes without saying that I respect your judgment—you bought this book—but I need to caution you not to overdo it. It's easy to get caught in the euphoria of "doing the deal" when you do this type of negotiation only occasionally.

*Guidelines for Successful Negotiation*

➤ Don't immediately agree to the offer. You'll brand yourself as a lightweight.

➤ Don't give ultimatums. If you adopt a take-it-or-leave-it attitude, they'll leave it.

➤ Don't be negative. Seek win-win resolutions instead; it'll disarm your opponent.

➤ Don't try to renegotiate a point that's already been agreed to. Trying to reopen a discussion once it is closed brands you as immature and may jeopardize the entire deal.

➤ Don't let the employer renegotiate anything unless you get a major concession.

➤ Don't discount the help. Let recruiters do their jobs. I once had a candidate who insisted on negotiating directly with the CEO instead of through me. The client and I wanted this guy badly and he knew it, but he never once asked about compensation. In the end, the candidate left $40,000 in base salary and $200,000 in options on the table, and that was just the initial package I'd been authorized to negotiate. The options alone turned out to be worth $1.6 million.

## ■ SUMMARY

You'd be surprised at the lengths to which some employers will go once they believe they have found their ideal candidate. It is absolutely essential to have the employer recognize your value before you begin to negotiate. If an employer understands your value and is convinced you can do the job, then the question becomes, "How much it will take to get you?" Deal from a position of strength and you might just hear Donald Trump say, "You're Hired!"

# Chapter 14

# Career Lancing

## All—Ways—Ready

Our deepest fear is not that we are inadequate. Our deepest fear is that we are powerful beyond measure. It is our light, not our darkness, that most frightens us. We ask ourselves, who am I to be brilliant, gorgeous, talented, and fabulous? Actually, who are you not to be? You are a child of God. Your playing small doesn't serve the world. We were born to make manifest the glory of God that is within us. It's not just in some of us; it's in everyone. And as we let our own light shine, we unconsciously give other people permission to do the same. As we are liberated from our own fear, our presence automatically liberates others.

—MARIANNE WILLIAMSON

Faced with a stagnant economy, you can pull in your horns and settle for an uninspiring routine job that doesn't challenge you, or seize the moment:

1. Assess your competencies and interests.
2. Select your Top 10 employers.
3. Detail your career history with an employer's needs in mind.
4. Network like the covert operative you've been trained to be.
5. Craft your marketing materials (resume, cover letter, follow-up scripts).
6. Organize yourself for highly effective and rapid response.
7. Plan and launch a personal Force Multiplier Effect.

301

8. Interview with confidence.

9. Negotiate like a pro.

10. Stoke your pipeline!

Guerrillas understand better than anyone how to position and market their skills; to search the world, cold-call prospects, get their attention, raise their value proposition above the background noise, and to keep at it tenaciously for however long it takes—be it weeks or months—and be intelligent enough to present their skill set in creative new lights until the persuasion works.

Guerrilla, the future is in your hands.

David Perry & Jay Conrad Levinson

# Bonuses

# About the Authors

**Jay Conrad Levinson** is the author or coauthor of more than 32 books in the biggest series of books on marketing in history. His ideas have influenced marketing so much that today his books appear in 60 languages and are required reading in many MBA programs worldwide.

Jay taught Guerrilla Marketing for 10 years at the extension division of the University of California, Berkeley. He was a practitioner of it in the United States, as senior vice-president at J. Walter Thompson, and in Europe, as creative director at Leo Burnett Advertising.

He has written monthly columns for *Entrepreneur* and *Inc.*, a syndicated column for newspapers and magazines, and online columns published monthly on the Microsoft and GTE web sites.

Jay has served on the Microsoft Small Business Council and the 3Com Small Business Advisory Board. In addition to books, he has produced a videotape, an award-winning CD-ROM, a newsletter, a consulting organization, and a web site.

Nicknamed the "Rogue Recruiter" by the *Wall Street Journal*, **David Perry** is a veteran headhunter, closing more than 1,000 projects, with a 99.7% success rate. He is a student of leadership and its effect on organizations ranging from private equity ventures to global technology corporations. David has developed an extensive knowledge of leadership, innovation, and technology. This ever-evolving expertise keeps him at the pulse of the most innovative and successful leaders.

He is frequently quoted on trends and issues regarding executive search, recruiting, and HR in leading business publications including the *Wall Street Journal*, the *New York Times*, *Fortune*, *Forbes*, *Canadian Business*, *Computerworld*, *EETimes*, and *HR Today*. He appears regularly as an executive search and labor market analyst on radio and television across North America.

David is the co-author, along with Jay Levinson, of *Guerrilla Marketing for Job Hunters 2.0: 1,001 Unconventional Tips, Tricks, and*

*Tactics for Landing Your Dream Job* (John Wiley & Sons, 2009) and *Guerrilla Marketing for Job Hunters: 400 Unconventional Tips, Tricks, and Tactics for Landing Your Dream Job* (John Wiley & Sons, 2005), and author of *Career Guide for the High-Tech Professional: Where the Jobs Are Now and How to Land Them* (Career Press, 2004).

He is immediate past vice chair of the Canadian Technology Human Resources Board and was on the board of directors for the Software Human Resource Council for five years. He is HR Policy Advisor for the Canadian Advanced Technology Alliance.

David graduated from McGill University in 1982 with a BA in economics and industrial relations. As a commissioned officer in the Canadian Forces Reserve (1980), he graduated first in his class and was awarded the Sword of Honor. He has been recognized as one of the "Top 40 under 40" entrepreneurs in Ottawa. He lives in Ottawa with his wife and business partner Anita Martel and their four children. David recruits globally. See perrymartel.com for more information.

# Index

# Free Job Search Resources